ALLEN COUNTY PUBLIC LIBRARY

FORT WAYNE, INDIANA 46802

You may return this book to any agency, branch,
or bookmobile of the Allen County Public Library.

GUIDE TO MARKETING FOR ECONOMIC DEVELOPMENT

GUIDE TO MARKETING FOR ECONOMIC DEVELOPMENT

Competing in America's Second Civil War

John K. Ryans, Jr.
and
William L. Shanklin

Publishing Horizons, Inc.

©Copyright 1986, Publishing Horizons, Inc.
 2950 North High Street
 P.O. Box 02190
 Columbus, Ohio 43202

Printed in the United States.

1 2 3 4 ◢◤ 7 6 5 4

Library of Congress Cataloging-in-Publication Data

Ryans, John K.
   Guide to marketing for economic development.

   Bibliography: p.
   Includes index.
   1. Industrial promotion—United States—Case studies.
2. United States—Industries—Location—Case studies.
I. Shanklin, William L. II. Title.
HC110.I53R9   1986   338.6 042   96-334
ISBN 0-942280-29-6

CONTENTS

LIST OF VIGNETTES

LIST OF ILLUSTRATIONS

LIST OF EXHIBITS

INTRODUCTION

Over 120 years ago, the United States was torn by a civil war that dramatically altered the course of history. It was strife that pitted state against state and sometimes brother against brother in a war claiming countless lives and living indelibly in America's collective consciousness. The Northern states ostensibly won, but the sectional war really did not end with the South's surrender at Appomattox. Today, the fighting between the states continues, but in a far more civilized form and for a different reason—economic development. In the Second War Between the States, the cannon, rifle, and sabre have been replaced with marketing concepts and techniques; some of the most intense marketing battles ever waged have been over attracting business corporations to states and communities. The first salvos in Civil War II were fired years ago when Southern states began luring Northern manufacturing facilities.

Just as surely as Civil War I realigned the balance of power in the United States for many years to come, so too is the more subtle and cerebral Civil War II creating power realignments among the regions and states. What is more, the Second War Between the States has more players. It is North, South, East, and West against one another and frequently against foreign nations; it is state versus state and community versus community. Sunbelt, Frostbelt, and Rustbelt are propaganda terms emanating from Civil War II. Organizations such as the Congressional Sunbelt Council and the Northeast-Midwest Congressional Coalition have been formed to advance the interests, in the federal Congress, of particular geographical sectors of the United States. And governors are widely held accountable now, by their electorates, for state economic development efforts meant to generate new jobs.

This book is about marketing's integral role in economic development. Marketing is often confused and considered synonymous with personal selling and advertising. Marketing encompasses these functions to be sure, but it is much more comprehensive in scope and far more strategic in perspective. Advertising and personal selling are tactical means by which marketing strategies are implemented. In our concept, marketing is basically the activity within an organization that is responsible for the discernment and fulfillment of needs and wants in the marketplace in the pursuit of organizational objectives. Naturally, these are not just any old needs and wants, but rather those within the organization's strategic competence to fulfill. In the private sector, the organizational objective is profit. In contrast, public-sector organizations usually look to provide a service of some kind for the common good. For a state or community, the objective of marketing programs in pursuit of industrial development is economic vitality and growth, as measured by the resulting level of business activity, job creation, and a rising standard of living for the citizenry.

Whether economic development strategy lives up to expectations or not depends largely on how well marketing does at discerning and then fulfilling the needs and wants of businesses looking to start up, expand, or relocate facilities. Of course, marketers are constrained by the resources available to them to formulate and implement economic development strategies. Moreover, the best marketing program conceivable cannot work miracles; it cannot attract high-technology industry to Appalachia or turn Alaska into a winter tourist mecca.

In its fundamental sense, economic development is a term describing the organized efforts of the public sector (states, cities, etc.) and the private sector (growth associations, chambers of commerce, etc.) to economically vitalize or revitalize states and communities, as the case may be, through industrial growth. Economic development also appropriately refers to regional or even national efforts to create growth and jobs. Some states and cities house tourism and exporting under economic development; but, in our view, these are peripheral economic development activities at best. To us, economic development is concerned with stimulating industrial growth—of manufacturers, distributors, retailers, service industries, and all other kinds of for-profit businesses.

Economic development has three main branches. First, the most publicized economic development activity is that of attracting business from elsewhere to locate in a state or community. The ongoing Sunbelt raids on Frostbelt manufacturing facilities are examples, as are foreign nations' enticement of U.S. manufacturing plants. The second branch of economic development is that of retaining the businesses a state or community already has and getting them to expand in those areas. This strategy is often overlooked in developers' zeal to attract business from other states or communities; however, it is an important one. It does a state or community little good to lure industry from other places and, in the process, alienate and perhaps lose the industry it already has. Third, economic development is concerned with fostering business start-ups. This entrepreneurial facet is crucial in the long-term scheme of things; most new jobs in the United States are being created by smaller companies. In addition, companies that start out in a community have a good chance of remaining there because a certain amount of corporate inertia and executive attachment are normally involved.

When economic development strategy is based mostly on luring business from other locales, it becomes a zero-sum game. That is, what one state or city wins in the way of new business, another loses. Second-place finishes in these kinds of battles count for naught. However, economic development based also on getting existing business to expand and on fostering business start-ups is not a zero-sum game at all. Every state and community can win at these games.

Today, there is a plethora of "how-to-do-it" books, pamphlets, and articles, often complete with checklists, to guide the marketer of state or community economic development. But, unfortunately, a good deal of this literature is largely conjectural and sometimes almost strictly anecdotal. Although some of this kind of information is no doubt useful and experience-tested, most of it can be criticized on two counts. First, too much of the "how-to" material is derived from small sample sizes—often the experiences of a single company, individual, or occupational group—which immediately calls into question its applicability across a diversity of state and community situations. Second, and even more problematic, the information is usually written from the viewpoint of a state, city, industrial realtor, or whatever or whomever, rather than from the perspective of the companies that are actually the decision makers in facility locations. As a consequence, the focus is on what "they think" a company wants in a location. In short, there is a dearth of representative information about what a meaningful cross section of companies indicate they want and avoid in perspective locations. And these are the opinions that matter most.

This book was written, therefore, to fill a real need in the area of marketing strategy and planning as it pertains to economic development. It goes beyond existing materials on the subject in that it has both a strong conceptual *and* empirical underpinning. The book also provides multiple perspectives; it offers the evaluations of all the key players in the economic development business. For instance, we surveyed or personally interviewed, or both, industrial realtors across the United States. To get at the entrepreneurial branch of economic development, we obtained the views of owners and operators of industrial incubators, again across the United States, whose role it is to facilitate business start-ups by providing low rent and technical and business consultation to entrepreneurs. The idea is for the fledgling businesses to eventually leave the incubator and go on their own. We also used the technique known as *content analysis* to see what various states and communities are currently emphasizing in their economic development literature. But, most importantly, we went straight to the horse's mouth—to companies, of all sizes and lines of endeavor, that locate and relocate facilities in communities throughout the United States and often abroad. We qualitatively and statistically analyzed and reported, in jargon-free terms easily understandable to the layman, what these companies had to say about different kinds of location decisions. For example, what do they really want in a community for a headquarters facility? What about a plant or subsidiary? How do high-technology location decisions differ from those of more traditional lines of business? What are some of the trade-offs between and among the factors that affect corporate location decisions? And how well does state and community promotional literature regarding economic development zero-in on these motivations of corporate location decision makers?

The first section of the book discusses such topics as what the Second War Between the States has meant in terms of economic development trends, what the states and cities are doing to promote themselves and to attract and encourage industry, how industrial realtors and incubator operators see economic development from their vantage points, and how the war has extended beyond U.S. boundaries to become an international "high stakes" game for industry.

The second section of the book looks at the particulars of such matters as fostering high-tech industry and what companies say they want in their headquarters communities and in locales and sites for plant and subsidiary facilities. The concluding section, Chapter 10, is devoted mostly to recommendations for how states and other political entities might do a better job of economic development.

We have also sprinkled vignettes throughout the book that serve as edifying examples of both success and failure in economic development efforts. For instance, how has Mentor, Ohio successfully overcome the "Rust Bowl" image so associated with the Midwest? How is Irvine, California fostering biotechnology? Or, what do industrial incubator operators say about their experiences? In addition, we screened thousands of advertisements by all types of economic development groups; the ones that best illustrate particular points and represent noteworthy examples of creativity and strategy are presented throughout this book.

We caution that this book is not a sure-fire recipe for success in the marketing of economic development. In all competitive endeavors, Civil War II in this instance, there will inevitably be winners and losers.

Nonetheless, this book can definitely assist many people in gaining a better appreciation for the essential ingredients underlying effectiveness in economic development and, thus, to become better at marketing it.

1

THE COMPETITIVE WORLD OF ECONOMIC DEVELOPMENT

EXECUTIVE SUMMARY

Can we help it if they love us? More important, can we help it if they don't? Many corporations have relocated here, and for most it has worked out well.

William H. Inman, *Texas Business*[1]

Although speaking of the Lone Star State, Mr. Inman could just as easily be talking about Florida or California or other recipients of the corporate moves we have recently witnessed. The Sunbelt has clearly been enjoying its place in the sun. In contrast, Governor Richard Celeste of Ohio feels that his state cannot successfully compete in the economic development scramble solely on its own. He has been quoted as saying that "...unless we [neighboring Great Lakes states] can join hands together, as states in a region where we can identify clear, common interests, then we're in deep trouble."[2]

Does this suggest, therefore, that there is no economic development battle occurring in the United States today, that the war is over? Hardly. In fact, Dick Celeste would be the first to disagree based on his recent proactive stance in attempting to attract the General Motors Saturn plant and others to Ohio. What his comment has signaled is a renewed effort by the Great Lakes area, especially the Council of Great Lakes Governors, to counter media references to the "Rustbowl" and "Frostbelt," an image the region hopes to shed. For example, a recent headline in *Business Week* reads, "A Software Success Story in the

Rust Bowl."[3] And, all regions are constantly searching for new, more effective strategies to bring to the battlefield.

In this book, the word industry is used in its broadest sense. The term includes virtually all types of corporate or business facilities (head-quarters, plants, warehouses, etc.) and other primary employers (hospitals, schools, etc.). Generally not included are service organizations, unless it is a service headquarters. It is important to note that corporate and business facilities typically attract more complementary facilities and services and thus produce a greater industrial multiplier effect (e.g., more ancillary employment). State and cities, of course, are virtually all engaged in some form of industry-attraction efforts. Their marketing programs involve nationwide advertising, personal selling (trade and investment promotion missions), and similar efforts. Further most have devoted considerable effort to packaging financial programs that they feel are necessary ingredients in remaining competitive. These programs are often quite innovative. It seems that certain financial program minimums have become the "table stakes" for entry into the scramble. One can make a strong analogy between the current city and state competitive bid for new industry and the competition found in the business world itself. This chapter makes that analogy by comparing the product life cycle of business and a city's life cycle.

The business world is actively involved in economic development, most generally, and appropriately, for self-interest reasons. Bankers, public utilities, industrial realtors, commercial park developers, and transport companies are among the industrial companies that have a direct, personal interest in economic development from the supply side and have become more aggressive in their efforts. It is not unusual to see a multipage advertising section in *Fortune* or *Business Week* extolling a city, such as Dallas, or even a country, such as Japan. In fact, the recent 60-page spread on Japan in *Fortune* may have established a Guinness record for such sections. Most of the advertisers in these special sections are corporations from the area, and predominantly the banks, and so forth, noted earlier. However, because all companies, except possibly direct competitors of the new industry, see some benefit from an improved tax-base in their community or state, this increasing strong business support for economic development is quite enlightened. This increased business involvement in state and city economic development is also reflected in membership in, and time devoted to, local chambers of commerce or other civic organizations, one of whose prime objectives is attracting or supporting existing industry.

Nationally, states and cities can choose from a broad range of organizations, whose primary purposes include economic development. Whether it is the National Association of State Development Agencies, or the National Association of Towns and Townships, each is involved in tailored lobbying, training, and other efforts in behalf of the constituents. Similar organizations are found for all the other direct or indirect participants in the economic development game ranging from developers (National Association of Industrial Office Parks) to architects (The American Institute of Architects). Finally, the competitive milieu of economic development is not complete without some recognition being given to foreign government efforts, both national and local, to attract industry. For many years, U.S. corporations tended to pursue overseas locations primarily to provide access to market opportunities in these locales, that is, a plant or subsidiary was built in Antwerp to produce goods for sale in Belgium and nearby countries. Since 1980, however, the strength of the dollar in world markets has had a multifaceted effect on corporate location decisions. Many U.S. firms now find it necessary to produce their goods or key components in lower-cost foreign environments, both to serve their overseas markets *and* to compete with foreign imports at home. Thus, a company in New England may find itself choosing between a site in the Sunbelt and one in Ireland for its new plant that will serve its American market, as well as the European Community. It is not surprising, therefore, that countries such as Ireland and Korea, as well as others, have stepped up their efforts to attract U.S. investments.

The time is at hand when one can expect to find a trade or industrial development mission from San Antonio stopping to say hello to their counterparts from Korea in the Seoul international airport. The Henry Cisneros party will be meeting in that country with potential investors for its Texas city, while the Korean mission will be en route to the States seeking direct investment for that rapidly developing Third World power.

∞

May 17, 1983, will long be remembered in the annals of the Lone Star State. On that date Texas, or rather its capital city Austin, wrestled *the* high-tech plum of the early 1980s from Atlanta, San Diego, Raleigh-Durham, and other premier U.S. cities. Microelectronics and Computer Technology (MCC), a consortium-sponsored computer research and development company, announced in mid-May that Austin would be its home. This announcement culminated a several-month confrontation involving more than half the states and 50-plus cities; it was a cause celebre for the victor and a smarting defeat for the losers.

Perhaps it seems overdramatic for us to draw our analogies for the current industrial development competition from warfare or sports. Terms such as "battle," "wrestle," and "struggle" may seem to be an exaggeration at best to those unfamiliar with the level of competition between cities, counties, states, and even nations for new industrial or commercial investment such as an MCC. But, after all, a governor or mayor's job may be tied directly to his or her ability to attract new industry, either from other locales in the United States or from overseas. Fueling this intense competitive effort is the real or feared sectoral unemployment that is so prevalent throughout the world today.

Take our Austin example or Pennsylvania's "win" over Ohio and other states in the bid for Volkswagen in 1976. Such successes represent new jobs, a spur to the local and state economies, and more. They also represent achievements that boost the city and state's morale and often can be turned into a "bandwagon" effect that brings other industrial development to a region. In addition, in the case of MCC, it represented an assurance that the "Silicon Prairie" would take its place with the more famous Silicon Valleys, Route 128s, and Research Triangles as technology centers of the future.

Thus, it is not surprising that the full resources of the state of Texas, including unprecedented cooperation between the University of Texas and Texas A & M, were brought to bear in the strategy to attract MCC. Leading businessmen, politicians, and research talents all played key roles in this effort; one publication even called it a "...victory for the whole Southwest."[4] The stakes were obviously high, but this Austin illustration is not unique.

What we are witnessing, in fact, is a level of competition rarely achieved in business itself. Most major industries today have reached the oligopoly stage in which competitors are few. Only the newer industries such as robotics and biotechnology, those yet to be "sorted-out," even begin to approximate the no-holds-barred aggressiveness that we find in the area of industrial development. And, this industrialization competition is not limited to the attraction of high-tech firms and their concomitant cadre of well-compensated, well-educated workers. The war relates to most any type of new industry or potential employer; a low-tech or service firm is preferable to no investment at all.

Just a few recent comments from the business press around the country serve to further emphasize the importance attached to this competition for new development, and its intensity. We read:

...some of the fiercest battles [new industry attraction] waged in the struggling Midwest, which desperately needs to replace dying industries with new ones and to keep healthy companies from fleeing.

Wall Street Journal[5]

[The Denver metro-area]...is fully aware of the battle to attract new businesses and jobs that is raging among cities and states across the country...

Rocky Mountain Business Journal[6]

Southern states have become true believers in international business, with each trying to outmaneuver the others for a larger share of the region's growing foreign investment.

Atlanta Journal and Constitution[7]

Regional efforts to attract new industries and care for existing ones run the risk of starting a zero-sum free-for-all in which states within a region compete with one another with no additional gains for the region as a whole.

New England Business[8]

Truly, the stakes are high and many areas of the United States see themselves vying for economic survival. It is small wonder, therefore, that military terminology in particular has been so commonly used by the press to describe what is taking place.

This chapter establishes a common background among our readers for the chapters that follow. In particular, it provides answers to questions such as, Who are the players in the industrial development game and what actions do they take to attract industry? What is the U.S. government's position regarding internal corporate shifts and direct investment from abroad?, and What forms might this much-sought-after investment take? Finally, this chapter briefly explores some current issues, such as the possible impact of state unitary taxes, enterprise zones, and the new incentive packages on corporate location decisions.

PLAYERS IN THE INDUSTRIAL DEVELOPMENT GAME

Prior to the 1970s, movie moguls seemed to delight in being able to use the phrase "...and a cast of thousands..." at the end of their list of credits. After assessing the numbers involved in economic development, we could well employ the phrase ourselves.

In the United States, states, counties, cities of all sizes, private business groups, chambers of commerce, regional and metropolitan bodies, and countless industrial realtors and land developers are engaged in industry-attraction activities. Often many of their efforts are being conducted within a relatively small geographic area and become redundant and counterproductive. However, increasingly it appears that at least the governmental bodies in a given area are recognizing the advantages of cooperation rather than a "survival of the fittest" mentality. The recent multipage Dallas-Fort Worth Metroplex advertisement in *Fortune* illustrates the clout that can be achieved through a complementary and cooperative effort.

ECONOMIC DEVELOPMENT AT THE STATE LEVEL

The primary economic development forces in the United States are found at the state level. Generally working independently from federal or regional programs, the 50 states find themselves at the forefront of the economic development struggle. Although many of them do devote a considerable share of their time and funds to serving in a coordinative and consultative role for their counties' and cities' development efforts, it is their own direct efforts that command their main attention. These direct activities may range from recruiting forays and advertisements in major media to the establishment of elaborate funding programs and infrastructures.

A March 1984 Stanford Research Institute (SRI) report prepared for Cleveland-based AmeriTrust Corporation states that a "high-growth" scenario for mid-America can only be achieved through "...coordinated public and private action to address deep-seated economic problems."[9] And, more and more it has been recognized that a state's public officials need the support of the state's commercial sector, if their economic development goals are to be achieved. As former Kentucky Governor John Y. Brown, Jr., so aptly stated, "...public and private sectors working together for the benefit of both."[10]

Thus, we see blue-ribbon committees of state influences working hand in hand with the governor in their efforts to attract new jobs and to revitalize or further strengthen their economy. Florida offers just one of many possible illustrations of such a group. To emphasize the importance of economic development, a number of states, including Indiana and Florida, have made their lieutenant governor the chief economic development officer. But, in every instance, the governor remains intimately involved in the process.

Other key individuals, businesses, and agencies generally involved in state economic development efforts include

- state departments of commerce and economic development,
- state port authorities,
- state legislative committees,
- the banking communities,
- key private-sector industrial developers and realtors,
- the public utilities,
- the major state university or universities,
- representatives of the state's leading industries.

Finally, the state economic development efforts also often involve county and city development organizations in an attempt to present a coordinated front to outside businesses.

This brief discussion of state efforts and participants hardly reflects the kind of imaginative economic development programs that are currently under way, programs such as those employing enterprise zones, university research parks, overseas economic development offices, and special entrepreneurial projects. In these activities the mix of actors often is different from the traditional group just noted.

But, the goals of state economic development efforts remain the same. As shown in Exhibit 1.1, some of the objectives reflect a defensive posture, while others are offensive in nature. However, it is only in the prioritization of these objectives that the states differ.

DEVELOPMENT AT THE CITY AND COUNTY LEVEL

Even the smallest municipalities have some unit labeled as their development authority, industrial development association, or economic development corporation. In many, of course, the organization or governmental body is led by a local volunteer or chamber of commerce head. In others, particularly the medium-to-large cities, the agency is directed by a full-time professional, who often has an extensive, trained staff. For example, the town of Hempstead, New York, a Long Island community of some 700,000 people, promotes its opportunities via a department of industry and commerce that includes several professionals.

The prime mover, of course, may well be the private sector in a city. The McAllen (Texas) Chamber of Commerce and the Scranton Plan (Pennsylvania) offer just two examples of extensive private-sector efforts to stimulate economic development. McAllen has a full-time professional economic development staff, as does the Scranton Plan through the Greater Scranton Chamber of Commerce. Playing a substantive role in the Scranton Plan is a group of 150 private and public-sector volunteers, who are involved in adding a "person-to-person" touch to their chamber's activities.

Similarly, county and metropolitan areas tend to have the same range of size and quality in their economic planning and development

EXHIBIT 1.1

State Economic Development Program Goals

Defensive	Offensive
Retain existing industry	Develop new and creative financing programs
Remain competitive with programs offered by other states	Attract new industry and accelerate growth of existing industry
Ensure infrastructure (transport systems, energy, ports, agencies) remains viable	Employ image-enhancement strategies
Remain visible (retain awareness level) via promotional efforts	Realistically target desired growth industries; match strengths with corporate needs
Coordinate city and county strategies	Coordinate (and enhance) city and county strategies
	Improve R & D (research and development) capabilities and training programs of area universities; perhaps establish university research parks

bodies. Although in some instances these groups have duplicated or competed with the municipal efforts, generally they have coordinated and complemented the city agencies or have provided a central impetus for all the cities in their jurisdiction. Madera County, California, illustrates the latter as it represents the cities of Chowchilla and Madera; these two cities joined with the county of Madera "...to form a professionally staffed Industrial Development Commission."[11] Especially noteworthy has been the success of the Indianapolis metropolitan area, and the state of Indiana. Although its county-government format may have helped, it has attracted, among other entities, an NFL team and a major Japanese direct investment (Sony Corporation).

PRIVATE-SECTOR DEVELOPMENT: INDUSTRIAL REALTORS AND DEVELOPERS

A heroic understatement would be that the private-sector plays an active role in the economic development battle. All of these private-sector elements have a special interest in their states', regions', or cities' successes, an interest that we view positively.

CHAMBERS OF COMMERCE AND GROWTH ASSOCIATIONS

There are numerous local and state business associations that focus much of their attention on assisting or directing their appropriate area's economic development efforts. For example, the California Chamber of Commerce has assisted local chambers, such as the City

ILLUSTRATION 1.1

Emphasizes support of a city program by a port authority.

of Fortuna Chamber of Commerce, in the preparation of community economic profiles and other industrial development materials. Similarly, these business associations may perform many of the industry-attraction activities we have already mentioned. For example, the Gainesville Area Chamber of Commerce ran an advertisement in the July-August 1984 issue of *Plants Sites & Parks,* as did governmental bodies such as the city of Norfolk (Virginia) and the state of Arkansas.

UTILITIES AND BANKS

A Vice President of Industrial and Corporate Development at Valley National Bank of Arizona described the bank's efforts on behalf of firms interested in expansion and relocation as "... helping companies to identify market potential, labor availability, tax and government structure as well as real estate and facility planning."[12] Similar efforts to encourage local economic development are offered by many banks throughout the country.

In addition, public utilities have an important stake in expanding current industry or attracting new industry to the areas they serve. Orange and Rockland Utilities (O & R), Pearl River, New York, illustrates the many specific services a utility might provide in an effort to stimulate industrial development. The services that O & R advertises include not only general information, but site-selection and development assistance as well. In a recent advertisement in the *New York Times* special Commercial Real Estate Report section, O & R indicated that it could provide

- site selection assistance, including helicopter flyovers;
- design and building construction (introduction to builders, contractors);
- financial incentives ("...knows how to finance plant construction...");
- energy-related information and expertise;
- training programs;
- regulatory application assistance;
- corporate relocation coordination;
- personal relocation consulting;
- detailed cost comparisons for locations within O & R territory versus outside locations;
- overall project coordination.

Such efforts on behalf of corporations, industrial brokers, and developers certainly demonstrate the interest that O & R and other public utilities have in their areas' economic development efforts.

ILLUSTRATION 1.2

Excellent example of city program support by a utility.

Rochester is an oasis for thirsty businesses.

You'll find the water your business needs in Rochester, New York.

We're in the heart of one of the most water-rich regions in the nation. Our section of New York State includes Lake Ontario, the Genesee River, the Barge Canal, the famous Finger Lakes and dozens of smaller lakes, rivers and streams.

We have a complete network of mains to bring you a plentiful supply of clean, clear water—today and in the future. And excellent sewage systems that are easily accessible.

But Rochester has more than a bountiful water supply. We have a superb workforce. Tax incentives. An abundance of available sites. And much more.

Find out why Kodak, Xerox, Sybron and many more companies call Rochester home—and why you'll like it here, too. Write Jack Clawson, Director of Area Development, Rochester Gas & Electric, 89 East Avenue, Rochester, New York 14649. Or call collect (716) 546-2700, ext. 4975. **RG&E**

Advertisement reprinted with the permission of Jack Clawson, Director of Area Development, Rochester Gas and Electric.

INDUSTRIAL REALTORS/
INDUSTRIAL DEVELOPMENT COMPANIES

Positioned at both ends of the economic development spectrum are a range of real estate or real estate-related companies. A number of private companies are involved in industrial site development, while the industries they hope to attract often employ national, regional, or local real estate firms to assist them in their relocation or location activities.

The Society of Industrial Realtors (SIR) was formed in 1941, and according to its literature, its members "...serve all of the functions of a real estate department for many industrial firms."[12] Among the members' possible site-specific services to its client companies are "...making site surveys; locating existing facilities or sites meeting specific requirements; selling or leasing land, plants and warehouses; counseling on design and construction; estimating value and arranging financing."[13] This organization, and those involved in one or more of the wide range of site-specific activities, include major industrial park developers, investors with large industrial real estate portfolios, and national and international lenders, as well as realtors. Another major association, the National Association of Industrial and Office Parks (NAIOP), numbers in its membership some 1,000 firms specifically involved in industrial and office-park development. These include such firms as land developers and planners, brokers, mortgage bankers, architects, and insurance companies.

Although there are several industrial realtors that are national in scope, the bulk of these firms cover only local or regional areas. Therefore, the more a corporation's relocation or location decision becomes site-specific, the more industrial developers, realtors, and so forth, tend to become involved in the economic development picture. A somewhat unique illustration of a regional industrial development company is offered by the Southern Pacific Industrial Development Company (SP). This company is involved in property development in the 14-state area covered by the railroad and owns some 70 industrial parks itself. According to the company, this total makes it the largest singly owned group of properties in the United States. It is involved in matching client relocation or initial location needs with possible sites within its area and may, in fact, handle the entire selection process. Interestingly enough, SP has indicated that it locates most of its customers on land owned by others.[14]

It is perhaps the multiplicity of *roles* played by the industrial realtors and industrial developers—two especially important private-sector actors—that sometimes creates confusion on the part of the general public. The state, county, and city economic developers have fairly clear objectives: (1) to entice outside corporations to relocate or expand into their area, and (2) to retain current area firms and assist them to grow. Ultimately, however, the corporations attracted to a given state and city must choose a particular site and in these efforts, they typically come into contact with industrial realtors or industrial development companies, or both. In other words, a corporation involved in relocating may work with a real estate specialist, such as The Benswanger Company (Philadelphia), from the outset or it may wait until it has chosen a given city or state prior to being involved with an industrial realtor or contacting an industrial developer. A company's real estate needs might involve purchasing a parcel of land to build a factory or warehouse, leasing space in an office complex, and so forth. And these are the sorts of activities that involve industrial realtors and industrial development corporations, perhaps with some facilitative assistance from the various public- and private-sector economic development groups.

Naturally, the various firms in this broad private-sector category, which even includes the major real estate developers of office space, vary greatly in size, financial strength, services, and types of clients. Trammel Crow Company, for example, has developed office space in 50 cities around the country.[15] Those involved in downtown development in major cities, such as New York or Chicago, may seem to have little in common with the industrial-site developer in a small south eastern city. However, they both might be dealing with a multinational corporation; the former is arranging for a major regional sales office and the latter a local warehouse.

INTERNATIONAL DIRECT INVESTMENT: A TWO-WAY STREET

In 1983, one of the authors participated in a trade program held in the Netherlands, hosted by the Netherlands Graduate School of Business and the Dutch government, that was attended by 200 or more Dutch businessmen. He was not surprised to find representatives from several American states, particularly Missouri and Louisiana, selling the opportunities of investing in and trading with their area. It has been a common practice of states to establish development offices overseas whose primary objectives are (1) to attract direct investment to their locale, and (2) to stimulate the exports of the state's agriculture and commercial sector. Similarly, states and cities will send economic development missions overseas with the same basic objectives. Both the Conference of Mayors and the National League of Cities have, in fact, encouraged such international activities.[16]

A recent U.S. Department of Commerce report has shown that the United States leads the world both in the inward flow of direct investment capital *and* the outward flow of investment dollars. In other words, while the United States is the prime recipient of investment from overseas, its own companies lead the world in investing outside their home country. Clearly then, foreign or international direct investment is an important two-way street.[17]

U.S. Government's Position: Unlike most free-world developed and developing countries, the U.S. government has avoided taking a proactive position in the race for direct investment. In fact, it does not appear to have well-formulated policies regarding international direct investment. On the other hand, the U.S. government, through the Department of Commerce, has been quite aggressive in stimulating and promoting U.S. exports.

Most countries have a policy of encouraging foreign direct investment, under certain prescribed guidelines, and often offer investors various incentives, both financial and nonfinancial. In the United States, of course, it is the various states that handle this function. However, perhaps the biggest difference is that many nations attempt to channel new investment to those parts of their country that lack an industrial base or have higher levels of unemployment. Japan, for example, offers incentives to companies willing to locate in its possibly less attractive northern island area, away from overindustrialized Tokyo and its other commercial centers. In this regard, the United States generally takes a very laissez-faire position and allows foreign direct investors to locate wherever they wish. Although this nonintervention in state economic development efforts undoubtedly has many pluses, it must be recognized that it does lead to a bidding for scarce resources in some locales (real estate and skilled labor, for example) and to long-term population shifts away from some cities and states.

Country Economic Development Activities: Part of this competitive economic development milieu includes another active, aggressive set of players—foreign governments. Although a France or an Ireland may not often be competing directly with U.S. cities and states for direct investment, they are often indirectly battling for the same investment dollars.

For example, the July-August 1984 issue of *Plants Sites & Parks* contained an eight-page special section on South Africa. Included in the special section were a discussion of industrial development opportunities in South Africa and several advertisements by South African public and private organizations. The latter were obviously also designed to attract investment in South Africa. The objective of such an effort by South Africa, of course, is not simply to get a firm in Richmond, Indiana, to relocate in Pietermaritzburg, although this aggressive South African city would likely welcome the Hoosier company. The objective is to get multinational companies to add South Africa to their list of countries where they have overseas subsidiaries. How, then, does this activity indirectly compete with the various states? Simply put, most corporations—even large corporations—have a limited amount of capital to devote to expansion. Therefore, the company's decision to expand may come down to building a new plant somewhere in the United States *or* to establishing a subsidiary in South Africa. In addition, of course, many companies now produce in foreign sites to gain access to particular markets or to access low-cost labor.

Some countries closer to the United States do compete directly with U.S. states, counties, and cities. If a northern company in the United States is seeking to move a plant southward to benefit from lower-priced labor, it might just move to even lower-cost areas such as Puerto Rico, Haiti, or Mexico. Or, a company may decide to locate a facility in Canada in order to be closer to a critical raw material used in its production process or to benefit from tax or other incentives some Canadian cities offer. Thus, the role of foreign country economic development efforts cannot be ignored.

THE DEMAND SIDE: COMPANIES RELOCATING

Every year hundreds, if not thousands, of companies relocate their corporate headquarters or establish new facilities—production plants, warehouses, sales offices, regional administrative offices, "back-office" operations, and so forth.[18] Others grow, but they simply add to their current facilities or acquire space nearby. It is the afore-mentioned, however, that receive the primary attention of the various economic development players. And, it is this group of companies that compose the demand side in our traditional supply-demand analysis.

There are, of course, a myriad of reasons that companies relocate or choose a particular site for their start-up or new facilities. Many are sound business reasons, while others tend to relate to emotional factors, and are highly subjective. One suggestion has been that corporate relocations generally are due to the whims or preferences of the CEO or president; undoubtedly there have been incidences where this has been the primary impetus for a move.

What has been surprising has been the lack of *real* data indicating the reasons for corporate moves of various types. There has been a plethora of research that has sought executive perceptions of various areas of the country ("attractiveness" or image studies) or has asked business people to rank their locational needs or factors that might trigger a move, or both. Recent research conducted for *Crain's Business Chicago*[19] and *Business Week*[20] are illustrative. But, in-depth research regarding firm locational decisions has been limited. Rather, states and cities tend to make the assumption that locational decisions are based on economic concerns and, therefore, offer a potpourri of financially-related incentives to draw industrial investment to their area. Yet, if such decisions actually are motivated merely by CEO whims or preferences, or if life-style or climate is the critical reason for such moves, these efforts are counterproductive both for the areas that gain the new investment and those who "fail to attract the firms."

The former would not need to reduce its taxes or provide other incentives, while the latter could keep upping the ante and creating confusion and dissatisfaction among existing local companies, and still not succeed.

Often, the basic reason for the establishment of a new subsidiary or a home office move may, of course, be based on economic factors. When Toyo Kogyo Company of Japan indicated it was moving closer to a decision on having a U.S. plant, no one questioned the firm's basic objective—the avoidance of U.S. protectionist efforts, including voluntary auto quotas. However, speculation was rampant regarding the factor(s) the company would consider when choosing a specific site within the United States. Its president was quoted as looking at three sites, including a vacant Ford plant in Detroit. Many discounted the latter, however, even though it was the only location he specifically mentioned, because Detroit was a UAW stronghold.[21] In other words, although a foreign firm, such as this Japanese company, may have a reason such as the avoidance of protectionism (tariffs or quotas) for entering the United States, its final location may be selected with an entirely different set of reasons in mind. In the case of Toyo Kogyo, the basic economic advantage of establishing in the United States could be obtained in any state and municipality.

It is our position in the book that too often the location decision has been oversimplified, as with the assumptions that all moves are economically driven or are chosen by the CEO. For example, "Even when a company makes a strong effort to resist political pressures, management is often accused of caving in to the preferences of an individual after a new location has been announced."[22] Although it may be human nature to make such an assumption, it is critical for economic development planners not to fall into such a trap. A single factor, such as the presence of a unitary tax law, may cause a state or city to be eliminated; however, it is rarely a single factor that leads to a final site selection.

In addition, it is our view that companies not only consider and weigh multiple factors when making their site-selection decision, but also employ different criteria for selecting a plant or subsidiary location than they do when making a headquarters move. Further, as the company moves through different stages of narrowing its alternatives, it may use different qualifiers. For example, one company may require a large water supply in order to produce its products. Once those areas with adequate water availability have been identified, then further screening using other factors can take place before that company's final decision is made. In other words, water availability is important in making the initial cut, but rarely if ever is it the primary location criterion.

As marketers, it is our intention to bring a demand- or consumer-oriented focus to the question of how companies make their location decisions. By knowing what companies want and their prioritization of these needs, states, cities, and so forth, can better assess what they can do to match them.

CORPORATE-LOCATION DECISIONS

Because of the extent of their holdings, many large companies have extensive real estate management departments or employ the services of outside real estate management firms or consultants, or both. On the other hand, some major companies have found it to their advantage to lease rather than own the bulk of their real properties, including their production facilities. Wang Laboratories offers just one illustration of a company that makes extensive use of office leasing; the computer company's rapid growth is cited as its reason for taking the lease route.[23] However, it must be recognized that leasing simply provides a good hedge in a most competitive industry. Typical company holdings may include headquarters and other office facilities; production plants; warehouse facilities; sales offices; laboratories; natural resource or raw materials sites, such as mines, agricultural lands, or oil or gas wells; and even retail operations. However, the primary attention of economic development groups is directed to acquiring headquarters or regional offices and production plants.

Naturally, the property needs of companies vary widely. They range from those of a Goodyear Tire and Rubber Company that has all of the types of holdings just listed, to those of a relatively new high-tech firm that may have its entire operations housed in a single facility. Each scale of company, however, has its own attraction for city, state, and other economic development organizations. Lawton, Oklahoma's acquisition of the ultramodern Goodyear production facility in the late 1970s and the NEC Corporation's 1984 decision to locate a manufacturing and assembly plant in Hillsboro, Oregon, naturally result in similar local plaudits, as would any investment of this magnitude. However, Pawtucket and Rhode Island economic development officials found considerable satisfaction in a Massachusetts high-tech company's (Augit, Inc.) selection of that Rhode Island community for just part of its R & D operations.[24] Although the company would employ less than 100 workers, lease its facilities, and is small in Goodyear terms, such an investment is seen as one more step in Rhode Island's high-tech strategy.

Because of this economic development group interest in the two major real estate decision areas—headquarters or plant location, or both—we have chosen these decision areas as the focal point of our research for this book. And, there are important economic (and marketing) reasons for this interest and the need for economic development programs in general.

VIEWING ECONOMIC DEVELOPMENT
IN PRODUCT-LIFE-CYCLE TERMS

ECONOMIC DEVELOPMENT PROGRAMS FROM A MARKETING PERSPECTIVE

New jobs, new wages, prosperity—these are seen as the hallmark of economic development. Even the most economically naive layman recognizes these desirable features of economic development efforts, although its many side effects may cause opposition to these activities.

The economic and political rationales for economic development appear to have been thoroughly explored in the literature of the field. However, there is a need to consider and explain economic development programs from a *marketer's* perspective, first by using a traditional product-life-cycle explanation, a cornerstone of marketing thinking, and then by adding the product-life-cycle perspective employed in our recent book, *Marketing High Technology*. What must be recognized is that every community or city has some current or original economic rationale for its existence. Further, there must be some generator of *primary employment* in the community or area. Although there are many residential or bedroom communities, they rely entirely on a nearby city with its generator of primary employment for their existence. Such primary employment producers can be a state or federal governmental facility—a military installation, state university, or state office center, for example—or a corporate headquarters or production facility, or a service company headquarters facility. However, it has long been recognized by urban economists that industrial (manufacturing) companies have the greatest multiplier effect on a local economy. City and state planners traditionally prefer to have a manufacturing company with both its headquarters and all or part of its production facilities in the community as the primary employment generator. The advantage of industry over a military installation, for example, is that it tends to attract complementary producers or suppliers, which provide parts, subcomponents, materials, and so forth, to the community. Although the headquarters of a major insurance company, a theme park, or a fast-food chain home office provides similar primary employment, it rarely generates the variety of complementary employment that industry does.

On the other hand, the purely residential or bedroom community may have a considerable number of local employment generators, such as service stations, fast-food chains, supermarkets, and motels; its sole raison d'etre is the primary employment base in a nearby city. If the major employer in the area closes, it's "house of cards" begins to collapse.

PRODUCT LIFE CYCLE

What do marketers mean when they talk about the product life cycle or, more specifically, the product life cycle for a given product such as Ivory Soap or Smucker's strawberry preserves? Basically, the product life cycle "...is an attempt to recognize [that there are] distinct stages in the sales history of the product."[25] And, thus, by identifying the appropriate stage of the product's evolution, the marketer is better able to define the marketing strategies and tactics it needs to employ.

Typically, the product life cycle has been presented as an **S**-shaped sales curve; one that moves through or is divided into four distinct stages. The concept recognizes that during a product's life, it moves from an *introductory* stage to a *growth* stage, then to a *maturity* stage and, finally to a *decline* period. Obviously, this description of a product's evolution is somewhat simplistic and not all products can be expected to follow this ideal **S**-shaped formal cycle (Exhibit 1.2).[26] As we have seen in the high-tech industries, for example, some products or breakthroughs move so quickly through the cycle that the stages are hardly discernible, whereas others may have a growth phase that is almost vertical over a fairly lengthy period of time.

But, regardless of the "neatness" of the cyclical pattern, the concept has proven extremely useful for marketing planners. To illustrate, the recognition that a product has reached the maturity stage indicates that most of its target market is familiar with it and that additional sales are likely to be repeat sales. In addition, the maturity stage is typically characterized by rather heavy competition, often price competition. Finally, the maturity stage strongly suggests the need to seek new markets or modify the product in an effort to regenerate the product and move it back on a growth pattern. Without the latter, the ultimate destiny of the product is decline. As shown in Exhibit 1.3, the product can either follow the dotted line (regeneration) or remain on the original curve that leads to decline, and ultimate elimination.

Is the product-life-cycle concept realistic or an academic exercise? Clearly the concept has shown time and again to be a realistic description of the evolutionary process for products of all types. Take the case of three recent Ford automobile models, the Mustang, the Maverick, and the Pinto, which were all introduced at about the same time. The Maverick and Pinto have both passed through the product life cycle, while the Mustang has remained a viable product, Yet, in order to keep the Mustang alive, Ford had to change both its form and its target market. Otherwise, it would have joined the others on the list of hundreds of major automobile models and companies that no longer are found in today's market.

Even America's number one global marketer, the Coca-Cola Company, recently found that its long-time lead product, Coke, was

EXHIBIT 1.2

Traditional Product Life Cycle

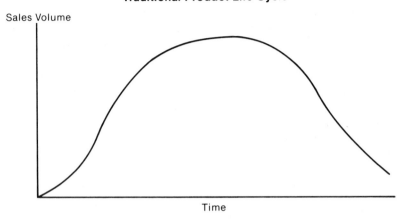

EXHIBIT 1.3

Product Regeneration

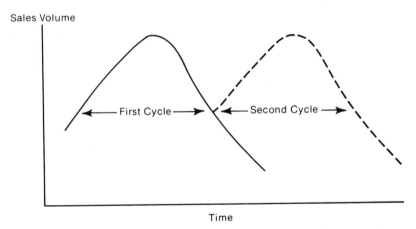

feeling the sharp pangs that come from a maturing market. The beverage company's attempt to sell its product to a different target market by altering the soft drink's flavor has been duly chronicled by the business media. Although one might fault its marketing techniques or execution, the fact remains that the company had correctly assessed the need to do something with its maturing leader. The list of product-life-cycle examples goes on and on, whether we are talking about single products or about brands, companies, or even industries. Some, such as the hula hoop, were recognized at the outset as fads, while others, such as the dirigible, appeared at one time to have virtually limitless life. Yet, each followed the predictable evolution.

COMMUNITY LIFE CYCLE

There is considerable similarity between the product-life-cycle concept and what we prefer to call a *community-life-cycle concept*. For example, let us begin by looking at a city that has one primary employment generator or industry. Basically, this could be the single major-company town—South Bend/Studebaker—or it could be a community that is considered the home base for a whole industry— Akron/automobile and truck tires.

In these single-company or single-industry communities, the life cycle for the community will closely parallel the growth of the company or industry through its maturity stage (Exhibit 1.4). But, its decline will be more gradual and the town will be much less likely to totally cease to be, because as the city's growth moves along with the company's or industry's, new service industries and complementary producers to the company or industry are attracted. This is the boom era for the community. However, as the company or industry matures and begins to flounder, there will be a lengthy period of personnel layoffs. Some of these former workers will leave the area, those who are most mobile or have the most marketable skills, or both, while others will accept other jobs in the community. (Human behavior being what it is, a number of individuals may be willing to take lesser positions, because "they love the environment," "have an attractive home," "want their children to complete their education," etc.) Even when the generator of primary employment finally closes completely, that is, Studebaker shuts down in South Bend or a military installation closes in Wilmington, Ohio, some individuals generally remain, although a few ghost towns do offer a worst-case scenario. Thus, in at least the short run, the community-life-cycle concept rarely follows the product-life-cycle concept to its bitter end; it just plays out a pattern of community frustration. And, unfortunately, there are and have been many, many communities whose whole raison d'etre has been a single company or industry.

Moving one step further in our consideration of the community-life-cycle concept, it is important to recognize that *every* town or city's employment base (and its tax base, etc.) is dependent on an amalgamation of the life cycles of its various sources of primary employment. The Route 128 and Silicon Valley communities are just as tied to their current growth firms and industries, as the Detroits and Clevelands are to their decaying ones. Take the community that has a military installation, some older-line capital-goods producers and a few new rapidly growing R & D-based companies. It is a diversified economy,

28

but one that still has a community life cycle, one that incorporates the life cycle of each of its primary employers. Although this diversified city is not subject to the same type of shock that the single-industry community experiences when a primary employer hits its decline, it still will not go unscathed. This has led many communities to take proactive steps that are somewhat analogous to those we have recently seen occurring in the product life cycles of some of the newer high-tech firms.

EXHIBIT 1.4

Community-Life-Cycle Concept

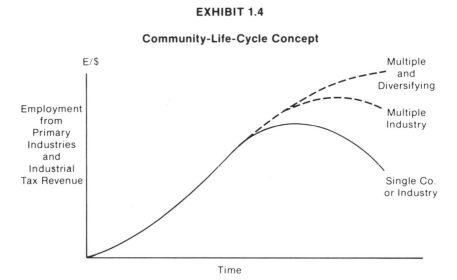

The rapid state-of-the-art change in industries, such as bio-technology, lasers, and microcomputers, has meant that before a product or process has completed its growth stage, new products or processes have been introduced that lead to a regeneration of the growth process, a regeneration that occurs well before current growth is over, much less the beginning of maturity.

This, in effect, is what aggressive economic development efforts should be all about. By careful planning, a community's life cycle could be more akin to the high-tech product life cycle. This would require it to attempt to attract new industry or encourage the further development, even regeneration, of existing industry, prior to the loss of any primary employment due to such an employer hitting its decline stage. A steady, planned infusion of new primary employment generating sources helps to offset the natural loss of those firms completing their life cycle, or those which have chosen to move. What must be stressed, however, is the need for the city's economic development group or groups to focus their attention on attracting primary employment generators. Although a new McDonald's may employ 35 workers, its ability to remain in business is dependent on the primary employment generators in the area, that is, the suppliers of the disposable personal income needed to buy a Big Mac.

Therefore, we suggest that a city's goal (and a state's objective for its cities) should be to constantly extend and regenerate its life cycle. Such a goal recognizes the finite life of almost any industry and makes it imperative for a community to estimate the current stage of each of its primary employers. As an illustration, suppose you have a city that has a research hospital, a university, and an air force base among its prime employers. You need to ask whether the military is becoming less dependent on the type of training being offered at your local base. If so, the installation may be approaching or may have reached the decline stage. Similarly, you need to determine to what extent your university's primary offerings or your hospital's research focus are remaining in the growth stage of their respective fields. This type of hard assessment is necessary to avoid some of the worst-case scenarios suggested earlier. Further, it not only indicates the need to step up new industry-attraction efforts, but may cause the community to take the lead in helping current primary employers become more state-of-the-art. For example, the university could be assisted in adding a research park or it might be helped in funding new research chairs to attract top-flight academics in highly relevant fields.

In summary, we often hear community representatives speak quite critically of economic development efforts. "We are happy with the way things are...we do *not* wish to expand the community further." Such a complacent view, of course, is fraught with risk. As the community's primary employment base evolves, the need for some form of regeneration increases. Perhaps by viewing a city or town in terms of its community life cycle and drawing on the experience evidenced by the product-life-cycle concept, the problems and worst-case scenarios that so many cities have experienced can be avoided.

Vignettes

GM WALTZES WITH TENNESSEE*

Tennessee's success in luring General Motors' Saturn plant to Spring Hill, near Nashville, was no overnight success: The state had been wooing GM facilities for years. In fact, Tennessee has a finely tuned economic development program meant to recruit business in the industrial northern states. Moreover, it has budgeted for the people and advertising necessary to implement its program.

Just why GM was persuaded to locate in Tennessee is not public information. Only GM knows for sure. Although Tennessee's incentive package was similar to the packages offered by a number of competing states, several other factors evidently made the difference:

- Location. Tennessee is within 500 miles of 50% of the U.S. population, minimizing automobile shipping costs.
- Right-to-work law. Even though GM and the United Automobile Workers have already negotiated a revolutionary agreement for Saturn workers, many of the nearby firms supplying Saturn will undoubtedly be nonunion, which will have a favorable cost effect.
- Work ethic. Saturn president William E. Hoglund confirmed that the sincerity, honesty, and attitudes of Tennessee's people were important considerations.
- Fresh attitude. GM was looking for workers without preconceived notions about how automobiles should be produced, which the traditional automobile manufacturing states would not have provided.
- Long-term commitment to educational improvement.
- Proximity to and competitive synergy with Nissan, also located in middle Tennessee, and its suppliers. General Motors was also impressed with Nissan's experience in the state.
- Lamar Alexander, the probusiness and businesslike governor, was a real plus.
- Tennessee's ranking of tenth in Alexander Grant & Company's study of manufacturing climates in the 50 states.

Interestingly, Governor Alexander did not participate in the Saturn "pitch" by various governors on the Phil Donahue network television show, nor did he personally visit Detroit. Tennessee under Alexander has avoided razzle-dazzle in favor of a more substantive, factual approach and low-key salesmanship, backed by truly professional advertising creativity and strategy. (For example, the accompanying advertisement entitled "Well, Saturn Finally Found Its Home...In Spring Hill, Tennessee," appeared in the *Wall Street Journal* on August 8 and 12, 1985; *USA Today* on August 5 and 9, 1985; the *New York Times* and the *Washington Post*, both on August 11, 1985; and the

Nihon Keizai Shimbun in Tokyo on August 8, 1985, all within a few days of GM's announcement.) Business people apparently find Alexander to be simpatico, not one to talk one way towards business and act another.

---

*Based partly on Karle, D. (1985, August 4). Fine-tuning pays off for Tennessee efforts. The *Plain Dealer*, p. 2B; What do businesses see in Tennessee? (1985, August 4). The *Plain Dealer*, pp. 1B-2B; and Holusha, J. (1985, August 4). Saturn division finds a home in the heartland. The *New York Times*, p. E5.

WELL, SATURN FINALLY FOUND ITS HOME... IN SPRING HILL, TENNESSEE.

Nobody can remember when there was more commotion about where to put a plant.

General Motors looked everywhere for the best place to put its $5 billion Saturn plant. The biggest corporation in the world was making the largest one-time investment in U.S. history.

Three banks of GM computers analyzed 1000 sites in 38 states. Then the top brass answered the bottom line question: *Where is the best place in America to build the highest quality car at the lowest cost, a small car that will compete with the Japanese imports?*

Their answer: Spring Hill, Tennessee, just 30 miles south of Nashville.

We are grateful for their decision, but no one here is much surprised. Nissan made the same kind of decision in 1980 when, after six years of study, it decided to put the largest overseas Japanese investment in Smyrna, Tennessee.

It worked. Now, Nissan makes 250,000 cars and trucks a year in Tennessee including the Sentra, America's largest selling small "import."

In fact, Tennessee has attracted ten percent of all the Japanese capital investment in the United States.

WHY HAVE THE LARGEST AMERICAN AND JAPANESE INVESTMENTS COME TO TENNESSEE? I CAN THINK OF THREE GOOD REASONS.

1. Tennessee is at the center of things— As a result, it costs less to make Saturn here and sell it everywhere in the USA.

We don't take credit for this advantage. We thank God and the Founding Fathers for putting Tennessee within 500 miles of three-fourths of the U.S. population. *GM's analysis—like Nissan's—showed that transportation costs are so important that you can't afford to be far outside the center of your market.* That's why Federal Express flies all its packages to Memphis every night: Memphis is America's Distribution Center.

See for yourself. Draw the circles any way you like and look who's at the center.

2. Just being in Tennessee does some things that orders from Detroit and Tokyo can't do —Here I'm talking about quality.

There's no delicate way to say this: tomorrow's jobs are coming to Tennessee because

Tennesseans still hold to yesterday's values and too many other places have lost them.

For example, we are careful with the dollar. Our taxes are among the nation's lowest. We have no payroll tax and no unitary tax. We have reduced our state debt 24 percent in six years. Know anyone else who has done that?

We still believe in rewarding people for doing

things well. Tennessee is the only state to pay teachers more for teaching well, although 26 other states are following our lead. Our legislature has invested $45 million in Centers and Chairs of Excellence at our universities. For us, Better Schools is Priority 1 through 10.

And we believe that giving people a choice is the American way. Memphis and other Tennessee school districts are bringing families back into the public schools by giving parents a choice of the public school their child attends. And our right-to-work law guarantees every Tennessean a choice about whether to join a union.

We won't be surprised to see a little friendly competition between Nissan workers making Sentras in Smyrna and Saturn workers, only 30 miles away in Spring Hill. We believe in that, too. Competition encourages efficient work practices, the lowest costs and the highest quality.

Thrift. Excellence. Choice. Competition. Yesterday's values helping to create an environment that is irresistible to companies who want tomorrow's jobs done right.

3. Then, there's Tennessee Homecoming '86 —You'll have to see this for yourself.

All next year we will celebrate the 3,000 places Tennesseans proudly call home. It'll be part history lesson, part family reunion and part good old-fashioned hoedown. I'm still trying to figure how I'm going to get to all of the 500 community celebrations that are already planned.

Minnie Pearl is co-chairman of Homecoming. She helped make a huge quilt with a patch for each place with a name in her home county. I took five of my fellow Governors to see it last August on Hickman County Heritage Day.

Alex Haley–the other co-chairman–is helping get together our literary festival for Tennessee writers and storytellers.

TOMORROW'S JOBS, YESTERDAY'S VALUES.

Peter Jenkins is also involved in Homecoming. You may remember that Peter and his wife, Barbara, walked across America in the 1970's, living and working with people for six years. After that walk they knew America as well as anybody. And guess where they decided to call home?

Spring Hill, Tennessee.

Probably for a lot of the same reasons Saturn and its employees will feel right at home there. Probably for the same reasons Rand McNally keeps mentioning Nashville and Knoxville and Johnson City and Kingsport and Bristol as among the best places to live in America.

For the same reason Komatsu put its new headquarters in Chattanooga and Florida Steel found a new home in Jackson.

In these complicated times it just makes sense to live and work in a place where the people who operate the world's fastest technology can keep their feet on the ground. Bill Hoglund, Saturn's new President, wants to be very careful about bringing in this new plant. That's good news for everybody in Spring Hill.

We are glad to be getting tomorrow's jobs, but that means we will have to work twice as hard to keep yesterday's values.

After all, that's what helped attract Saturn here in the first place. We know they will want to work right along side us to preserve the way we live.

NOW, WHAT ABOUT YOU? IF YOU'RE LOOKING FOR A HOME, TRY TENNESSEE.

The largest *American* investment found a home in Tennessee.

The largest *Japanese* investment found a home in Tennessee.

What about a home for your new investment? Here's my telephone number: (615) 741-2001. I hope you'll call me about it today.

We may even get you interested enough to come to Tennessee Homecoming '86 and find out about Tennessee and Tennesseans for yourself.

Lamar Alexander
Lamar Alexander
Governor

Tennessee
We're proud of our country

THE NETHERLANDS, IRELAND, AND BELGIUM: THREE PROACTIVE EUROPEAN COMMUNITIES

ECONOMIC DEVELOPERS

As U.S. companies continue to internationalize in ways ranging from outsourcing to a matrix of wholly owned subsidiaries, the industrial and economic development programs of foreign governments become of increasing interest to American business (and public- and private-sector economic developers). While a few countries have attained reputations as mere tax havens or short-term solutions to U.S. competitiveness problems, others offer solid, long-term opportunities to smaller and medium-sized companies. These latter, unlike their multinational corporation counterparts, have heretofore served overseas markets primarily via exports and made little, if any, use of foreign production to remain competitive in the United States.

Especially noteworthy in the 1980s has been the effort of key European Economic Community (EEC) countries to attract "foreign companies," particularly U.S. companies. In contrast to the Koreas, Taiwans, and Mexicos that use lower-cost labor as their primary incentives, many EEC countries have wage rates comparable to those in the States. And, in fact, some have socially-oriented labor rules that may put them, to some extent, at a labor disadvantage. So what do these countries have to offer? One thing, of course, is virtually duty-free access to a dozen or so primary markets, a marketplace comparable in buying power to the United States. This is a critical advantage for many U.S. companies that have been forced offshore by the superdollar. Possibly equally important, however, is these countries' understanding of a business's needs and desires. To illustrate this current proactive economic development effort by a few EEC countries, we have selected Belgium, although we were tempted by the excellent advertising programs of Ireland and the Netherlands to pick those countries. Belgium, however, has been extremely "demand-side tuned," especially in the programs that it offers to the high-tech and smaller to medium-sized firms, and, thus, is the focus for this vignette.

BELGIUM

One statement in the Belgian Ministry of Economic Affairs' attractive brochure, *New Economic Opportunities in Belgium,* really capsules our raison d'etre for selecting Belgium. Under the heading, "A Market Oriented Industrial Policy for the Renewal of Our Industrial Structure and Export Based New Growth," is the following:

Restoring the competitive edge of our enterprises and putting our public finances on a sound footing are the necessary prerequisites for the success of measures aimed at reconversion and industrial renewal. Under the motto 'adapt to change' new investments have been created for the fundamental overhaul of our industrial structure on a market oriented basis.

Translated into action, this has meant that the Belgians directed their attention to determining the *needs* of the types of companies they wished to attract. Highly desirous of new technology, as are all developed and developing countries, Belgium took the extra effort to determine what smaller, more innovative companies need during their earlier growth periods. These are the kinds of needs, in fact, that have been characteristic of Route 128, Silicon Valley, and Research Triangle companies.

Because a critical early-on concern is capital—venture capital— "...the Belgian government has worked out an intensive aid scheme to encourage venture capital in Belgium. The aid scheme consists of fiscal measures in favor of all parties involved, from the innovation company down to those providing the venture capital and even the private investor." What is now in place is an impressive set of tax incentives, including tax-free enterprise zones, that are especially appropriate for the smaller enterprise. Couple these tax benefits with a wide range of other investment incentives, a strong transportation system, and duty-free access to the EEC, and the Belgium package is formidable.

In addition, the Belgian government has aggressively sold this package in the United States, a further extension of its proactive efforts. For example, the Commercial Officer of the Consulate General of Belgium, Chicago, and a representative from the Port of Antwerp, participated in the 40th Annual Cleveland World Trade Conference in May 1985.

ILLUSTRATION 1.4

Campaign designed to show Ireland's strength, historically and today.

School of Engineering, Trinity College, Dublin

IN A 16TH CENTURY IRISH UNIVERSITY: 21ST CENTURY KNOWLEDGE.

The Irish.
The Irish have always had a hunger and respect for education. Today, over 40% of our college students choose science and technology.
Ireland.
A member of the European Common Market. Noted for its favorable government attitudes towards business. The most profitable industrial location in Europe for US manufacturers.

Ireland. Home of the Irish. The young Europeans.

IDA Ireland ❖
INDUSTRIAL DEVELOPMENT AUTHORITY

IDA Ireland has offices in New York (212) 972 1000; Chicago (312) 644 7474; Cleveland (216) 861 0305/6; Los Angeles (213) 809 0081; Menlo Park, Calif. (415) 854 1800); Houston (713) 965 0092; Boston (617) 367 8905; Fort Lauderdale (305) 785 9430; Atlanta (404) 351 8474

This announcement is published by IDA Ireland, 9 Grand Central Towers, East 45th Street, New York 10017, which is registered under the Foreign Agents Registration Act, is amended, as an agent of the Government of Ireland. This material is filed with the Department of Justice where the required registration statement is available for public inspection. Registration does not indicate approval of the contents by the United States Government.

REPUBLIC OF IRELAND

"WE'RE THE YOUNG EUROPEANS."

Advertisement reprinted with the permission of John Lyons, Director, North America—IDA—Ireland.

ILLUSTRATION 1.5

Using location as an important asset.

Right in the Center.

Put your company right in the center of the $3 trillion European market. The Netherlands. You'll discover the distinct advantages more than 1,000 U.S. companies now get by doing business from The Netherlands: Tariff-free trade to the EEC. Easy access to other markets in Europe, the Middle East and Africa.

One of the world's most extensive and cost-efficient transportation and distribution networks. A well educated, highly productive, multi-lingual work force. Attractive investment incentives and readily available financing.

In other words, one of Europe's most sophisticated international business communities. But what else would you expect from the country multinationals such as Philips, Shell and Unilever call home?

For further details, write to the Center: The Netherlands Industrial Commission, One Rockefeller Plaza, New York, New York 10020. Or call (212) 246-1434.

The Netherlands

Circle Reader Service Card No. 135

PACIFIC NORTHWEST: TOKYO TO TIMBERLAND

The Portland, Oregon/Vancouver, British Columbia area is one of the most scenic in all North America. Recently, it has been alternately dubbed "the Timberlands" and "the Silicon [Rain] Forest," as it attempts to balance the forces of economic and industrial development with a genuine desire to remain environmentally "whole." Oregon, in particular, has wrestled with the ongoing conflict between quality of life (nature/frontier style) and the need to attract jobs to the state. Even in the early 1980s, Oregon retained the image of being the most environmentally-sensitive state, as well as having an upper-New England-like independence. And, Oregonians seemed to have little tolerance for or understanding of the kinds of smog, traffic, and other woes that had beset its neighbor, California.

By 1982, however, it became apparent that changes in Oregon's outlook were needed if the state was to solve its unemployment problem. Oregonians "...knew they did not want their state to become another Silicon Valley...but maybe it could be another North Carolina."[27] What we have seen since that time are moves that would undoubtedly have been considered shocking in the 1970s, for example, Oregon's modification of its unitary tax in response to Japanese business insistence. Still, such actions have a strong ring of pragmatism when one notes the devastating problems in the state's lumber industry.

What has happened in Oregon offers an excellent and unfortunate illustration of the community-life-cycle concept in action, but only on a statewide basis. To a great extent, Oregon has been dependent on a single commodity—lumber. As competition began to sap this commodity's local strength, the downward slope of its life cycle was mirrored in the state's economy. In the face of what the *New York Times* calls the "flight from the timberlands,"[28] the growing presence of Japanese electronics companies have helped to fill the void in Oregon and its more northern neighbors. The state's current efforts to diversify its industry, such as through electronics, to become less dependent on the volatile lumber market, represents a start. This is the kind of action other single-industry communities and states need to take to survive over the long haul.

REFERENCES

1. Inman, W.H. (December 1984). The Texas Draw. *Texas Business*, p. 49.
2. Hall, M. (January 1985). Governor Celeste's mid-term review. *Ohio Business*, p. 43.
3. Rothman, M. (September 2, 1985). A software success story in the Rust Bowl. *Business Week*, p. 82.
4. Naisbitt, J. (1982). *Megatrends*. New York: Warner Books.
5. Lancaster, H. (1983, December 28). Competing by states to lure firms turns into a fierce struggle. *Wall Street Journal*, p. 1.
6. Meadows, J.B. (1984, March 26). Selling the metro area with style. *Rocky Mountain Business Journal*, p. 11.
7. Saporta, M. (1984, February 24). Foreigners welcome in Dixie [Southeast Economic Survey section]. The *Atlanta Journal and Constitution*. p. 16E.
8. Brooks, S. (1984, April 2). How huge U.S. deficits affect regional growth. *New England Business*, p. 45.
9. SRI International. (1984, March). *Choosing A Future: Steps to Revitalize the Mid American Economy Over the Next Decade*, p. 2. (Menlo Park, CA).
10. New local economic push in Kentucky *Plants Sites & Parks*, January-February 1983, p. 33.
11. Literature provided the authors by Robert E. Tremaine, Executive Director, Madera County Industrial Development Commission.
12. Callahan, J.J. Letter to author, October 27, 1982.
13. Society of Industrial Realtors® brochure available from the Society of Indusrial Realtors®, 777 Fourteenth Street, NW, Washington, DC 20005.
14. *Southern Pacific: Putting industry on the right track*, p. 5. Brochure available from Southern Pacific Development Company, One Market Plaza, San Francisco, CA 94105.
15. Wald, M.L. (1984, May 13). Back offices disperse from downtowns. (commercial real estate report). The *New York Times*, p. 58.
16. Robbins, W. (1984, June 24). Cities going where the business is. The *New York Times*, p. E3.
17. U.S. Department of Commerce. (1984, August). *International direct investment: global trends and the U.S. role*. Washington, DC.
18. Wald, p. 60.
19. Goodman, J.E. (1984, September 17-23). Chicago image poor among execs' study. *Crain's Chicago Business*, p. l77.
20. Hillkirk, J. (1984, October 5). North Carolina top pick for new industry. *USA Today*, p. 1.
21. Woutat, D. (1984, March 16). Toyota moves closer to establishing auto plant in the U.S. *Wall Street Journal*, p. 8.
22. Harding, C.F. (1982, September/October). Company politics in plant location. *Industrial Development*, p. 19.
23. Corporate real estate investment: The undiscovered road to higher profits. *Site Selection Handbook*, February 1983, p. 10.
24. R.I.'s 'Greenhouse' down but not out, *Plants Sites & Parks*, September-October, 1984, p. 117.

25. Kotler, P. (1980). *Marketing management: Analysis, planning, and control* (4th ed.). Englewood Cliffs, NJ: Prentice-Hall, Inc. 1980.
26. Kotler, p. 290.
27. Brennan, S. (1984, June). Life in the Silicon Rain Forest. *Inc.*, p. 114.
28. Sharp, K. (1985, June 16). An exodus from the timberlands; A regional report: The Pacific Northwest. *New York Times*, p. F17.

2

TRENDS IN ECONOMIC DEVELOPMENT: A LOOK AT THE FUTURE

EXECUTIVE SUMMARY

Economic development is a dynamic field. If there are any doubters, a look at the number of current trends should resolve their skepticism. There is a continued escalation in the type and quality of programs that are being developed by U.S. cities and states, as well as by overseas economic development organizations. Two words seem to best capture what we have seen during our extensive review of current programs, *sophistication* and *professionalism.* There is, of course, considerable room for growth and improvement; this is reflected in the trends.

We have identified 11 trends that we feel are having, or will have, a major impact on economic development. These range from the increased importance that is now being given to fostering local start-ups and local expansions to international joint ventures between foreign and U.S. states or cities, or both. (The latter are formed for the mutual assistance of the companies in each locale.)

Two trends are especially noteworthy. One is the rapid growth in importance of business incubators, some of which are formed with private-sector funding; others are started by public-sector capital. Because business incubators are designed to assist high-potential new businesses during their formative and often most difficult months and years, their establishment is most compatible with city and state industrialization efforts. The business-incubator concept has captured the fancy of business and government officials at all levels, and their numbers seem to be increasing exponentially.

Even more dramatic is a 12th trend we have identified, one we have chosen to term a *megatrend*, a la Naisbitt. This is the increased impact that foreign economic development efforts, when coupled with a U.S. corporate mindset that says "let us explore new production locations wherever feasible," can be expected to have in the coming years. Countries such as France, Japan, and Ireland are taking, or have taken, proactive development steps designed to ensure their niche in future worldwide industrial expansion. Like U.S. cities and states, their target is often the high-technology industries. And, their efforts often place them in direct competition with potential expansion sites in the states. (To date, there is little to suggest that U.S. corporations have become so multinational in philosophy that they evaluate foreign sites when they are considering headquarters-type moves.) Given the type of incentive packages, and so forth, that foreign governments can offer to direct investors, this relatively new and dramatically increasing form of competition can be considered formidable.

An important attribute of economic development, and one that offers promise that a marketing orientation can become "accepted practice," is that the field (and those comprising it) are flexible. Practitioners, in fact, would seem to be more wedded to change than to tradition. Perhaps the only exception is that many economic planners still see financial considerations to be preeminent (or all-important) to corporate-location decision makers.

Economic development is characterized today by a number of trends and likely future activities; some may be viewed positively and others may have negative implications for state and local planners in particular. This chapter considers a few of those trends that may chart new avenues for the field. These trends include back-office decentralization, start-up support (and corporate retention efforts), unitary tax repeal (and other prohibitive legislation), private research consortia, and enterprise zones. The remainder of the chapter focuses on one overriding trend, a trend that we feel may have the single greatest impact of all on city and state economic development efforts—the growing attractiveness of establishing foreign production subsidiaries and its corollary, the growing aggressiveness of foreign country and city industrial development efforts. This trend has been exacerbated by the current "superdollar era," the evolution of the European Community, and the increase in foreign competition for markets in the United States.

TREND 1: BACK-OFFICE DECENTRALIZATION

Many companies have begun to decentralize some of their routine home-office activities from high-cost central-city locations to regional sites, that is, they have found it advantageous to pull back from metropolitan centers. Operations such as the accounting department, the data-processing division, and the billing group illustrate the "back-office" activities that are included in such decentralization efforts. Technology improvements have made headquarters-related moves, such as American Express' shift of its credit-card processing operations from New York City to Phoenix and Ft. Lauderdale, feasible.[1] However, it is the higher space-rental costs in central-city office locations and the difficulty in attracting office workers to such downtown sites at a reasonable cost that has also given the impetus to this trend. With the present increases in new and existing prime-space costs in cities such as New York, Chicago, and San Francisco—relative to small communities nationwide—this trend will continue.

Further fueling such moves have been some bolder actions by states. South Dakota, for example, changed its state law to eliminate the interest ceiling, and thus enticed "...Citibank to move its entire credit-card division from Manhattan to Sioux Falls."[2] These are not isolated examples. Part of the raison d'etre for major city, downtown locations was "cultural." There was the belief that "competent office workers could only be found in the New Yorks, Chicagos, and L.A.s" and that "good employees would not move to the sticks." Now, however, some of these cultural beliefs have proven to be myths and we see moves such as Harcourt Brace Jovanovich's shift to Orlando and those of Citibank and American Express.

TREND 2: SUPPORT FOR LOCAL START-UPS/ INDUSTRY RETENTION

Economic development groups, chambers of commerce, and so forth, still hope to catch "the big fish"; an announcement that a large domestic or foreign firm is looking for a plant site will draw as much (if not more) attention today as it did in the past. However, we now find that states and cities are increasingly looking for ways to help an existing local company expand or remain viable, and to assist new entrepreneurial ventures to get under way. Some states and cities, in fact, have formed venture-capital groups.

A major criticism that was often voiced over the years by local companies was that a city or slate was using its tax dollars to offer tax incentives to outsiders, and let the locals "be damned." To illustrate, Ford was perhaps rightly indignant a few years ago when Ohio and the Cleveland-area communities were offering Volkswagen "the moon" to locate there while Ford was a leading local employer having a tough time competing costwise with foreign auto producers. Now numerous communities, such as Syracuse, New York,[3] have been directing attention to local corporate retention and start-ups. It is a simple recognition that retaining firms who already have a commitment to an area and which have growth potential may be a more attractive community investment than constantly engaging in battles for outside firms, and often achieving a "low hit rate." Such efforts, of course, can be mutually exclusive, and there appears to be excellent advantages to employing a dual strategy.

TREND 3: UNIVERSITY RESEARCH PARKS

When we studied the high-technology industries, we noted that "...the hubs of high-tech innovativeness in the United States are proximate to the 'finest research universities.' "[4] This fact has not been ignored by economic developers and has led to a proliferation of public and private high-technology research centers that are tied to local universities. Certainly, a hallmark of Silicon Valley, Route 128, and the Research Triangle has been the access to major research-oriented universities. One is somewhat trapped in a "chicken-and-egg" situation when trying to determine which comes first, the research-orientation of an area or the university-related involvements.

To some, however, the answer is clear; Virginia felt it necessary to carve out a university-research base where none was in place.[5] In other instances, the university or universities developed their own research park, either with or without public funding. Yale and Rensselaer Polytechnic Institute offer prime illustrations of private schools establishing such research parks.[6] As the efforts to obtain the industries of the future—the high-tech industries—expand, there will be a concomitant increase in university research parks.

TREND 4: UNITARY TAX REPEAL

A particularly onerous form of taxation employed by a dozen or so states (1984 figures) is the unitary tax. This form of tax "...involves a formula in which a state determines a multinational company's (MNC) base income...from the value of its products produced in the state and from a percentage of [its] worldwide sales, after factoring in such items as payroll and property."[7] This taxing method has been sharply criticized by MNCs as a form of double taxation; it has led some companies to avoid investing in states that impose such taxes. Indiana and Oregon are recent examples of states that have replaced their unitary tax laws, and several other states are considering such repeals. Perhaps the most interesting feature of the repeal "pressures" has been the lobbying efforts of the Japanese business community and the impact these efforts have had on state legislatures. What is suggested by this tax brouhaha is that state legislators and corporate leaders need to work more closely as corporate tax legislation is developed. In other words, a type of business-government economic marriage, like the one that has been followed in Switzerland for years, might be appropriate in the United States.

TREND 5: PRIVATE RESEARCH CONSORTIA AS INVESTORS

Just as Silicon Valley's success led to a plethora of clones—the Silicon [Rain] Forest and the Silicon Prairie, for example—the computer-related research joint venture of 19 companies as Microelectronics and Computer Technology Corporation (MCC) in Austin, Texas, appears to be setting a similar trend. Such consortia have the effect of producing a level of R & D funding that is comparable to that generated by similar groups in Western Europe and Japan. To local economic developers the attraction of such a consortia investment is somewhat akin to a blue-collar worker winning a $20 million state lottery. In a single coup, the city and state becomes a future state-of-the-art leader in a form of technology, plus it makes a most positive impact on 19 or 11 (or whatever) individual leading companies. It is small wonder that the battle waged and won by Austin has marked it as

U.S. growth center for the next decade. With R & D costs spiraling to the point that few corporations, even the GMs and IBMs, can stand alone, such consortia will increase in the years ahead and offer real opportunities for economic development groups. The recently proposed defense-industry software consortia is a case in point.[8]

TREND 6: INDUSTRIAL DEVELOPMENT/ HIGH-TECH BACKLASH

We would not suggest that interest in industrial development will abate or that there is any national ground swell toward less industrialization. However, there has been some increase in the number of economic development dissenters or critics, individuals who feel that economic development has failed to achieve its promises. To some extent the miracles to be achieved from new industry have been oversold, particularly in terms of the time required for its effects to be felt. Undoubtedly, much of the MNCs' criticism in the developing world has resulted from the failure of such companies to provide "instant utopias." The same can be said for a new plant or a research park in a U.S. community.

Of course, there have always been those who failed to see economic development as progress. Witness the lengthy political struggle that occurred in Austin, Texas, during its environmentalist local government era. However, much of the criticism seems to be directed toward the real glamorous investments, the high-tech companies. Complaints in Massachusetts have been that a company may be high in technology but still low in terms of its total employment. At the other end of the country, some residents in famed Silicon Valley have said that "enough is enough in terms of crowding". Others found chemical waste levels to be an unexpected "bonus" from smokeless industry. In particular, history has suggested that expectations often run too high and, thus, some continued dissatisfaction can be expected. Similarly, even Houston has found it necessary to affect some development-related control; the benefit of growth seems inevitably to be crowds.[9]

TREND 7: ENTERPRISE ZONE ACCELERATION

States have been much quicker to accept and adopt the enterprise zone (EZ) concept than has the federal government, although the latter first promoted such programs. Basically, EZs are designed to redirect the flow of both new investment and reinvestment toward pockets of high unemployment or scarce development. Benefits of EZs are perceived to include the increased hiring of the disadvantaged, site improvement, a semblance of private urban renewal, the restoration of an economic and tax base, or the development of a new center where none previously existed; and a general social improvement in the affected environment.

National governments have long used incentive packages to "balance" development activities. Many U.S. business people have rigorously complained about the barriers to investment in Japan. However, in fact, Japan to a great extent welcomes investment in particular areas of the country, but makes it more difficult to establish business in overcrowded locales such as Tokyo and Yokohama. France is another country that has used incentives similar to those offered by EZs in order to shift investment flows to pockets of underdevelopment and unemployment. In particular, Paris is the focal point of French concerns; everyone (business and worker alike) seems to be attracted by this most sophisticated of cities. The French government was concerned that Paris was drawing too many unskilled, unemployed workers from the hinterland, and that national development efforts were needed to stem the flow, that is to make it attractive employmentwise to remain in a city such as Grenoble, for example. Similar examples could be given for most major developed and developing countries; Brazil's construction of Brasilia in an effort to lure population swells away from Rio and Sao Paulo is a case in point.

If all of this sounds familiar, it should! We have seen similar intracity/intrastate, and interstate migrations of workers in the United States over the years, but there have been limited organized federal-level efforts to correct for the resulting socioeconomic imbalances. (Perhaps some might include the NRA and WPA legislation in such efforts, but these were relatively short-term, problem-specific acts.) The proposed federal EZ legislation introduced in 1980 by Congressmen Jack Kemp and Robert Garcia was an initial step in this direction.

Regardless of what will happen at the federal level, it appears that the EZ trend will continue. Nearly half the states already have enacted some form of EZ legislation, although individual laws do vary widely in form. Some states, such as Oklahoma, have no specific limit to the number of EZ designations, although most set maximum numbers. Also, they vary widely in the specific incentives offered. The typical legislation, however, does focus on some form of tax inducement, such as credits or elimination, and regulatory relief as a means of encouraging businesses (often smaller) to operate in specific areas and to hire and train disadvantaged workers.[10] The Louisville EZ, one of four Kentucky zones, illustrates why some cities have been enthusiastic about the legislation. During its first year of operation (mid-1983 to mid-1984), it attracted 25 businesses and generated (or preserved) 670 jobs.[11]

TREND 8: FORMAL INTRASTATE OR INTERSTATE PROGRAMS

Any discussion of economic development trends would be remiss if it failed to include the new, and highly sophisticated, intrastate and interstate regional development programs now under way. These point to a future level of cooperative effort that has either been unheard of or has met with limited success in the past. The ever-present danger in these regional efforts, regardless of whether they are in-state or bridge states, lies in the possibility of jealousy or self-interest driving a wedge between participants. The lessons gained from international-level regional integration offers us important insight in this regard. Both the East African Community and the Central American Common Market failed because some members saw others getting a "bigger share of the pie." A true test of a regional development effort occurs when State (or City) A gets a major invest-ment, but States (or Cities) B and C do not. As this pattern is repeated, even the tightest alliances will be tested.

The Ben Franklin Partnership Program fostered by the Pennsylvania Department of Commerce and the Baltimore-Washington Common Market offers examples of such regional efforts. The Pennsylvania plan establishes four regional advanced technology centers (North East Tier, Southeast Pennsylvania, Western Pennsylvania, and Cen-tral/Northern Pennsylvania). Each of the four centers unites the efforts of the state, the local area business, and area universities to attract new businesses or upgrade existing industry.

On the other hand, the Baltimore-Washington Common Market seeks to blend the economic and life-style attributes of two major cities and related suburbs into a most marketable package. Calling itself the "Land of Pleasant Living," the Common Market presents an economic unit that ranks fourth among metropolitan areas. (This regional association is an alliance of the business communities in 17 contiguous counties of Maryland and Virginia, as well as the District of Columbia.) Again, the concept appears good and, in fact, the association could serve as a model, if it is successful. Our only caveat lies in the potential self-interests of the participants; it can only be determined to be successful when it has been tested.

TREND 9: INCREASED INTERNATIONAL JOINT EFFORTS

For years the "sister city" concept, for example, the special cultural bridges between cities or states in the United States or those in South America or East Europe for example, has in practice been akin to neighbors exchanging favorite recipes. The primary objective typically has been to build goodwill which, needless to say, is a very worthwhile objective. However, the economic results of these efforts would certainly not be sufficient for us to feel that they deserve discussion in a book on economic development, or much less, to cite as the basis for an important trend in the field.

What is an important economic development trend, however, is the new state-to-foreign-country, state-to-foreign-state, or city-to-foreign-city linkages that are now being formed or are likely to be formed in the future. The mechanisms are now in place for relationships between U.S. states or cities and their foreign counterparts that could range from an exchange of high technology or market information, or both, and distribution assistance, to co-production. Regarding the latter, for example, a city in the United States could create an assembly plant where companies from a particular French city could send their disassembled products or components for assemblage. This would permit the French producers to enter the United States under a lower tariff arrangement; generally lower duties are paid on disassembled products. In return, the French city could provide a similar arrangement for its counterpart U.S. city. The potential for these types of joint efforts seems unlimited. A current illustration is the complementary arrangement between Baden-Wuenttemberg, a West German state, and Indiana.

TREND 10: SURVIVAL/COMMON FOES CREATING STRANGE BEDFELLOWS

Only a super optimist could look at the current level of often over-zealous competition between states, between counties within a state, between cities within a county, and even between different "growth" organizations in a single city, and see hope for future cooperative efforts. And frankly, the evidence we see to-date is not sufficient for us to predict such a trend. But, there are glimmerings.

First, how dysfunctional has this conflict been? Rarely does the news of such competitive warfare hit the media; individual turf battles between differing economic groups typically go on behind the scenes. It has not been unusual for a community to have multiple civic groups concerned with industry attraction, local economic improvements, and so forth. But, a first question often is, Who speaks for the community or county? At the state level, the governor's public role can hardly be more than one of attempting to attract a given company to his or her state, not to a specific city. As an example, consider Ohio Governor Richard Celeste's recent efforts to attract General Motors' (GM) new Saturn division to his state. In commenting on his formal discussions in Detroit with GM officials in late January 1985, Celeste said, "I came here to learn about Saturn and express the strong interest of the state of Ohio ... in providing a home for [it]." Further, he pointed out that "... he hadn't promoted a specific Ohio site, and wouldn't, but he would offer the Ohio Department of Development as a clearing-house in the dozen-plus Ohio localities coveting the plant."[12] This is consistent with the role that we generally see for a governor, but the situation may call for more direct action.

Quite often it is difficult for a governor to remain aloof from the intrastate rivalry, often a battle for his or her support. Both a unique example of cooperation and one of confrontation was offered during the MCC location search, which ended with the selection of Austin, Texas. The cooperation evidenced by the state of Texas (governor's office); the city of Austin; and other city, state, and university officials demonstrates the rewards from cooperation. Yet, a reported Colorado intrastate rivalry prevented such joint efforts there.[13] On the other hand, efforts are under way for a more coordinated front in the Denver metropolitan area.[14] And, the Great Lakes states are beginning to jointly attack some of their problems; they are seeing the aggregate advantages of the whole offsetting some individual state competitive disadvantages.

Although still embryonic, the Denver metropolitan united front; the new efforts in the Great Lakes; and other examples suggest a new cooperative spirit that may be a trend. However, to-date the examples of noncooperation still seem to far outweigh examples of cooperation.

TREND 11: "WILDFIRE" DEVELOPMENT OF BUSINESS INCUBATORS

As nearly 400 people gathered at a Small Business Administration (SBA) conference on business incubators in San Antonio on November 30-December 1, 1984, it was obvious to most, if not all, the attendees that the incubator concept had captured the imagination and attention of both public- and private-sector economic developers. However, business incubators per se are not new; for example, Broome County, New York, was in the incubator game for many years. What had changed was the nature of, the impetus for, and the complexity of business incubators. And, this change was dramatic; it was a concept that had found its time.

The business incubator appears to have originally been designed merely to provide low overhead costs for small businesses or start-up firms. The emphasis was on converting unused or outdated physical facilities—a warehouse or an abandoned plant site—into low-cost rental units. And, to a great extent, the emphasis was on identifying new rental prospects for the previously "nonrentable" property. Gradually, the number of joint services that could be provided for these business "apartment" dwellers became apparent, and secretarial, copying, telephone switchboard, and similar services were introduced as part of the parcel.

Today, however, the impetus has changed to one of assisting high-potential firms get started. The motivation for private-sector incubator owners can range from the profitable management of the facility to a longer-term relationship with the start-ups. (The latter could include venture-capital involvement or a future equity position or both.) Although the public-sector incubator management may seek to "break-even" (at a minimum) via rental charges, its major objective is the development of successful firms that will become taxpaying, job-creating new businesses and industries for the community.

Undoubtedly, the public officials in every community even envision the incubator, whether public or private, hatching at least one company that will become tomorrow's Xerox, Eastman Kodak, or IBM. For that reason, some incubators, both private and public, have been especially targeted toward the attraction of start-up high-technology companies.

Keeping an accurate scoreboard on the number of incubators that are currently in operation has been difficult. A recent SBA publication identified some 51,[15] including such well-known incubators as Georgia Tech's Advanced Technology Development Center, the Utah Innovation Center, and the Rubicon Group, Austin, Texas. Control Data Corporation (CDC) has been especially active in the incubator field; they have started 10 themselves and franchised 6 others.[16] (Whether this particular private initiative of CDC is representative of a trend itself will be interesting to follow in the future.)

As we began to closely follow the increased interest in the incubator concept, it became apparent that this was one of the easier trends to predict; we see the number of incubators, especially private-sector-financed ones, continuing to rise sharply throughout the latter half of the 1980s. First, cities and states have begun to recognize that it is easier to retain existing industry than it is to acquire new industry. And, as the economic development costs to attract the outside firm from overseas or via domestic relocation spiral, the advantage of helping locals will become even more obvious. The incubator concept is designed to build from within and allow a promising start-up to prosper. If this is accomplished, a natural bond between it and the community has been established. Second, many states have initiated steps to improve their R & D base by funneling new funds into university engineering and scientific programs. The diffusion of this academic talent leads to "scientific entrepreneurs," who have the ideas and even the patents, but need that initial boost that an incubator can provide. Thus, an incubator, much like the university-research-park idea, is a natural outgrowth of this increased attention to high-tech education and research. Third, we are approaching, and some feel we have reached, a point where the availability of venture-capital funds, at least for start-ups, has exceeded its demand. A continued and increasing linking of venture-capital groups with incubators can be expected; often the venture-capital group will even be the source of funding for the incubator itself. And, fourth, private-sector economic development firms, such as the railroads, major developers, and industrial realtors, will continue to see the incubator as another "outlet" for the real-property holdings they own or represent. An analogy would be the conversion of a large home to an apartment building, but here we are witnessing the conversion of an unused plant to a business or industry apartment complex. Further, these apartment complexes (or incubators) may be eligible for government funding or tax relief, or both, depending on their location (in an enterprise zone, for example), the state's or city's economic development programs, the criteria used in selecting occupants, and other factors. (A good information source, and one illustrating what one state [Illinois] has available for incubator support, is *Starting a Small Business Incubator,* published jointly by the U.S. Small Business Administration and the Illinois Department of Commerce and Community Affairs.)

During late 1984 and early 1985, we conducted a survey among the 51 small-business incubators that had been identified by the Small Business Administration.[15] Some 34 (or roughly 67%) cooperated by providing us with extensive information on their operations. These results, other studies, and business and public-sector comments all lead to the same conclusion—the incubator concept is alive and well and will be an important force in the future.

A SINGLE MEGATREND: INTERNATIONAL ECONOMIC DEVELOPMENT—A TWO-EDGED SWORD

John Naisbitt coined the term *megatrend* to describe the supertrend, the kind that will shape our economic destiny in the years to come.[17] Such a trend is occurring in the economic development area and has multiple dimensions. One is tied all or at least partially to the ongoing strength of the dollar in the world marketplace and the other to the ongoing battle among countries for national growth. Like the two-headed dragon of mythology, the so-called superdollar has dramatically set the course for international direct investment flows for now, and for the foreseeable future. Such a trend-setting impetus, when combined with the existing heavy world competition for investment, suggests a long-term megatrend.

THE SUPERDOLLAR IMPETUS

Direct investment overseas by U.S. producers and service organizations has typically been an outgrowth of their international involvements. In fact, U.S. foreign direct investment was particularly high in the post-World War II era and led to the term *multinational corporation* (MNC) that was used to describe companies such as Goodyear, Ford, Caterpillar, ITT, Gulf Oil, Coca Cola, and Citibank. And, European companies such as Fiat, Dunlop, Unilever, Philips, Barclays, Siemans, and Peugot, have also carried the same distinctive designation because of their overseas expansion, as have the Japanese giants.

Similarly, many smaller companies in the United States and abroad have made somewhat less-dramatic expansion overseas in response to growing markets. Although not in the class of the MNC, these companies have accounted for a part of the continued expansion of U.S. foreign direct investment.

Now, however, we see a new movement overseas by U.S. companies, many of which had previously been content to export and had no thoughts of foreign subsidiaries.[18] Rather, these moves have been precipitated by the superdollar. At the same time, a countermove is under way as many companies overseas have selected this time to invest in the United States.

U.S. COMPANIES AND THE SUPERDOLLAR

The superdollar, or high-valued dollar, has made many export doors close to U.S. producers. Company after company, especially those in business-to-business marketing, have horror stories about how they have lost long-time customers overseas, simply because they were priced out of the market. For example, consider a small U.S. exporter of motors used as components in major appliances. Such a company finds itself unable to compete effectively with a French or German competitor in European markets. The value of the dollar against the mark and franc, coupled with the tariffs in the European Community, makes this U.S. company's motors too high-priced.

However, this small producer of motors, and other U.S. companies with the same competitive problem, do have an alternative. They can build a plant and manufacture all products in one of the European Community countries. Let us say that the company chooses to build a plant in Ireland. What advantages does a direct investment offer? Consider the following pluses for the company:

- Its prices are now competitive and are no longer dollar-inflated,
- It has duty-free access to the European Community,
- It has reduced transport costs,
- It has lower wage rates,
- It receives an Irish investment-incentive package.

With such advantages, it is small wonder that many companies have opted for investing overseas (either a wholly owned or joint-venture arrangement), or have entered into a licensing agreement.

To the foreign investor, there are a number of equally attractive reasons for investing in the United States. These include:

- The opportunity to earn superdollars via profits from their subsidiary,
- Direct (duty-free) access to the large U.S. markets,

- The avoidance of the pressure (and sometimes voluntary quotas) the U.S. exercises on some governments over "the U.S. balance of trade" problem,
- The access to the United States' strong R & D base and research universities,
- The opportunity to negotiate with state or local governments, or both, for investment incentives.

In particular, the size and viability of the U.S. market alone has been sufficient to make it the most popular place to invest, much less the superdollar and investment-incentive pluses. This investment may take the form of acquiring an existing firm, a joint venture, or a subsidiary or licensing agreement.

The superdollar will undoubtedly be a force for the foreseeable future. But, even if it is not, the momentum for these trends to continue are in place. In fact, the factors are in place for a quickening of the international competitive pace for direct investments.

ACCELERATION OF INTERNATIONAL COMPETITION

The pace of international economic development competition is quickening. Further, the nature of the competition is dramatically changing, but in a way that is almost *imperceptible* to most observers. Consider the following:

- The United States continues to be the most attractive market for investment in the world. However, the major European, Japanese, and other developed countries' producers are already here. They will *expand* their U.S. operations, but once here they tend to make location decisions much like U.S. companies. The next big wave of direct investment from overseas will come from medium-sized specialty producers home-based in developed countries and from the new MNCs from the developing world. Such investment (or U.S. entry) is, therefore, more apt to be in the form of licensing agreements or joint-venture arrangements. This will mean that state and local area economic development groups will increasingly be involved in finding local (U.S.) companies willing to serve as partners or licensees as part of their development-attraction process. This category of potential investors is much larger than the first wave (developed-country-based MNCs), but will offer a greater challenge to economic development groups.
- The desirability of attracting foreign direct investors seems to have become more apparent now to public economic development groups at all levels. The number of state and city trade missions going overseas has grown; the *New York Times* reported in a June 24, 1984, article that Mayor Andrew Young of Atlanta has visited Nigeria, Tunisia, Saudi Arabia, the United Arab Emirates, Sweden, Finland, Korea, Jamaica, and Trinidad, and is generally "...viewed

as the leading traveler among mayors..."[19] Such missions generally have a twofold purpose—attracting direct investment and stimulating exports of the city or state manufacturers. For several years, a number of state development groups have had development offices in key overseas locations. An early, dramatic example was Governor James Rhodes, of Ohio, who established an office in Beijing, China, following other offices in Brussels and Tokyo. Now cities have begun to follow this pattern and, in doing so, often go head-on-head with foreign development groups also seeking either to keep their investors home or go after third country-based producers.

- The recent federal legislation permitting U.S. companies to establish foreign sales corporations (FSC) has the potential effect of making the Virgin Islands, other U.S. possessions, and a number of Caribbean countries more attractive to U.S. corporate investors. Under the legislation, which became effective January 1, 1985, American companies can exempt a portion of their federal corporate taxes (16% to 30%) by handling the transactions portions of their exports through offices located *outside* the U.S. Customs Zone. (The U.S. Customs Zone includes the 50 states and Puerto Rico.) Although these countries (Virgin Islands, Guam, etc., as well as the Cayman Islands, Bahamas, Panama, and the others to be determined) are not necessarily competing with U.S. states and cities for location, relocation, and plant-site dollars, we must recognize that companies do not have unlimited investment funds. Thus, some companies are quite likely to move part of their production to these low-cost countries as well. It is simply too early to determine the impact of this legislation, but its potential must be recognized.

- The activities of select foreign countries and cities designed to attract direct investment is increasingly competing with U.S. state and community economic development efforts. This is especially true when these competitors are located in close proximity to the United States or when the trade barriers between the United States and the foreign countries is minimal, or both. In an advertisement in *Plants Sites & Parks* (July-August 1984), Huron County (Ontario, Canada) puts this competition in perspective by saying "...We are close to the enormous Great Lakes market of both Canada and the U.S.." Similarly, Puerto Rico has been employing its proximity and its unique status to its advantage.

Further, U.S. manufacturers are more and more often finding it necessary to try to serve their export markets from locations outside the United States for reasons unrelated to the FSC legislation. As long as the *superdollar* phenomenon[20] is with us, many companies cannot compete for overseas sales via exporting from the United States. Rather, they may produce or do assembly work in a country such as Ireland to gain duty-free access to the European Economic

Community markets, or in Mexico or Taiwan to take advantage of lower wage rates. And Ireland, for one, has recognized its advantages, coupled them with special incentives, and made itself a competitive force in world investment circles. Again, this type of investment outside the United States impacts funds available for investments in the United States.

What these and other international competitive actions suggest is a trend toward more aggressive intercountry strategies pitting this country's states and cities against their foreign counterparts. Clearly, the stakes are high and the economic development efforts of all parties are requiring more sophistication. One implication of this international competition is the need for international marketing expertise on the part of our state and city economic development groups, as well as U.S. industrial real estate companies. The need to know the implications of FSC legislation, foreign and U.S. tariff and nontariff barriers, and cultural considerations alone make such expertise essential.

OTHER "FUTURISTIC" TRENDS

As industrial development experts know, there are many, many trends or new activities that could have been mentioned. Those selected trends seem to have the greatest potential for longevity, and are also the most general in nature. For example, a number of the venture-capital plans that states and cities are devising today are extremely exciting. However, today's state-of-the-art venture-capital plan will likely be replaced tomorrow by a newer and even more exciting development. Although we do see that states and cities will increasingly offer financial incentives and low-interest loans for start-ups and new investors, the exact form of the these fundings will continue to evolve.

Although not new, another trend that will continue and increase is the substitution of the long-term lease for outright ownership by many companies. Evidence suggests that this will be especially true for center-city headquarters locations, although leasing is also widely employed for other regional and local offices and plant sites. This trend can be attributed to the aggressiveness of office- and industrial-facility developers and their access to funds, to the corporate advantages of leasing over ownership, and, particularly, to the nature of the location and relocation that is now occurring. Regarding the latter, newer high-tech firms' office, production, and research facilities; service organizations' office space (accounting, legal, fast-food, etc.); and regional sales and back offices of major corporations account for much of the location and relocation activity. Many high-tech companies, for example, favor leasing because of the difficulty in predicting their longer-term space needs and the desirability of putting all their available funds into R & D, which often has a greater long-term financial return. A study of annual reports of high-tech companies, such as Massachusetts-based Adage, Inc.,[21] indicates the extent to which leasing is being employed.

Among other trends are the ever-increasing independent economic role being played by cities; the more careful targeting of prospective industries, rather than using the old "shotgun" approach; the greater role or involvement of area business leaders in state and city economic development activities; and an increasing aggressive posture from affected regional utilities, banks, and so forth. The latter have begun to actively promote their area and to offer assistance of various kinds to prospective investors. Finally, our research among the commercial and industrial real estate community indicates that they will become involved much earlier in the corporate-location decision process.

Vignettes

INCUBATOR SURVEY EXECUTIVE SUMMARY*
FEBRUARY 1, 1985

BACKGROUND

Possibly no area of industrial or economic development is receiving more attention today than the business incubator. Recent momentum, of course, has been generated by articles in the business press (*Venture, Planning*, etc.); by cities and states with an increased interest in retaining or supporting local businesses, or both; by the renewed role of the entrepreneur (and venture capitalists) on the U.S. scene; and by the series of incubator programs and seminars sponsored by the Small Business Administration. In reviewing what had been written on the topic, the authors and researchers became aware that most of the available information on small-business incubators was based on individual cases and incidents rather than on empirical research covering the entire "industry." In fact, many basic questions, such as, What services are typically included in the tenant's rent and what services are provided only on a fee arrangement? needed to be answered to obtain a more complete picture of incubator policies and practices. The authors decided to conduct an independent study among incubator directors and managers to provide such answers. The remainder of this Executive Summary is based on the responses of the 34 incubator executives who participated in our survey.

INCUBATOR DEMOGRAPHICS

The incubators in our study ranged in size from 1 to 120 tenants. Nearly half (49%) had fewer than 10 tenants and only five incubators reported having over 30 tenants. The majority of the incubators, except those in the start-up phase, had over a 75% occupancy rate. Although many of the incubators were too new to have developed reliable statistics on their "success rate"—the percentage of former tenants who outgrew the incubator and proved to be viable "on their own"—those able to provide such data all reported success rates of 50% or higher. Based on the tenant-mix data that was reported, the bulk of the tenants in incubators fell into one of three categories. Three-fourths (75%) of the incubator executives indicated that lower-tech or light-industry tenants were included in their incubators, while over half (54%) had service-industry tenants. Ranking third in importance were high-tech specialists (43%), followed by high-tech generalists (40%). The remainder were typically either lower-tech or heavy-industry tenants, or pure research firms. Interestingly, only 28% of the incubators were reported to be focused on a particular type of tenant—high-tech or service, for example—but nearly 70% concentrated on start-up firms in general. On the question of who has the responsibility for approving new tenants, over two-thirds (68%) reported that this decision resides with the incubator director or manager. In the remainder of the incubators, tenant final approval is a board of directors' decision. Finally, among our respondents, 40% reported being public incubators; 33%, private incubators; and the remainder, public or private combinations.

SERVICES

According to our findings shown in Exhibit 2.1, relatively few services are automatically provided to incubator tenants, that is, included in the tenant's monthly rent. Only such services as a business library, small conference room, and onsite general management consultation are provided by a majority of the incubators as part of the rent. Most, however, do make available the following onsite services: receptionist/-switchboard (73%), computer services (79%), financial consultation (63%), stenographic-duplication (85%), mailroom (60%), marketing consultation (64%), and business furniture and equipment rental (70%). (These latter may be included in the rent or provided on some type of fee basis.) On the other hand, few of the incubators report providing onsite access to legal, advertising, marketing research, technical library, and technical consultation services. While not offered onsite, referral information, typically at a fee, is available on most other services that may be needed by tenants.

SUMMARY AND CONCLUSIONS

First, based on the study findings, it would be wrong to attempt to stereotype business incubators; they vary more widely in size, focus, services provided (those included in the rent), or offered (for a separate fee), and tenant mix than has previously been suggested. Second, there is no regional pattern in terms of these characteristics. Third, most of the specialists that incubator tenants may need, for example, accountants, lawyers, marketing researchers, and technical consultants, are available via referral rather than onsite access. Fourth, the bulk of the business incubators, whether public, private, or a combination of both, work mainly with start-up firms and do not attempt to track these new businesses after they leave "the nest." Fifth, the incubators normally have a mix of tenants, three-fourths with lower-tech and light-industry tenants and over half with service-industry tenants in this mix. With the current national attention on high-tech start-ups, this finding was especially noteworthy. And, finally, fewer saw venture capital as playing an integral role in tenant attraction than might have been expected.

*This summary is based on the findings of a mail survey of incubator directors conducted by Ryans and Shanklin during December 1984 and January 1985. All 51 incubators listed in the U.S. Small Business Administration's *Incubators for Small*

EXHIBIT 2.1

Services Provided to Incubator Tenants

Service	Included in Rent (%)	Separate Incubator Fee (%)	Separate (Outside) Provider Fee (%)	Not Provided (%)
Receptionist/ switchboard	46	12	15	27
Onsite computer assistance	18	49	12	21
External mainframe access	6	21	24	49
Programming assistance	6	21	27	46
Onsite accounting firm	9	—	31	60
Referral/access to offsite accounting	24	6	37	33
Onsite financial consultation	40	12	8	40
Financial referral/offsite access	24	3	33	40
Library-business	61	—	12	27
Library-technical	36	—	12	52
Onsite technical consultation	21	9	15	55
Technical consultation referral/access	24	6	36	34
Stenographic/ duplicating	21	49	15	15
Mailroom/shipping	40	15	5	40
Onsite general business consulting	55	15	18	12
Onsite marketing consultation	37	9	18	36
Marketing consultation referral/access	24	3	36	37
Onsite marketing research firm	9	—	21	70
Marketing research firm referral/access	18	6	36	40
Business furniture and equipment rental	15	37	18	30
Onsite legal firm	—	3	18	79
Legal firm referral/access	12	3	46	39

Business, dated October 1984, were included in the sample, and 34 (or 67%) provided responses to the highly structured questionnaire employed in the research. This Executive Summary was sent to those directors (respondents) who requested a copy of the study findings.

EXHIBIT 2.1 (Continued)

Service	Included in Rent (%)	Separate Incubator Fee (%)	Separate (Outside) Provider Fee (%)	Not Provided (%)
Onsite venture capital firm	12	3	12	73
Venture capital firm referral	15	6	45	34
Large conference room/ special facilities	30	15	3	52
Small conference room	52	12	6	30
Onsite advertising agency	6	—	13	81
Advertising agency referral/access	12	—	38	50

Note: Percentages in this table have been rounded.

DIRECT FOREIGN INVESTMENT: INCENTIVES OFFERED TO ACHIEVE ECONOMIC DEVELOPMENT GOALS*

Plant- and office-site location decisions are becoming increasingly more international. A recent survey of executive *Business Week* magazine subscribers indicated that 33% of the respondents would consider plant- or office-site locations in foreign countries.**

The trend toward expansion overseas has been growing at a steady rate since World War II. Factors encouraging companies to grow beyond national boundaries range from developing sources of supply for raw materials and other goods obtained less expensively abroad, to tapping a new profitable market. Such business motivations are stimulated by a vast array of incentive plans offered by foreign countries anxious to host and reap the benefits of a new business enterprise.

Most countries actively involved in attracting foreign investors, have very specific economic goals they hope to fulfill. Exhibits 2.2 and 2.3 show the types of industries most welcomed abroad and the economic goals most frequently stated.

Countries that are experiencing unbalanced growth will most likely offer greater incentives to potential investors if they will locate in a lesser-developed part of the country. Countries in need of more exports offer special considerations to investments that create export markets.

The incentive packages offered to obtain the host country's objectives range from tax incentives to labor-training grants. Exhibit 2.4 lists the most commonly-offered incentives. It is interesting to note that specific areas of the world offer similar incentives. This is, of course, due to the competition.

Specifically, the Asian countries seeking economic development by hosting international investments have the same tax incentives and accelerated depreciation benefits. A quote from an investment brochure published in Taiwan's Science Based Industrial Park states, "The Republic of China on Taiwan, Singapore, Hong Kong and South Korea are crowned by the press as the 'four little dragons of Asia.' Their rapid growth and development surprised many people...we are clearly competing against the three other little dragons for high quality investors. This pamphlet is prepared for you to see where Taiwan stands..."

The 10 most frequently mentioned foreign countries to be considered a potential site for a plant or office space location in the *Business Week* study are Mexico (24%), Great Britain (15%), Ireland

(11%), West Germany (8%), Japan (7%), Singapore (7%), Brazil (6%), South Korea (6%), Taiwan (6%), and France (5%).

Exhibits 2.3 and 2.4 outline the economic goals of the aforementioned countries and the associated incentives offered to foreign investors to achieve those goals.

*Vignette prepared by Lori Mitchell, a doctoral student at Kent State University.
**From a survey of executives that subscribe to *Business Week* magazine. The survey consisted of 526 respondents, a 53% response rate. The study was completed between January 16 and February 27, 1984.

EXHIBIT 2.2

Types of Industry Desired by Country

Industry	Mexico	United Kingdom	Ireland	Taiwan	Singapore	Korea	France	Brazil	Japan	West Germany
Nonelectrical equipment	X			X	X					
Electric machinery	X			X						
Electronic equipment	X		X		X					
Chemical industry	X			X	X			X		
Advanced technology	X	X		X	X	X	X			X
Pharmaceuticals			X		X					
Health care			X		X					
Consumer products			X	X				X		
Automotive components				X	X			X		
Optical				X	X					

EXHIBIT 2.3

Economic Development Goals

Goal	Mexico	United Kingdom	Ireland	Taiwan	Singapore	South Korea	France	Brazil	Japan	West Germany
Balanced/Regional growth	X	X	X				X	X	X	X
Increased exports		X		X	X	X	X	X		
High technology	X		X		X	X				X
Increased skill levels			X		X					
Labor-intensive projects		X	X				X	X		

EXHIBIT 2.4

Investment Incentives Commonly Offered

Incentive	Mexico	United Kingdom	Ireland	Taiwan	Singapore	Korea	France	Brazil	Japan	West Germany
Tax holiday				X	X	X	X	X		
Tax incentive for export					X	X				
Investment tax credit				X						
Depreciation benefits			X	X		X	X		X	X
Grants		X	X							
R & D grants/ Innovative support		X	X	X	X					
Loans	X	X	X		X		X	X	X	X
Labor-training support		X	X		X		X			
Factories		X	X	X						
Industrial parks			X	X					X	
Import-duty incentives				X				X		

REFERENCES

1. Wald, M.L. (1984, May 13). Back offices disperse from downtowns. The *New York Times*, p. 57.
2. Posner, B.G. (1984, October). *Inc's. Fourth Annual Report on the States, Inc.*, p. 129.
3. Dempsey, K.B. (1984, July-August). Cities enticing firms. *Plants Sites & Parks*, p. 7.
4. Shanklin, W.L. & Ryans, J.K., Jr. (1984). *Marketing high technology.* Lexington MA: Lexington Books, Inc.
5. Carlson, E. (1984, June 5). Virginia plans research site to serve its high tech firms. The *Wall Street Journal*, p. 37.
6. Phalon, R. (1983, December 19). University as venture capitalist. *Forbes*, pp. 82, 87, 89, 91 and 93.
7. Schuler, S.D. (1984, August 1). Oregon votes to abandon unitary tax in victory for multinational companies. The *Wall Street Journal*, p. 10.
8. Stipp, D. (1984, October 9). Eleven concerns that develop software for defense mull joint research venture. The *Wall Street Journal*, p. 2.
9. Reinhold, R. (1984, September 16). Houston tightens reins on growth. *Cleveland Plain Dealer*, p. E1.
10. Revzan, L. (1983, December). Enterprise zones: Present status and potential impact. *Governmental Finance*, pp. 32-33.
11. Houx, C. (1984, August 20). Enterprise zone aims to be best in the nation. *Business First*, p. 1.
12. Suddes, T. (1985, January 25). Celeste pitches Ohio to GM chiefs for Saturn plant. *Cleveland Plain Dealer*, p. 10.
13. Hillkirk, J. (1984, October 23). Colorado weighs hi-tech price tag. *USA Today*, p. 3B.
14. Meadow, J.B. (1984, March 26). Selling the metro area with style. *Rocky Mountain Business Journal*, p. 11.
15. U.S. Small Business Administration. (1984, October). *Incubators for small business.* (Washington, DC).
16. Demuth, J. (1984, November). What can incubators offer? *Venture*, p. 80.
17. Naisbitt, J. (1982). *Megatrends.* New York: Warner Books.
18. Buskirk, B., Cort, S.G., Ryans, J.K. Jr. (1985, April). How to survive the superdollar crisis. *Business Marketing*, pp. 68, 70, 72, 76, 77.
19. Robbins, W. (1984, June 24). Cities going where the business is. The *New York Times*, p. E3.
20. The superdollar. (1984, October 8). *Business Week*, pp. 164-167.
21. Adage, Inc. Annual Report 1984, p. 32.

"WE'RE NUMBER 1": THE STATE'S BATTLE CRY

EXECUTIVE SUMMARY

As the recent Saturn, Toyota, and other industry-attraction battles have proclaimed, the states have heightened their aggressive efforts to attract new business, to get established businesses to expand, and to foster entrepreneurial start-ups. For many years, the states have taken the point position in behalf of their cities and counties or parishes in the industry-stimulation game. But, the reason for today's increased state concern is obvious. Some 36 states have shown a *decrease* in manufacturing employment from March 1979 to March 1985. Illinois alone lost 324,000 factory jobs, while six-digit losses were also recorded by Ohio, Michigan, Indiana, Pennsylvania, and New York.

With this bleak national picture, it is little wonder that many governors find themselves virtually acting as state public relations people; they tend to spend more time on economic development efforts than any other activity. And, nothing puts governors in good or bad stead with their populace more quickly than their industry attraction or expansion record. It is small wonder that a group of governors *competed* on the Phil Donahue Show in the slim chance that they might grab the brass ring (or rather the 6,000 jobs promised by Saturn). Spanish galleons may provide the gold for today's underseas explorers; but for a governor, give him or her a new auto plant and a successful political career follows close behind.

What has become increasingly popular are the state rankings and ratings provided by various publications and research organizations.

Pittsburgh's number *one* rating in Rand McNally's *Places Rated Almanac* brought that city a wealth of publicity, but Florida's first place showing in the Alexander Grant & Company study perhaps did even more. While only the "Steel City" enjoyed the benefits of the former, every city from Pensacola to Miami was able to bask in Florida's success. Again, however, these have placed further pressures on state economic developers; a low ranking increases their level of promotional difficulties because of its "image-influencing" effect. What is often ignored by rating watchers is that the ratings use different criteria and have different objectives. For example, *Inc.* magazine is concerned with support for small business and entrepreneurs, while the Alexander Grant & Company is concerned with general manufacturing climate.

Although state economic development programs have become more sophisticated, the incentive packages that they offer are becoming increasingly standardized. In fact, it is becoming quite difficult to offer something unique in the case of financial incentives due to the level of competition that exists. In some variation, most state incentive packages include state or local tax relief or both, job training, site preparation, and industrial bonds. Less frequently offered, but becoming more popular, are state venture capital, enterprise zones, high-tech university parks, and start-up assistance. With the incentives themselves becoming more difficult to use as the basis for state differentiation, more attention is now being given to *image* enhancement.

Of special importance in terms of image is the first contact between the state and a company seeking information on investing in that state. Employing content analysis, we evaluated the promotional materials of some 41 cooperating states. Based on our criteria, the top 10 states, in terms of the promotional material they sent in response to initial inquiries, were Alabama, Rhode Island, West Virginia, Delaware, Florida, Mississippi, Kentucky, Illinois, Oklahoma, and Michigan. However, many other states were close in terms of promptness of response and quality. Although such promotional materials may *not* play a critical role in a state's ability to attract investment, the initial inquiry response materials do tell the inquirer a great deal about its business orientation.

∞

In the year 2025, marketing historians will likely remember the decade of the 1980s for some of the classic struggles for market share, brand awareness, and corporate image leadership that took place. They will speak eloquently via their 3-D wall screens to their students, as they describe the confrontations between Coca-Cola and Pepsi, Hertz and Avis, GM and Toyota, McDonald's and Wendy's, IBM and Apple, and Florida and Oregon. Why would they mention these two states—Florida and Oregon—or any states in the same breath with GM and Toyota?

What we are witnessing today, and what historians will be describing in the future, is the "battle between the states," a confrontation not unlike the famous Pepsi versus Coca-Cola comparative advertising free-for-all in Dallas a few years ago. But, the prizes these states seek tend to be much grander than those sought in the "taste-test" warfare. They seek to recruit firms which, through headquarters relocation or the construction of productive facilities, will add employment and tax revenue to their states. And, maybe the states are even hoping for a bit more. Wouldn't it be nice, for example, to be ranked number one or in the top 10 in one of the annual polls or, in this case, the annual rankings by *Inc.* magazine, Alexander Grant & Company, and *Business Week?* Such a ranking would undoubtedly enhance the state's image and reflect a level of awareness that state economic development groups hope to achieve.

Is every state engaged in this classic struggle? Yes, all states engage in economic development efforts, but to widely varying degrees. Some emphasize the attraction of outside industry, while others focus to a great extent on promoting the output of existing firms or on encouraging internal growth and development. Further, a number devote the major share of their economic development efforts to tourism or to export promotion, or both. Although *recruitment* and *fostering exports or internal growth* are not totally mutually exclusive, they do call for widely different marketing objectives, strategies, and tactics. And, some frankly question the ability of a state economic development body to effectively handle such multiple missions, even when the efforts are handled by different divisions.

This chapter discusses the current competitive efforts states are taking to attract industrial development and foster growth by existing firms. It also considers why the governor's office plays such a key role in state efforts and considers the various *rankings* and what they suggest in terms of the direction being taken by state programs. Finally, it presents the results of a detailed content analysis study of some 41 state programs that we conducted for this book.

WHAT ARE THE STATES OFFERING?

In sharp contrast to the early 1970s when then Governor Tom McCall eliminated the budget for the state's economic development program,[1]

Oregon has recently become proactive in seeking industry. In fact, Oregon is credited with obtaining $500 million worth of new high-tech corporate development in the latter half of 1984.[2] Part of this new industrial growth can be attributed to the state's dropping of its unitary tax regulation in mid-August 1984, but much of it can be credited to new attitudes, attitudes translated into reducing the barriers that had been thrown up in the "isolation era."[3] Still, Oregon is a long way from matching the development programs and incentives that can be found in such states as New York, Florida, or perhaps even South Dakota.

The economic development efforts of the proactive states—the most aggressive ones—not only call for matching the programs of the other states, but also creating product differences that give them an edge. Often the efforts of states relate to changing tax or other state regulations that impede a firm's competitive ability or moving that state ahead of its competition. For example, South Dakota altered its banking laws and therefore attracted credit operations from the money centers. But, the state efforts often go well beyond merely passing enabling legislation or eliminating restrictions. Some form of industrial revenue bonds or loans for site acquisition, equipment, site improvement, or capital construction are commonplace in a state's incentive portfolio.[4] Creative differences and pluses for the more proactive states center on such considerations as the way in which the loans are state-taxed, if at all, or on the state's ability to harness private-sector funding to complement its own financing efforts. The Ben Franklin Plan in Pennsylvania is just one example of the latter. On the other hand, a few states have taken only minimum (or no) advantage of available federal funding, such as the Urban Development Assistance Grants, that could be used to their cities' advantage. This lack of awareness or initiative has led, in part, to the establishment of the National Development Council, "...a private, nonprofit organization that helps state agencies learn the ropes of creative financing."[5]

What states offer in terms of financing and other pluses, and the extent to which they appear to be proactive, depends to a great extent on the type of industry or business we are considering. Are we talking about attracting or assisting small businesses, high-tech firms, *Fortune 500* subsidiaries or plants, or even headquarter relocations? For example, Kansas was ranked number 9 in a recent *Inc.* magazine study of the optimum states for small businesses[6] and yet, in a *Business Week* study of its readers, only 2% indicated that they would consider Kansas for a new plant site.[7] The former obviously was a ranking in terms of the state's interest in attracting or assisting small business, while the latter survey included executives from a broad cross section of manufacturers in terms of size, industry, and so forth. Naturally, the two surveys are not directly comparable, but the results do suggest that the incentives that are deemed important to small business may not be as appropriate for business in general. And, a few years can make a big difference in how a state may be viewed in terms of its economic development programs; the programs that catch the imagination are constantly changing. Mississippi makes an excellent case in point. The state was extremely active in industrial-revenue bond financing in both 1982 and 1983[8] and primarily due to this same factor was ranked among 10 states that *Inc.* called "...great homes for small companies..."[9] in 1981. However, Mississippi fell to 49th in the most recent *Inc.* report,[10] primarily on the basis of its capital resources. Evidently, the capital resource considerations that were most important 2 or 3 years ago changed as other states began to offer small business-specific financial-incentive programs. It was not a question of Mississippi offering less, but rather the programs that other states are now offering, and what is now considered important by small business (as represented by *Inc.*).

Today, a new and quite significant plus is venture-capital funding. Private venture capital, per se, is readily available in many parts of the United States and, in fact, some venture capitalists report excess dollars available. Yet, many venture-capital groups specialize in high-tech or particular industries and these private-sector funds are certainly not evenly dispersed around the country. To illustrate the latter, *Business Week* reported that venture capitalists provided $364 million to start-ups in southern California alone in 1983[11] and Houston now has over 20 venture-capital groups with $250 million in funds.[12] Further, not all start-up and expanding companies want to turn to venture capitalists, and other sources of private funds may not be available. These factors have led several states to "fill the gap." Again, the scoreboard changes quickly, but the *Inc.* report identified some 15 states currently having a venture-capital program.[13]

Tax exemptions or temporary (or permanent) tax moratoriums play an integral role in most state economic development programs. Several states, such as Alaska and, more recently, Ohio, make a point of not offering tax advantages to newcomers that are unavailable to existing companies. Other states, however, use certain tax concessions only as an attraction tool. According to *Industrial Development,* a tax exemption on raw materials used in manufacturing is perhaps the most widely employed industry tax incentive. At the other extreme, only a handful of states now offer tax exemptions to encourage research and development.[14] However, this type of tax exemption is one that can be expected to come into increasing vogue, as states move toward seeking industry (or to encouraging existing industry to be state-of-the-art). Tax incentives are often also employed to direct investment to blighted areas or to encourage training of workers in certain classifications. Enterprise-zone legislation offers excellent examples of using tax exemptions to direct investment to pockets— often urban—where jobs and site improvements are badly needed.

Virtually every state has a program of grants or low-interest funding for a wide range of land acquisition, site improvement, equipment, and related initial or expansion costs. For example, when Ohio announced that Honda would construct a new facility at Marysville, Ohio, it indicated that the Japanese auto producer would be provided with a $1.5 million grant for plant-site improvement.[15] Since this general type of state program has become quite commonplace, it has moved from being an incentive or special attraction to an expectation on the part of corporations, especially the direct investor from overseas. The only competition seems to be in the terms or the amount of the grant.

More indirect, but perhaps equally important to many corporations, are the state efforts to "beef up" their higher education programs. One approach has been to establish university research parks at their major state (or sometimes private) universities. Florida has established research parks in conjunction with three of their major universities— the University of Florida, the University of Central Florida, and the University of South Florida. The latter two universities are located in major metropolitan areas—Orlando and Tampa, respectively—and indicate the state's response to urban needs. Recognizing the same need and the desirability of access to the federal funding agencies, Virginia has chosen a bit different route. While desirous of establishing a major "university-type" research center in heavily populated northern Virginia (the Washington, DC metropolitan area), the state plans to develop a separate operation (Center for Innovative Technology) from any single university and to instead draw on the facilities of several schools.[16] Increasingly, states are trying to build strong linkages between their universities and the private sector. In particular, efforts focus on making the state's higher education programs responsive to the special needs of current and prospective industry. The University of Arkansas (and the state of Arkansas), for example, established an individualized program to train workers for a new biotech subsidiary (and complementary industries) coming to the state. Similar, though often less company-specific programs designed to meld public higher education research and training more closely to local company interests have been announced, or are under way, in Kansas, Nebraska, Montana, Alabama, New Jersey, and a host of other states.[17] Perhaps we should point out that for many years state technical institutes (junior-college level or below) have provided trade-related education; this is not new. What is new is the effort to make the state 4-year and graduate-related universities more responsive to the needs of the state's private sector. Historically, agricultural colleges and some engineering colleges in major universities have worked with the private sector on individual or joint programs, but other arms of the academic community have tended more toward independent or grant-related research. These latter often have prided themselves in *not* modeling degree-related programs to conform in any way to private-sector needs. For this reason, the current efforts to better link higher education and industry are

ILLUSTRATION 3.1

Combining a famous emotional/psychological appeal ("I Love New York")
with impressive factual information about the well-known and respected
corporations that are already located in New York State.

"Made in New York" folder cover reprinted with the permission of the New York State
Department of Commerce. "Made in New York" is a registered service mark of the New
York State Department of Commerce.

noteworthy and will bear closer examination in the future to determine if the programs are successful. (We are reminded of a recent discussion with an economic development program official, who described how an engineering department in a major university in his state had willingly added several faculty members as an accommodation to a new high-tech firm being constructed near its campus.)

Finally, the business and social environment represents the most intangible (and nebulous) offering that states are now actively promoting. Be it business climate or quality of life, environment tends to be a factor more subjectively judged than tax concessions or industrial-revenue bond availability. And, it is easy to draw a parallel between the image efforts of a state and the corporate advertising and promotion of a corporation. The various former subsidiaries of the AT&T system are currently working hard to develop a separate identity and awareness, while still retaining some of the carry-over image from their former parent. A good example is US WEST, a holding company composed of Mountain Bell, Northwestern Bell, and Pacific Northwest Bell. Its image is one of an aggressive marketer seeking to increase the awareness of its name. The company is running an extensive advertising campaign in publications such as the *Wall Street Journal* (p. 22, January 16, 1985). Similarly, many states are promoting their business climate or quality of life, or both, in an effort to change or reinforce their image and to heighten awareness. To illustrate, Delaware avoided any possibility of vagueness or ambiguity by using the headline "...They Like The Climate..." in a November/December 1984 advertisement.[18] It then listed six leading corporations with facilities in its state. South Carolina, on the other hand, sought to reinforce and retain its quality-of-life features while stressing other factors in an advertisement headed "...Don't Let The Charm of South Carolina Be The Only Reason You Locate Here."[19] South Carolina was, in effect, telling us it is more than a pretty face. Many states might like to have some of the images that South Carolina feels it conjures up in the corporate mind. However, too much attention to climate or any particular quality of life factor can, of course, be negative if the state is seen as having little else to offer. Yet, with data increasingly supporting the importance of quality of life, and executives often talking of good or bad business climates, a continued heavy emphasis on these two location and relocation factors can be expected. Parenthetically, we might mention a Washington state advertisement in *Business Facilities* that targeted *both* business climate and quality of life with a headline, "Executive Privilege in Washington" and an office with a view of its artwork theme.[20] Particularly on the increase is the use of testimonials by business executives, often from firms that recently located in the state and featuring executives citing their companies' reasons for locating there. What substantiates the claim of a good business climate may be difficult to determine and, therefore, a testimonial may avoid this dilemma. As the other incentives to locate or relocate continue to "even out," more use of such image-advertising techniques, so widely used in industry, can be expected.

STARTS AT THE GOVERNOR'S OFFICE

IS THE GOVERNOR THE KEY?

Is it correct to say that the governor is the key individual in the success or failure of his or her state's economic development programs? To a great extent, the answer is *yes*. Before critics retort that a governor's power is limited, that this view is simplistic, that the governor cannot change the weather, and so forth, let us consider why the governor's role is so important in today's state economic development matters.

To many private-sector leaders, a state's business climate is reflected by its governor's attitudes toward business. And there is considerable evidence to support this belief. Typically, it has been the governors that have taken the lead when antibusiness legislation, such as unitary tax laws, have been repealed or when high-tech education centers have been established in their states. On the negative side, business has also been quick to take note of those governors who seem to automatically turn to the corporate world first whenever added tax revenue is needed, or those who have been the principal industry critics on environmental issues. Thus, when such positives or negatives take place, it should be expected that the governor making the statement has given his or her image (and the state's business climate image) a push in the same direction.

It should be added that this view—that the governor's attitude and the state's business climate are the same—has been reinforced by the members of the governors' club themselves. For example, when commenting on the economic development aggressiveness of a neighboring state (South Dakota), Minnesota's Governor Rudy Perpich is quoted as saying, "...South Dakota was smart enough to change its banking laws...you have to tip your hat to Governor William Janklow on that one."[21] Governor Perpich was in effect giving his counterpart in South Dakota all the credit for that state's legislative climate.

Additionally, governors have been so willing to make public announcements that would be deemed positive to business, that it is not surprising that they carry the burden of the negatives as well, even when they do not announce them. Often equal or greater media attention is given to companies leaving a state than to those which are added. To illustrate, one Ohio corporate head received congratulatory notes from 12 governors when his company make the *Inc. 500* in 1983, but none from his own governor.[22] Who gets credit for this perceived rebuff and therefore for a perceived negative business climate that was causing the executive to consider building a plant in Texas—Governor Richard Celeste. Celeste is the one that makes the announcements, such as Honda is adding a new plant in Marysville, Ohio, so it is small wonder that the angry executive sees him as the responsible party.

The point is that rightly or wrongly the governor is going to be seen as making the key economic development decisions, those that shape the state's image as a friend or enemy of business. Further, as the chief elected official of the state, the governor is responsible for establishing the *tone* for the state's relationship with business, even if he or she is not actively involved in economic development matters. And besides tone, the governor is also responsible for prioritizing economic development along with everything ranging from highway safety to state mental health programs. Because of this, the governor is the key to the state's efforts.

WHO SPEARHEADS THE STATE EFFORTS?

Given this key role, we are increasingly seeing the governor, or in some cases the lieutenant governor, becoming intimately involved in his or her state economic development efforts. This reflects the growing priority that so many top state officials (and the voters) are now assigning to attracting new jobs and to increasing the state's industrial- and private-sector revenue base.

There are, of course, many potential positives associated with the governor's office playing such a lead role. For example, it

- signals to state officials and employees that economic development is truly a high-priority activity;
- increases the likelihood that the governor's office will make certain that the state's developmental programs are adequately funded;
- assures economic development officials access to the governor's office when his or her presence at negotiations is needed;
- demonstrates to prospects (corporate executives in locating and relocating firms) that the state deserves a "good-business-climate" reputation;
- offers needed prestige for dealing with foreign corporate executives, that is, the latter often are accustomed to dealing with top government officials in their home country.

In many instances, the involvement of the governor's office reflects a tone that subsequently pervades all of the state's economic development programs. When John Y. Brown, Jr. was the governor of Kentucky, he made it clear by his actions and support that "business had a number one spot" in the state's priorities. Using his background as the president of Kentucky Fried Chicken for credibility, Governor Brown's state's slogan became "...Kentucky & Co. The State That Is

ILLUSTRATION 3.2

Confronting a perceived negative head-on

Oops.

Who'd have thought that Arkansas was such a secret.

Apparently a lot of people. Including American business leaders. That's what we discovered when Governor Bill Clinton commissioned Yankelovich, Skelly and White to conduct a special research project on business attitudes about Arkansas.

The results of that research showed that American business knows Arkansas is a terrific state, a great place to live and work, with a strong, productive work force. But it also showed that many of Arkansas' strongest assets—transportation, cost of doing business and the like—aren't credible, partly because many people don't believe we are where we are.

"So," said Arthur White, "you've got to get out there and tell everyone where you are!"

Well, where we are is right in the center of the country. Just look down there at the map with the state shaded in. That's Arkansas. Smack dab in the middle of the sunbelt. Right between Texas and Tennessee. In other words, once you know where we're located, Arkansas is a great business location.

The research also tells us a lot of other positive things we think you'll like about Arkansas. And we'll be sharing more of them with you each week in *The Wall Street Journal.* Right here, every Thursday.

So come visit us again next week when we'll tell you about Arkansas' excellent water transportation network.

Unless you enjoy paying more for transportation than you have to, we think you'll like what you'll learn about doing business in Arkansas.

Governor Bill Clinton / Arkansas Industrial Development Commission / One State Capitol Mall / Little Rock, Arkansas 72201 / (501) 371-6000 / Telex 536433 AIDC LRK

Advertisement reprinted with the permission of James Sharkey, Director, Ind. Div., Arkansas Ind. Dev. Commission.

Run Like A Business." This tone is similar to the one now strongly reflected in the Robert Orr/John Mutz team in Indiana. And it raises the credibility of its slogan "...Government Listens (to business) in Indiana," when changes such as the recent repeal of the state's unitary tax occur.

Without editorializing, we need to indicate that a trained business observer can tell rather quickly whether a state's chief executive is truly supportive of business or merely likes to reap the harvest, that is, announce the state's economic development news. For example, do the governor's announcements themselves put the new company or the state or governor's kudos first? Recently, we noted that one governor's press release on a new state acquisition waited until the fourth paragraph to bother to mention the company's name, even though the firm was investing nearly $50 million. By the fourth paragraph, the governor's name had been mentioned twice and the state three times, even though the company had been ignored.

Regardless of whether it is the governor or the lieutenant governor who is the lead economic development *elected* official, it is clear that in successful programs there is more often a direct reporting line from the economic development office to the top. And, increasingly, the individual actually managing the office or department is a professional rather than merely the recipient of a political plum. This represents a trend and philosophy that gets our vote!

INTERSTATE COOPERATIVE EFFORTS

Regardless of whether we are talking about economic and social problems or the weather, there is a tendency to generalize on the basis of regions of the country. Terms, such as the "Industrial Midwest" (or Smokestack America) and the "Sunbelt," on the one hand, or the "southern accent" and New England "pragmatism" on the other, have long been part of our stereotyping. In fact, to most Americans a reference to the Northwest conjures up scenic wilderness, rushing streams, and similar natural beauty, in contrast to the desert Southwest. Similarly, problems tend to be seen as regional concerns whether they are plant closings or agricultural droughts.

The point is that we think and frequently report regionally. This would suggest, therefore, that states in the various regions work together to solve a whole range of mutual concerns, such as economic development or tourism. To illustrate, because states rely heavily on tourism and often have a limited number of attractions, one would expect that several Midwest states or Southwest states would have joint promotional campaigns in Britain, Germany, or Belgium to attract tourists to their area. But, this does not happen. Similarly, states in the same region rarely work together to solve their economic development problems or to present a unified front either to attract industry or to fight common foes. Interestingly enough, when states have worked together, the results can be dramatic. A case in point was the Great Lakes Commission's success in "cleaning up the Lakes."

How might states in a region cooperate and still give their "best shot" at attracting new business and industry, or retaining existing firms, to themselves? To begin with, often a state's biggest problem is its image and level of awareness, and the image and level of awareness of its region. Negative regional stereotypes, for example, might best be countered through regional advertising and promotion. Would Michigan be better off by stating in its European promotions that "Michigan is not like the rest of the Rust Bowl," or by working with the rest of the Midwest to develop an image and an awareness in Europe that is positive? Similarly, a region's combined resources often are far more extensive than any of its states viewed individually. A three- or four-state grouping may present a significant upper-income market, population base, or concentration of scientists and research universities that can match or outstrip some of the glamour states. Whether state alliances will ever occur on more regular and long-term bases in the future is questionable. A more credible scenario seems to be continued conflict such as the verbal battle that took place between the governors of South Dakota and Minnesota in 1983.[23] Similarly, four Great Lakes governors were reported to have been unable to forge an agreement not to "raid each other's industry,"[24] which naturally raises doubts about regional willingness to work on more positive joint programs.

STATE RANKINGS AND RATINGS

Florida placed number *one* in Alexander Grant & Company's 1983 state rankings, while North Carolina topped *Business Week's* 1984 rankings and Connecticut headed *Inc.'s* 1984 list. Because such differences have been used by critics to question the legitimacy and value of these and other rating systems, let us take a closer look at the game of ratings and decide whether or not they may be useful to corporate decision makers, industrial realtors, and others, including the states themselves.

There are a number of publications and organizations that are now providing detailed data on the individual states. Generally, these data are presented in comparative form. And, often the states are ranked 1 through 50 (or sometimes the contiguous 48) in terms of each criterion (viewed separately), or the states are given an overall ranking based on a weighted aggregate of all the criteria, or both. Each publication and organization employs somewhat different bases for its ranking or assessment and has its own distinctive objective or purpose for providing the service. Further, the methodology used in gathering the data is typically quite different. Let us consider some of the better-known systems which we will review in no particular order.

BUSINESS WEEK'S SURVEY

Business Week (BW) conducts its plant-site-selection research among a random sample of its executive subscribers, that is, individuals at the chairman-of-the-board, president, vice-president, owner, or partner level. This research is conducted periodically by *BW*, and the findings from 1976 and 1980 are included in the 1984 report, along with the most recent data.[25] This permits the reader to note changes in the attitudes and decision-making criteria that may have occurred over the years. The 1984 study was administered by McGraw-Hill Research, the research arm of *BW*'s publisher. Some 53% of the 1,000 executives sampled (or 526 executives) responded to the 1984 survey, which was conducted by mail.

The results of this current survey are reported in a publication entitled, "Business Week's 1984 Plant Site Selection Survey of Management Subscribers in Industry." Presented in this report are the executives' views on questions such as

- which areas (of the country) they would most likely consider, if their company was going to select a new plant site;
- which states they would most likely consider;
- whether they thought that their company would be in the market for a new plant site in the next 5 years.

Further, the executives' opinions on the importance of a number of individual site-selection factors were presented. In addition, a wide range of decision-making information, such as the titles of the individuals involved in site selection, and current and future company "intentions" data were included.

The *BW* research offers several pluses to the user. First, it represents a focus on the *demand-side*—what company decision makers look for and whether companies have an ongoing plan for location and relocation. Second, it is longitudinal, that is, it has been repeated periodically and, therefore, response differences can be traced. Third, the methodology is sound. (The only key assumption required is that *BW* readers are representative of the business community.) Fourth, it obtains information on foreign locations, as well as the states.

In particular, we think this *BW* study will assist the economic development groups in planning their marketing strategies, and assist corporations by providing them with the views of others on questions they must answer. In this regard, the *BW* study is the closest to the type of research we conducted for this book.

ALEXANDER GRANT & COMPANY STUDY

For the past 5 years, Alexander Grant & Company (AGC), a Chicago-based CPA firm, has published a business-climate study. As with the preceding four studies, the current version (1983), published in 1984, focuses only on the 48 contiguous states and relies on quantifiable factors in producing its assessment of each state's business climate.

The current AGC study is published under the title, *The Fifth Study of General Manufacturing Business Climates.* Like the *BW study,* the AGC study is notable in the rigor of its methodology, but is otherwise quite dissimilar to the *BW* research. Before describing the differences between the *AGC* and *BW* studies, however, let us provide a brief overview of the AGC methodology. (For a detailed look at the methodology employed in the AGC study, published by Alexander Grant & Company in Chicago, Illinois, refer to pages 7-14 of the document.) Basically, the AGC study employs a model that incorporates 22 measurement factors that have been deemed by manufacturing associations as "...the important issues relating to a manufacturer's location and business success." Not only have the manufacturers' associations chosen the factors, but their combined judgment was used in establishing the *weight* of each factor. Whereas the selection of the factors (and their weighting) may seem subjective, once those factors have been identified (and weighted) the remainder of the evaluation process followed for each state is totally objective. For the past 3 years (1981, 1982, and 1983) the measurement factors remained the same, but the weightings assigned to them changed. This latter is due to changes in their relative importance as assigned by the manufacturers' associations.

The 22 measurement factors are classified by AGC into one of the following five categories:

- state and local government fiscal policies
- state-regulated employment costs
- labor costs
- availability and productivity of labor force
- other manufacturing-related issues (energy costs, environmental control, and markets)

To illustrate, *debt* is one of the 22 factors and is included in the "state and local government fiscal policies" category. The figure representing debt in the model is "state and local government debt per capita" and is obtained for each state from U.S. Department of Commerce, Bureau of the Census reports. For most of the 22 factors, equally reliable federal or state data are available and for the remainder, special studies are conducted for AGC. Therefore, this research is objective and the information sources are reliable.

Like any research, critics might raise certain questions about the

AGC study despite its obvious objectivity and the reliability of its sources. Some might question, for example,

- its weighting system; are the views of the state manufacturing associations representative of manufacturing firms in general?
- the number of factors included in the model and whether or not these are the most relevant factors to include?
- the absence of qualitative factors; are there quality-of-life factors that should be included?

With the very rigorous and consistent methodological approach that was followed, the AGC study sought to overcome these first two criticisms. Regarding the third criticism (quality of life), the researchers recognized this potential weakness, but said, "...no single, quantitative composite factor is available, as the definition of quality of life is distinctly subjective."[27] To have included a nonquantifiable factor would have reduced the research's objectivity.

In contrast to the *BW* study, which is highly subjective, the main strength of the AGC study is its cold objectivity. However, although there appears to be merit in varying the factor weightings annually (the importance of factors do change), it makes it a bit more difficult to trace state changes. For example, a state may make dramatic improvements in one category or factor, possibly even as a result of a low AGC ranking; however, it might not improve its national ranking, because that factor now carries a *lower weight*. We see the AGC study as playing a useful role in providing data for the pragmatic side of the location and relocation decision, especially for labor-intensive, industrial concerns. However, more information is needed to complete the picture.

Clearly, the AGC studies do draw considerable attention. While Florida was ranked number one in both 1983 and 1982, there was a great deal of "shuffling" that occurred among the top 10. For example, South Dakota moved from number 14 in 1982 to number 2 in 1983. In contrast, North Carolina slipped from number 3 (1982) to number 10 in 1983 and South Carolina fell from the 5th spot in 1982 to the 15th position in 1983. Such dramatic shifts downward do not go unnoticed, and do not occur without drawing the ire of those who feel victimized.

INC. STUDY

Unlike the *BW* or *AGC* studies, the *Inc.* research explores only the small-business climates of the 50 states. However, *Inc.* does not limit its study or studies to manufacturing firms and, in fact, includes services in its annual ranking of the *Inc. 100*.[28]

According to *Inc.'s* 1984 "Report on the States," there is a growing state attention being given to the attraction and retention of small business.[29] As more and more states have taken specific actions to encourage the small-business community, dramatic shifts in the state rankings have occurred over the 4 years of the report.

Methodology: There are several methodological similarities between the AGC study and the *Inc.* report research. Like the AGC study, the *Inc.* report is based almost entirely on quantifiable data. Further, a weighting system is employed that gives different weights to each of the five categories of factors that make up the overall rankings that are assigned to each state.

However, there are many distinct differences between the AGC study and the *Inc.* report. The latter's report research may be characterized as follows:

- *Inc.* compares all 50 states;
- *Inc.* examines *only* small business-specific concerns, that is, "...important, quantifiable factors that contribute to the general climate for small business..."[30]
- *Inc.'s* factor categories, but *not* its weighting system or overall methodology, is detailed in the article presenting its findings;
- *Inc.* considers in detail the availability of state programs, such as venture capital and loan guarantees, as well as the deployment of U.S. Small Business Administration programs, in its rankings;
- *Inc.* considers the availability of assistance to small business, such as advisory offices and councils, in its rankings;
- *Inc.* relies on government reports and telephone interviews.

Further, again like the AGC study, *Inc.* provides at least partial rankings of the states on individual business-climate categories, as well as the aggregate, weighted rankings. For example, it offers the top 10 in terms of state support, business activities, labor, taxes, and capital resources. In addition, the AGC study and the *Inc.* report have similar views on questions such as unionization and taxes; both are considered negative.

Report Use: How might the *Inc.* report be used? It undoubtedly provides considerable information for the small firm. The data that it provides in a single source alone makes it useful; all the information presented can be found in published sources, but would require a great deal of time and experience for a small businessperson. To illustrate, the information regarding the states presently offering venture-capital programs is *quite important* to the smaller entrepreneur and might be difficult for him or her to obtain.

Perhaps least significant to the small businessperson is the state rankings. *Inc.* itself admits that the rankings have shifted widely over the last few years, as the factors being measured change and the involvement of the states becomes more intense. However, the rankings do offer some leverage for encouraging the lower-ranked states to improve their small-business programs. Then Governor Jay Rockefeller could not have been too pleased with West Virginia's

90

number 50 ranking, nor could Mississippi gain succor from West Virginia's plight after plunging from the top 10 in 1981 to the 49th position in 1984.

For business, of course, the *Inc.* report provides only part of the story. As with the AGC study, it offers little qualitative information on such factors as quality of life. And, even business climate itself requires some qualitative assessments, such as the governor's attitude toward business and the support provided the economic development department.

INDUSTRIAL DEVELOPMENT LEGISLATIVE CLIMATE REPORT

For the past 18 years, *Industrial Development* (ID) has provided an annual "Legislative Climate" survey. This year the publication, perhaps a bit contemptuously, states that its purpose in its annual survey "...is not to draw up yet another ranking of the states or to proclaim any 'top ten' for their sunny business climate." The publication adds:

Rather, what is attempted here is a presentation of information that is as up-to-the-minute as possible for practical use by facility planners and students of both economic development and the site selection process.[31]

While not wishing to be drawn into the controversy, we do see *ID* achieving its purpose.

Although offering no ranking of the states, *ID* provides a state-by-state assessment of financial-assistance programs, tax-incentive programs, special services for industrial development, incentives for pollution control, industrial-revenue bond eligibility and uses, and so forth. By carefully examining each comparative table, the reader can determine what *specific* state and federal programs are available in the individual states. (This breakdown also includes the availability of certain city and county programs in the states.) Further, the *ID* report's elaboration of various programs (and their current status), such as enterprise zones, in the discussion portion of the *ID* report is especially valuable.

As with the *AGC* study and the *Inc.* report, the annual *ID* report presents only the "facts." Here, the attention is more on program availability than on quantifiable factors, such as SBIC financing per 1,000 population (*Inc.* report) or value added by manufacturing employees per dollar of production payroll (*AGC* study). Its strength (and value) to businesspeople and economic development groups lies in *comprehensive coverage*—the specificity and depth of program assessment that it has presented in comparative form.

OTHER RELATED SERVICES

Business Facilities publishes an annual *Site Seekers Guide* issue, which includes lists of business associates, site consultants, port and railroad officials, state and city economic development officials, and so forth. The 1984 issue including more than 5,000 economic development contacts. Thus, for those seeking more specific information than that supplied by the *AGC* study, *BW* study, *Inc.* report, and *ID* report, the *Site Seekers Guide* issue indicates where to obtain the information. Other related up-to-date information sources and listings are included in the other monthly issues of *Business Facilities* and in *Plants Sites & Parks*. The latter has been especially useful in its state reports that are included in each issue.

Venture magazine now publishes an annual plant site directory in the form of a special advertising supplement. The most recent example (*Venture* 1984 Plant Site Directory) presented a listing of information sources, as well as articles discussing industry trends. *Venture* magazine's interest, as well as that of other publications, suggests that the number of state ratings and special advertising sections offering economic development information is increasing. However, it has been the *BW* study, the *AGC* survey, and the *Inc.* report that have attracted so much interest and controversy because of their rankings.

RANKING CONTROVERSY

Major college football has perhaps unwittingly added considerable fuel to the rating/ranking game, because the annual winner of the number one spot is decided by the polls (coaches and press). (The 1984 "off-the-field" battle between Brigham Young and others has really climaxed this struggle.) However, our penchant for wanting to see who is number one has led also to the *Fortune 500* ranking, the *Inc. 500* ranking, the Miss America contests (and similar beauty pageants), the rent-a-car warfare, the hundreds of awards shows, and even a movie entitled "10."

Not surprisingly, the media have been prompt in recognizing the news value of the state rankings. *USA Today,* for example, published a colorful map indicating the results of the 1984 *BW* study.[32] Concomitantly, the importance attributed to the rankings resulted in challenges to the published results of some of the studies and reports. Seeing his state's ranking slip seven notches (from 3rd to 10th) in the *AGC* study reportedly did not sit well with North Carolina's director of industrial development. The *Wall Street Journal* published his criticisms along with its own questions about some of *AGC* study findings. Particularly noteworthy was the reported response from the Alexander Grant & Company executive in charge of the study. He said, "There's a danger with people taking the rankings and saying, 'We're first,' or 'We're third.'" [Rather]... "what it tells you is what states are generally good and generally bad."[33] With the public's increased interest in economic development, however, the importance assigned to the rankings themselves can be expected to grow.

RANKING: A FINAL COMMENT

Each of the ranking systems has its own niche in the market. The *BW* study is the only one focusing on the demand side; for example, what does the business community have to say about locations? Who makes the site-selection decision? The *Inc.* report offers an assessment of state factors that are important to small business, while the *AGC* study ranks states in terms of their general *manufacturing* business climate.

With these differences in their purposes, there is little value in comparing their findings. For example, there would be little or no reason to expect that a state would rank the same in all three studies. (Interestingly, only Texas did rank among the top 10 states in the latest version of all three studies.) Rather, the value of each study or report lies in the provision of data on key factors that may be important to a particular corporation's (or group of corporations') location decisions or to the states themselves in improving their offerings for special segments of the business world. Further, most firms will need information or opinions on other factors that are not included in these studies. Some are quality-of-life factors; others may be company-specifics or the type of information found in the *ID* study.

MARKETING STATE ECONOMIC
DEVELOPMENT PROGRAMS

State marketing efforts are increasingly taking on the sophistication of the large consumer or business-to-business marketers. Undoubtedly, the closest parallel that can be drawn is between state economic development programs and the corporate marketing efforts of the business-to-business producer. Like the latter, state economic development programs are being marketed to domestic and foreign industry, and to the corporate executive in particular.

Just as corporate marketing is concerned with "selling the company" rather than its individual products, so the state is typically concerned with "selling the state" rather than its individual cities or the goods of any particular company in the state. Let us consider the problem faced by a "...company called TRW" in 1974 and see how it parallels in a number of ways the problems faced by many states. Although it was already a large company, TRW's problem was its relatively low level of awareness and virtually no image—neither positive or negative—among business and government leaders. The company's marketers realized that to effectively continue to market its products to business in the United States and overseas, it needed to first build the awareness and image of the company itself. What TRW subsequently undertook was a massive corporate (not product) promotional and marketing effort that included its now famous slogan: "Tomorrow is taking shape...at a company called TRW."[34] Was it successful? By 1979, TRW had moved from among the unknowns to being among the most recognized firms in its business-to-business category, and with the added sales and stock value that such recognition produces.

Many states face a problem similar to TRW whether they wish to admit it or not. Most in the United States and many overseas can list all (or a good part) of the 50 states. However, which states come to mind when the domestic or foreign executive is considering a corporate headquarters move, a plant location or relocation, or a subsidiary site? Further, when a state does come to mind, what is the image it produces in the executive's mind? Even if a state has neither a low awareness nor an "unknown" image problem, however, the marketing strategy it will follow is still akin to that of a firm's corporate campaign. Typically, the state is focusing on getting the corporate executive to consider it among the company's location alternatives. To achieve this objective, the state economic development officials need to present the state's pluses in a way that is attractive to the corporate decision makers. Similarly, when working to build the state's export trade, the state officials can only be product-specific if the company selling the product has no in-state competition. Rather, they are more involved in developing a vehicle by which the state's manufacturers, agricultural sector, and so forth, can effectively present their products to potential customers. In terms of foreign markets, this involves trade missions or the development of overseas trade offices in key locations, or both. Finally, with the exception of state-owned facilities, state tourist-promotion efforts involve selling the attractions of the whole state and developing the broad idea that Kansas or Montana or New Jersey is a good state to visit.

On the strategy implementation side, we see the state economic development marketers employing the same quality promotional efforts and media that are used by their business counterparts. One is not surprised to see a 60-second Ohio economic development commercial on television, a full-page advertisement for North Carolina and Michigan in *Inc.*, or an advertisement in the *Wall Street Journal.* They have become commonplace. Equally commonplace is the use of trade missions, often led by the governor, and possibly the use of trade offices. Minnesota, for example, has offices in Sweden and Norway.[35] Particularly noteworthy have been the quality of the state advertisements in the economic development industry's equivalent of trade journals, *Plants Sites & Parks* and *Business Facilities.* Add to these media the extensive direct-mail and trade-show efforts of the states, and the level of marketing support for the various economic development programs becomes more obvious.

Naturally, however, marketing includes much more than media advertising, brochures, and personal selling (trade offices/trade missions/trade shows). Marketing involves extensive planning, marketing research, and market-segmentation efforts. For example, the decision on where to locate the state's overseas trade office or the selection of target industries requires extensive planning, segmentation, and control efforts.

What we feel to be the first marketing stage for a state economic development organization, however, is something even more basic. We feel it requires the organization to evidence a demand orientation, a sense of responding to the customers' needs. In this instance the customers are the companies—the company decision makers—that are considering relocating their headquarters or building new plants, now as in the future. An appropriate question, therefore, is whether the state economic development organizations respond in terms of the customers' needs, that is, do they build their marketing programs in a way that facilitates the corporate decision-maker's job? Because the various states often use their media advertising to invite corporate inquiries, one way to answer this question, at least in part, is to analyze the content of the initial promotional materials the states send these corporate inquiries. It should be noted that often these initial materials mark the first direct contact these executives, through corporate inquiries, have ever had with the state's government and, thus, can have a significant image impact.

STATE PROMOTIONAL PACKAGE CONTENT ANALYSIS

We conducted a content analysis of the basic direct mail promotional package that each state provides to inquiring corporations, specifically to (1) determine whether or not it evidenced a "demand orientation," and (2) assess the initial impression that their promotional materials make.

As a measure of demand orientation, we felt that the states should include materials that relate to factors that traditionally have been viewed as important to location decision makers. And, we felt that the information should be in a form that would be convenient to the users, rather than convenient to those preparing the data. Second, we wanted to recognize the importance of the first impression or perception that the state's initial package creates with the corporate location decision maker. Here we were not concerned with appearance alone, however. Most states now produce attractive, four-color brochures or booklets. Rather, we focused on questions such as whether the state "showcased" its strongest points or assets and whether the state developed or centralized its assets around a core image or theme. Because the corporate decision makers are probably reviewing the materials from several states, a core theme or image increases the state's chances of being remembered.

METHODOLOGICAL MATTERS

We employed content analysis in reviewing both the state and city materials. While this technique is sometimes seen as highly subjective, it actually involves a disciplined and rigorous analysis of the material under review. Prior to initiating the content analysis, a highly structured format was developed against which the materials were judged. In this case, a list of eight traditional location decision-making factors was constructed and this list was used in the review of the individual state's materials (see Exhibit 3.1). Also, a separate overall quality rating was given. As suggested above, the basis for that rating included the existence of a core theme or consistent image; an assessment of whether the materials appeared to be specifically prepared and organized for inquiry response ("or appeared to be a 'throw-in'"); and the relevance of the package "as a whole." To ensure equity and comparability, the same individuals were involved throughout the content-analysis process from the establishment of the measurement factors to the individual state content assessments.

There were 41 states that cooperated with the authors by providing their promotion material package, the one they send to corporations making an initial inquiry, either through a "bingo-card" response or letter of request. However, economic development officials in all 50 states were contacted by us and were requested to provide the materials.

THE CONTENT ANALYSIS RESULTS: OUR "TOP TEN"

At the outset, we should note that all 41 states had some strong and weak points in their promotional packages; none was perfect. Further, our content analysis focused on content of the promotional package, which is quite different from an evaluation of a state's economic development program. From a content-analysis perspective, the availability of the best possible financial-incentive package would not offset the failure of the state's information package to make the reader aware that it was available.

Given these caveats, we could hardly resist identifying the states that came closest to matching our criteria; each provided extensive coverage of the factors and were strong in their presentation quality. In fact, each can be characterized to a varying degree as ranking high in

- visual effect or impression
- manner of presentation
- ease of finding and locating information
- quantity and quality of information

Our rating of all 41 states is presented in Exhibit 3.2. However, in fairness to the various cooperating states, we did not list them by name, especially since some of them were in the process of producing new materials at the time of our request and others indicated that they preferred to send extensive materials only after obtaining detailed information on the corporate prospects. The latter, in particular, were likely "penalized," because their second mailing is the most critical one.

EXHIBIT 3.1

Category-Specific Factors in Location Decision Making

I. Site-specific
  1. Transportation
    a. Rail
    b. Highway
    c. Trucking
    d. Air
    e. Bus
    f. Port
    g. Rapid transit
  2. Water
  3. Soil
  4. Space
  5. Zoning
  6. Buildings
  7. Utilities
  8. Price
  9. Topography
  10. Climate
  11. Drainage/flood control
  12. Housing
  13. Communications
  14. Security
  15. Advice/development services
  16. Natural resources/raw material
  17. Ethnic Breakdown

II. Financing
  1. Industrial revenue bonds/ tax exempt bonds
  2. Lease agreements
  3. Grants
  4. Low interest loans
  5. Loan guarantees
  6. Private financing
  7. Municipal bonds

III. Economic factors
  1. Diversification of industry
  2. Banking
  3. Income
  4. Infrastructure
  5. Location in terms of markets
  6. Demographics
  7. Retail sales
  8. Economic indicators
  9. Growth
  10. Wage rates
  11. Stability
  12. Building permits

IV. Tax Base
  1. Rates
  2. Gross receipts
  3. Foreign trade zone
  4. Tax exempt financing
  5. Target job tax credit
  6. Real property net taxable value

  7. Business fees
  8. Employment tax credits
  9. Valuations
  10. No state income tax
  11. No local income tax
  12. Periods of exemption
  13. Investment tax credits
  14. Tax advantages for renovation

V. Quality of life
  1. Religion
  2. Education
  3. Recreation
  4. Arts
  5. Museums
  6. Media
  7. History
  8. Quality of life
  9. Parks
  10. Libraries

VI. Employment
  1. Availability
  2. Training
  3. Extent of unionization
  4. Employment/unemployment statistics
  5. Employment by category/ distribution
  6. Work stoppages
  7. Labor relations
  8. Work Ethic
  9. Labor-force participation rates
  10. Referral service/job placement

VII. Incentives
  1. Tax exempt industrial revenue bonds
  2. Foreign-trade zone
  3. Tax exempt financing
  4. Port of entry
  5. Period of tax exemption
  6. Job incentive programs
  7. Free services
  8. Freeport status
  9. Grants

VIII. Companies
  1. Large industries
  2. Listing of employers, numbers employed
  3. Targeted companies
  4. Dollar sales by business categories
  5. Distribution/types of industries
  6. Number of companies located in vicinity

Source: Various publications including *A Guide To Industrial Site Selection*
by the Society of Industrial Realtors, 1979.

Alabama No. 1: Whereas the Crimson Tide of its major state university did not rank number one in football in 1984, the state's economic development promotional package topped our list. A few sample comments from our rating forms suggest why.

- Most of Alabama's presentation is coordinated around a single theme—"Alabama is cut out for business"—and employs a logo of the state surrounded by a dotted line.
- Individual brochures carry this theme forward—"Alabama's tax benefits are cut out for business," "Alabama's financings are cut out for business," and so forth.
- Virtually every factor is covered and is given equal stress; "...you don't get the feeling one factor is stressed over others." "The information is presented in a thorough, visually appealing manner."

Alabama's high overall rating results as much from its thoroughness, consistency, and obvious design for the business reader, as it does from any single, imaginative theme or superior artwork or design. It offers just a solid piece of work, one that would impress a "no-nonsense" executive.

Next Nine: The remainder of the top 10 all ranked close to Alabama and were characterized by pluses. Bunched especially close were Rhode Island, West Virginia, and Delaware—the holders of positions two through four. Each relied on a consistency of presentation and a level of quality that was just behind Alabama's. Rhode Island scored especially high with its presentation of the companies that have moved to the state, while West Virginia could have crowded Alabama for the top spot with more follow-through on its theme, "West Virginia the Challenge."

Following in order after Delaware were Florida, Mississippi, Kentucky, and Illinois. Florida's use of comparisons with other states on several key factors was impressive, as was Mississippi's consistent reference to its "distribution-center" strengths. Kentucky's plus was its presentation of incentives and its organization of the materials, while Illinois made a particularly impressive and well-coordinated visual impression in addition to its thorough, yet easy to follow coverage of the factors.

Rounding out the top 10 were Oklahoma and Michigan. Oklahoma's format provided a helpful summary of the state's key assets, while Michigan was particularly strong in its incentive presentation.

Special Mention: We could point out strengths or key pluses in virtually every promotional package; the differences between the top 10 and bottom 10 are relatively narrow. Here are just a sample of the comments our research produced about special features of a few of the other states:

EXHIBIT 3.2
Subjective Assessment of States' Key Economic Development Factors/Categories

	MW 3	E 3	SE 3	E 4	E 5	MW 4	SW 1	MW 5	E 6	MW 6	W 2	SE 4	SE 5	E 7	SE 6	W 3	E 8	SE 7
I. Site specific	C	C		A	A	B	B	B	B	C	C	B	A	B	C	B	C	C
II. Financing	C	C		B	C	B	C	C	C	A	C	A	B	C	B	C	D	C
III. Economic factors	C-D	B-C		A	C	B	B	C	C	C	C	B	C	C	C	B	B	C
IV. Tax base	C	C		B	C	B	B	B	C	B	C	A	B	C	B	A	B	B
V. Employment	B	C		B	A	A	B	B	B	B	C	B	B	B	B	B	B	B
VI. Incentives	B	C		B	C	A	C	B	C	C	D	A	B	C	B	B	C	C
VII. Companies	D	A		A	B	D	D	D	C	C	D	D	C	C	D	D	D	D
VIII. Quality of life	B	C		B	C	B	B	B	C	C	C	D	D	B	B	B	D	C
IX. Overall quality	B-C	C-D	C	A	C	C	C	B-C	C	C	D	B	B	D	C-D	D	E	C-D

Assessment rating scale (emphasis):
A = Strong; B = Above average; C = Average; D = Below average; E = Not mentioned or poor.

State Code: E = East; SW = Southwest; SE = Southeast; W = West; MW = Midwest and numbers = specific state in the region.

SE 3 provided only a partial package to an initial inquiry.

EXHIBIT 3.2 (Cont'd)
Subjective Assessment of States' Key Economic Development Factors/Categories

	SW 2	E 10	SW 3	E 11	SW 4	SW 5	W 5	SE 9	MW 9	MW 10	MW 11	MW 1	SE 1	E 1	MW 2	E 2	W 1	SE 2
I. Site specific	C	C	C	C	C	C	C	C	D	D	D	D	C	C	C	C	C	C
II. Financing	C	C	C	C	C	C	C	C	C	C	C	E	C	C	B-C	C	C	C
III. Economic factors	B	C	C	C	D	C	B-C	C	C-D	D	D	D-E	D	C	C	D	C	D
IV. Tax base	B	C	C	C	C	C	C	C	C	B-C	B	B	C	C	C	C	C	C
V. Employment	B	C	C	C	C	C	C	C	C	C	B	B	C	C	C	C	C	C
VI. Incentives	B	C	C	C	C	D	C	C	B	B-C	C	C-D	C	C	C	C	C	C-D
VII. Companies	C	D	D	B	D	C	B-C	D	D-E	C	D-E	D	D	C	C	D	D	D
VIII. Quality of life	C	C	C	C	D	B	C	C	B	C-D	C-D	C	C	C	B-C	B	C	D
IX. Overall quality	B	A	C	C	B-C	B-C	B-C	B-C	B-C	C	C-D	D	A	A	B	C	D	D

Assessment rating scale (emphasis):
A = Strong; B = Above average; C = Average; D = Below average; E = Not mentioned

EXHIBIT 3.2 (Cont'd)

**Subjective Assessment of States' Key Economic
Development Factors/Categories**

	MW 8	SE 8	E 9	W 4	MW 7
I. Site specific	C	B	C	A	C
II. Financing	B	C	B	B-C	C
III. Economic factors	C	B	B	C	C
IV. Tax base	B	C	C	C-D	C
V. Employment	B	C	C	B	C
VI. Incentives	B	C	C	C	C
VII. Companies	C	B	C	D	C
VIII. Quality of life	C	C-D	D	D-E	D
IX. Overall quality	C	B	C-D	C-D	B-C

- Maine. "...the brochure, A Profile in Capability, should be an 'effective selling piece'..." "Major corporations located in Maine are used in discussing state attributes and top executives cite their reasons for choosing Maine."
- Iowa. "...a publication entitled, *Iowa's Quality of Life As Compared to the Nation and Other Midwestern States,* indexes easily quantifiable quality of life components." It lends itself to quick reading and offers comparative data.
- Virginia. "...featured the advantages it offered corporate headquarters [especially high-tech] in terms of key considerations, including business costs, business intangibles and quality of life." Well documented.
- Minnesota. "...especially impressive set of guides and directories to assist the company in finding information."
- Indiana. "...the organization of its economic development materials, which focused on six categories of legislative support it provides industry."
- Colorado. "...its manual entitled *Doing Business in Colorado* carefully outlines the essential steps (requirements) for operating in the state."
- Alaska. "...the detailed booklet regarding *Establishing A Business in Alaska* offers a most useful set of guidelines."

- California. "...California's advertising follow-up material entitled *The Californias* is perhaps the single most impressive direct mail brochure that was received by the authors."

Viewing the state materials in aggregate, a few observations might be made that would be useful to state economic development officials. These are:

- States could resist including materials that have little likelihood of being relevant to the corporate decision maker;
- The use of a central theme or an index helps the busy reader follow the materials more easily;
- A set of executive overview materials, highly concise and pointed, can be most impressive, especially when used with a larger mailing (Indiana's "A Case for Indiana" that we received in response to a "bingo card" is an excellent illustration);
- The types of materials provided should be consistent: Never include several brochures each suggesting that a *different* industry is the state's highest priority; this raises questions of sincerity and credibility;
- Make the package appear to have been developed particularly for the location decision maker, not just an omnibus package on "what's happening in _____" that could be sent to legislators, travel agents, high school civics classes, and so forth;
- Personal letters are important and should all be signed personally; a stamped signature or an obvious reproduction suggests little enthusiasm in the state's response.

Finally, we suggest trying to avoid an overuse of pictures of the governor. This was, in fact, possibly the major weakness in the Alabama package. And, as an addendum, we would recommend that states take a look at some of the impressive promotional materials being put together by several of the U.S. and Canadian cities, as well as foreign locales. Coming to mind immediately are those provided by the Industrial Development Commission of Mid-Florida, Inc.; the Broward County Development Board; the Washington-Baltimore Common Market; and the North of England Development Council (Newcastle).

ILLUSTRATION 3.3

Important tie-in with all direct mail materials.

THE CALIFORNIAS RANK FIRST
IN THE WORLD IN FULLY-IMPROVED
BUSINESS PARKS.

We make it easy.
We can offer you more choices in cost, size and location of turn-key facilities than any other state, any other nation.

We make it easy.
We're investing almost $5 billion annually for infrastructure to support you, to supply you.

If you'd like to know why 400 industrial companies expanded in The Californias last year, write the California Department of Commerce.

We make it easy.

THE CALIFORNIAS
California Department of Commerce
Office of Business Development P.O. Box 9278 Dept. 410
Van Nuys, CA 91409

Vignettes

THE BEN FRANKLIN PARTNERSHIP PROGRAMS*

Pennsylvania's Ben Franklin Partnership Challenge Grant Program for Technological Innovation established four advanced technology centers around the commonwealth—at Bethlehem, Philadelphia, Pittsburgh, and University Park. The partnership links private and educational resources, particularly research capabilities, to make Pennsylvania's traditional industry more competitive in international markets and to spin off new, small businesses on the cutting edge of technological innovation. It also provides resources to address educational and training needs and supplies entrepreneurial development services, including the provision of small-business incubator facilities.

Each of these four centers engages in joint research and development efforts with the private sector in specified areas. For example, the North East Tier Advanced Technology Center, which is based at Lehigh University, specializes in research and development in CAD/CAM (computer-assisted design/computer-assisted manufacturing), polymers/materials, solid state microelectronics, and biotechnology. This center includes 22 private and public colleges and universities, 86 industrial labor and financial organizations, four small-business development centers, and 21 economic development or local government groups and organizations, as well as foundations. By contrast, the Advanced Technology Center of Southeastern Pennsylvania, made up of Philadelphia-area organizations, concentrates in sensor technologies, human adaptability in space, biomedical technologies, and technology to benefit the handicapped.

The Ben Franklin Partnership is managed by a 15-person board that encompasses private-sector, small-business, education, labor, and legislative representation. Its main charge is to foster and maintain Pennsylvania jobs in advanced technology enterprises, to improve productivity among Pennsylvania's existing firms, and to diversify the Commonwealth's economy into high-technology areas. In addition to the R & D work of the four technology centers, the partnership has supportive programs, such as research seed grants to small businesses seeking to develop or introduce advanced technology into the marketplace and a computer profile of research capabilities in the Commonwealth in both the private sector and colleges and universities.

---

*Information for this vignette adapted from various promotional publications of the Ben Franklin Partnership Programs.

GEORGIA CAMPAIGN: TARGETING ATTRIBUTES

Too often states and cities are unable to resist the old advertising temptation of "filling all the white space." For economic development organizations with limited budgets and much to communicate, this temptation is doubly acute. We have seen all-too-numerous quarter-page advertisements in national publications that give the "27 reasons why you should locate in _____." Not only do these advertisements defy all readership research (except those for supermarket specials), they additionally fail to target their messages to particular audiences.

By matching their pluses with target-market needs and by avoiding the temptation to cram all their benefits into one advertisement, states and cities can effectively communicate. The advertisement for the state of Georgia in the accompanying illustration provides an excellent example. This advertisement and the total campaign recognizes the (state's) pluses, uses targeting, and shows an impressive use of white space. Was the campaign successful? We asked for comments from H. M. Parker, Jr., the account supervisor of the state of Georgia account at Pringle Dixon Pringle, an advertising, marketing, and public relations agency based in Atlanta, Georgia. He said:

> The state campaign ran for a period of six months using the creative concept as exhibited. The campaign was designed to create image presence and to generate qualified response. In less than four months, it was obvious that the objective had been achieved based on the high number of inquiries.

ILLUSTRATION 3.4

Use of white space to emphasize a single point.

GEORGIA. Where the climate's right for business.

Move, relocate, or open branch operations in Georgia and you'll enjoy more than a strategic, pro-business sunbelt location featuring low corporate taxes. You'll enjoy the weather.

Because the temperate Georgia climate provides a perfect recreational environment year round. So bring your business in out of the cold. Bring your business to Georgia. For further information call Bob Lewis at 404-656-3572. Or write: THE GEORGIA DEPARTMENT OF INDUSTRY AND TRADE, 230 Peachtree Street, N.W., Box 1776, Atlanta, Georgia 30301.

GEORGIA .U.S.A.
The Strategic Market

REFERENCES

1. Brenner, S. (1984, June). Life in the Silicon Rain Forest. *Inc.*, p. 112.
2. Hillkirk, J. (1984, November 13). States find it hard to recruit firms. *USA Today*, p. 1B.
3. Brenner, p. 114.
4. The fifty legislative climates. (1984, January/February). *Industrial Development*, p. 8.
5. Bailey, D.M. (1984, September 3). A race for development funds. *New England Business*, p. 82.
6. Posner, B.G. (1984, October). Inc's Fourth Annual Report on the States. *Inc.*, p. 110.
7. *Business Week.* (1984). *Business Week's 1984 Plants Site Selection Survey of Management Subscribers in Industry* (p. 14). New York.
8. The fifty legislative climates, p. 6.
9. Padda, K. (1981, October). Report card on the States. *Inc.*, pp. 93-94.
10. Posner, p. 110.
11. The high-tech renaissance in southern California. (1984, September 17). *Business Week*, p. 142.
12. Venture capital rides in Texas. (1984, September 16). *New York Times*, p. F8.
13. Posner, p. 110.
14. The fifty legislative climates, p. 6.
15. Ohioline advertisement. (1984, December 11). *USA Today*, p. 4B.
16. Carlson, E. (1984, June 15). Virginia plans research site to save its high-tech firms. *Wall Street Journal*, p. 37.
17. Dempsey, K.B. (1984, November/December). States increase high-tech educational opportunities. *Plants Sites & Parks*, pp. 1, 11-15, 70-75, 108-111.
18. Delaware advertisement. (1981, November/December). *Plants Sites & Parks*, p. 81.
19. South Carolina advertisement. (1984, November/December). *Plants Sites & Parks*, pp. 108-109.
20. Washington advertisement. (1984, November/December). *Plants Sites & Parks*, p. CZ.
21. Blank, D. (1984, September 25). Inquiry topic: Minnesota. *USA Today*, p. 11A.
22. Khan, J.P. (1984, October). An ache in the heartland. *Inc.*, pp. 116-117, 118.
23. Posner, p. 129.
24. Carlson, E. (1983, July 12). Great Lakes governors split over truce on industry raids. *Wall Street Journal*, p. 35.
25. *Business Week*, pp. 1-23.
26. Alexander Grant & Company. (1984). *The Fifth Study of General Manufacturing Business Climates*. Chicago: Alexander Grant & Company.
27. Ibid, p. 7.
28. Ketchum, Jr., B.W. (1984, May). The Inc. 100. *Inc.*, pp. 155-166.
29. Posner, p. 108.
30. Ibid, p. 108.
31. The Fifty State Climate, p. 7.

32. Hillkirk, J. (1984, October 5). Top states for new plant sites hold their own. *USA Today*, p. 5B.
33. Carlson, E. (1984, April 17). Business-climate ratings stir debate over study's methods. *Wall Street Journal*, p. 35.
34. Hise, R.T., Gillett, P.L., & Ryans, J.K., Jr. (1984). *Marketing: Concepts, decisions, strategies.* Houston: Dame Publications, Inc.
35. Minnesota and Wisconsin: Trade activitists. (1984, November 12). *Business America*, p. 19.

4

CITY ECONOMIC DEVELOPMENT EFFORTS: BATTLING ON THE FIRING LINE

EXECUTIVE SUMMARY

Harry Truman's famous "buck stops here" desk plate could well serve as the motto for city economic development executives. State efforts can go a long way in fostering the appropriate business climate, creating necessary legislation, and providing key contacts. However, as communities have increasingly come to recognize, there is no substitute for effective *local* efforts.

In some instances it is the county, or perhaps two or three counties, that take the lead at the local level; the Industrial Development Commission of Mid-Florida, Inc. (Orlando-area), and Broward County (Fort Lauderdale) provide prime examples of such county-level leadership. But, by and large, we find a community-level group, either public-sector, private-sector, or a blend of the two, that is the principal champion of the Richmonds, Dallases, Atlantas, New Bedfords, Belens (New Mexico), and so forth.

What cities in effect have come to recognize is that states cannot really carry the economic development burden for them. Although a governor can support efforts to attract industry to the state, it is necessary for him or her to avoid touting any single location. Unless the company being sought narrows the list in some way, for example, it will only locate near a river or must have a certain type of rail access, the state economic group will typically provide relatively equal support for all of its interested communities. This recognition has given the impetus to city efforts not only to attract domestic investors, but to engage in overseas industry development forays as well.

In targeting new industry or business development, it is important for cities to seek a realistic balance in terms of industry and employment "types." While many major metropolitan areas, especially those in the Midwest, have suffered during recent recessions, it is not surprising that cities such as Minneapolis, Columbus, and Indianapolis have fared reasonably well. These are not single-industry towns, nor are they solely dependent on manufacturing. They are able to balance service, business, government, education, and medical care along with manufacturing. Obviously, states can have only one capital, but when seeking growth it is important for cities to also provide for economic diversity. For example, a number of communities have started business incubators or research parks themselves, or have cooperated with private-sector groups in their development. Channeled properly, these efforts to support high potential start-ups represent an important step in such diversification activity.

Part of our research for this book involved the use of content analysis to examine the promotional materials a select group of cities provide to inquiring companies. Unlike the state analysis, the cities were not rated by name. Rather, we simply wanted to consider the level and quality of the materials of a sample of cities so that we could illustrate the possible strengths and weaknesses of such offerings. We offer several suggestions based on this analysis. However, the major weakness we noted was the failure of these cities to address *any of their image problems.* Most had some potential negatives that they could address. In fact, this reply to inquiries was their one opportunity to address them, but they tended to emphasize their positive and hope that the negative would be ignored or go away.

Finally, another problem for many cities has been their inability to get their "act together." Although we did not research this particular problem, there is continued evidence that cities too often have multiple economic development groups, each vying to represent the city. This divisive, often highly dysfunctional, competition clearly hurts community developmental efforts, because it is usually obvious to knowledgeable outsiders.

∞

Bloomington/Normal, Illinois and Springhill, Tennessee, may now be approaching "King of the Hill" status in terms of industrial growth, but the proactive promotional efforts of the Omahas, the Beloits, the Brownsvilles, and the Scarboroughs (Ontario) demonstrate that other cities have not conceded the battle. In fact, never has the competition between cities (and counties)* been greater, or the stakes higher. Why is this true? Are the cities merely duplicating their state's economic development efforts?

A state development organization is primarily concerned with competing with its counterparts in the other 49 states. It may encourage a prospective industrial investor to locate in one area of the state, but typically this will happen only if it is apparent that a particular city or county has the best chance of attracting the particular company. Otherwise, the state economic development agency will generally promote the whole state and is equally satisfied if a company decides to locate or relocate in any of its communities. South Dakota, for example, promotes all of its cities, not just Rapid City or Mitchell. Thus, the states are attempting to assist cities by creating an awareness of the state, providing financial and marketing support, establishing a competitive legislative posture, and offering complementary programs. The next question is one the cities must answer. Is this state effort alone sufficient to enable a Beloit, Wisconsin, a Rangeley, Maine, or a Santa Maria, California, to attract new industry or business? Increasingly, the answer appears to be *no!* Today, as always, it is the city or local area that is really on the front line in the economic development war. The final corporate-location decisions involve choosing from among acceptable cities and making a site-specific selection. Therefore, a city cannot afford to remain aloof from the process. In other words, regardless of whether the relocating or locating corporation (1) selects a state and then selects a city in the state, or (2) narrows its decision to a select number of cities in more than one state, the company's site-selection decision ultimately is a local one. To city officials in Beloit or any other city, the only difference is whether it must compete with a Milwaukee in its own state or with a Rockhurst (Illinois). In the latter instance, the state will aggressively assist Beloit, while in the former it will normally remain noncommittal. In either event, city officials have become all too conscious of the fact that second place offers no consolation to the loser or losers.

---

*At the local level, cities and the counties in which they reside may work together or may have separate economic development efforts. For our discussion purposes, we will use the term *cities* to refer to all the various types of local efforts. The reader should recognize that this is merely for convenience, however, because counties in some instances play a *critical* role at the local level. For example, Broward County, Florida, takes the lead in the economic development efforts of that area of South Florida.

ILLUSTRATION 4.1

Addressing an obvious negative perception.

WHY WOULD ANYBODY MOVE TO ANDERSON, INDIANA?

Reason #1 *Believe it or not, our locally-established manufacturing wage rate is 17 percent below the statewide average.*

Anderson has always received a bad rap for high industrial wages. We are proud to be the home of two divisions of General Motors. Premium wages paid at those plants are established by national contract, and they are much higher than local rates. The average manufacturing wage established by Anderson-based employers is only $8.41 per hour. And many capable people are happy to work at that rate.

Reason #4 *Anderson's location gives you all the advantages of operating and living in a big city, without suffering from the big city blues.*

Land, labor, and utilities are inexpensive in Anderson. And you won't have to drive for several hours to get to and from work. We are only minutes from the hub of the nation's interstate highway system. So getting your product to your markets is fast. And it's inexpensive. Living in Anderson, you can enjoy the social and cultural environment of a small city. At the same time, you have easy access to the sporting and commerical opportunities of Indianapolis. So why put up with the crime, pollution, high costs and the rough life of a big city? Especially when you don't have to.

Anderson.

Come for the business, stay for the people!

Eleven cost-cutting reasons for moving to Anderson are described in the FANTUS Company's report on our city and will be discussed further in this information series. For further information, **call collect:** Bob Kamm, Anderson Corporation for Economic Development, 317/642-0264; or Tony Demos, City of Anderson, 317/646-9655.

INDIANA Produced in cooperation with the Indiana Department of Commerce Lt. Governor John M. Mutz Director

Given the competitive environment, communities of all sizes find themselves engaged in efforts to stimulate industrial economic development. Since early 1982, we have been closely monitoring numerous community economic development programs, especially their marketing strategies and tactics, vis-a-vis their promotional materials and advertising efforts. Dozens of cities, for example, have provided us with the types of materials they mail to corporations that make inquiries about such factors as their economic programs.

In this chapter, we will draw upon this ongoing research as we explore the current state-of-the-art in city and local economic development programs. Questions such as, What promotional and marketing efforts are the cities employing?, How important is the quality-of-life factor?, and What types of incentives are being offered?, will be considered. Further, we will explore how cities can be more *specific* in terms of their "pluses" than can state and regional economic development groups, and how these *pluses* have been tied directly to investor needs by some cities.

Finally, we will present the results of a content-analysis study of the informational materials offered to prospective investors by some 25 cities. This latter research paves the way for our later recommendations on marketing economic development programs.

ILLUSTRATION 4.2

Creativity in attracting attention in a small-size advertisement.

Any way you slice it.

Columbia, Missouri, tempts new industry.
    And the reasons are many: Columbia is a prime location to reach the mid-continent heartland. Columbia offers a large, available work force — and no manufacturing unions. Our cost of living is below the national average. And we offer financing through industrial revenue bonds. Slice yourself a piece of Columbia. Ask us for the statistics.
    CONTACT: Robert D. Black, Columbia Economic Development, P.O. Box N, Columbia, MO 65205
    (314) 874-7214.

©Copyright 1983

Ripe for the picking.
COLUMBIA
P.O. Box N   Columbia, MO 65205   (314) 874-7214

Advertisement reprinted with the permission of Robert D. Black, Columbia Economic Development—State of Missouri.

COMMUNITY ADVANTAGE

Many cities have only recently come to recognize their necessary role and their particular advantage or advantages in the economic development game. For years, they appeared satisfied to have the state take the lead; they merely supported the state efforts whenever they were called upon. It was the states that had economic development offices overseas, arranged for trade missions, and ran the advertisements in *Business Week, Fortune,* the *Wall Street Journal,* and the airline magazines, while the cities merely responded to industrial inquiries stimulated by the states.

Perhaps we have overstated the historic situation a bit, but it makes a critical point. Cities, especially the larger ones, now have started to shed their secondary role and are taking steps to at least complement the states' efforts. More and more often, however, they have moved beyond the complementary stage, and have taken the initiative to chart their own course. San Antonio, through the direct influence of Mayor Cisneros, illustrates how a city can become bold enough to move beyond state efforts. The cities have the advantage of being able to be more specific about their offerings in terms of benefits, services, and so forth, than can anyone else. Naturally, each city is unique. Toledo and Cleveland are both in Ohio, but share little in common besides Lake Erie. Each has its own peculiar combination of industries, socioeconomic groups, quality-of-life factors, and so on. With the exception of John Denver, most see Toledo as an aggressive self-starter, while Cleveland too often seems bent on ignoring its potential. (The long delay in its domed stadium effort illustrates the latter.)

Further, a city is often able to turn more directly to its own constituency for support than is the state. After all, it is the local retail community, the local public utilities, the local banks, and the local real estate firms that will benefit most directly from the infusion of new payrolls. Therefore, when Dallas wants to have a special advertising section in *Fortune,* it is small wonder that included among the firms participating in the sponsorship are such companies as a bank and an industrial realtor.

From a marketer's perspective, the difference between the states' and cities' role in economic development can be described conceptually in terms of a continuum that ranges from "abstract" to "concrete." Of course, many of the special financial programs are state-developed and maintained, plus a number of the federal finance or tax-related programs are channeled through the states. And, some states offer corporate tax relief for a period of time, and this concession is typically more significant than when a city offers such an incentive alone. These state offerings would hardly be considered abstract, nor would capital and site improvements. Given all these caveats, it still is clear that states must operate more on the abstract end of the continuum, while the cities can develop marketing strategies and tactics that are more concrete. For example, Florida state economic development promotional materials can speak in terms of "more than 140 Florida enterprise zones," while individual Florida cities can say, "We have an enterprise zone." As another illustration, the city of Oakland (California) provides a straightforward list of Oakland-specific employment and business development services to inquiries.

Another way of contrasting the states' and cities' role in economic development is through use of corporate marketing efforts as an analogy. During the 1984 Olympics, Beatrice Foods did extensive *corporate advertising*. This corporate advertising was designed to enhance Beatrice's image with the general public and to build its corporate awareness, that is, increase consumer awareness that Beatrice is a formidable corporation. On the other hand, Beatrice does product marketing in behalf of its various products; this product advertising is designed to sell the specific product. Now, comparing Beatrice Foods and state and city economic development efforts shows that Beatrice Foods' corporate advertising program is comparable to a state's marketing objective, while a Beatrice product advertising is comparable to a city's.

WHAT CITY PROGRAMS CONTAIN

Initially, we must recognize that the types of economic programs vary widely and range from those cities that merely respond to inquiries to those cities that even have teams crisscrossing the United States (and the world) seeking potential industrial and business investors. Based on our research experience, it is difficult to identify a typical city economic development program.

However, most state-of-the-art city programs tend to incorporate a number of the following features in their economic development offering. Some of these programs are federal-sponsored or co-sponsored, state-sponsored or local public- or private-developed. In any event, their availability at the local level all requires some degree of local initiative.

- Financial packages for (1) existing area firms or start-ups, and (2) outside corporations seeking to relocate or establish a subsidiary (or other major facility);
- Job training (company-specific, general training, or both);
- Tax relief (property tax reduction or corporate tax reduction, or both);
- Capital improvements, such as site development (and construction) and transportation access (rail sidings, connecting highways, and so forth);
- Site-location assistance;

ILLUSTRATION 4.3

Use of testimonials by business executives.

"A Rewarding Lifestyle Was The Most Important Consideration In Where We Located. That's Why We're In Palm Coast, Florida Today."

Robert Brownlee, Sr. Exec. V.P.,
Chairman of Board. Simon Fuger,
Exec. V.P., Sec. & Treas.

The key to Cardiac Control Systems' future success was its ability to attract and retain high-quality employees to manufacture its advanced heart pacemaker product. Cardiac had to offer not only a good working environment, but a good living environment, too.

Palm Coast offered five miles of beautiful beach, golf, tennis, swimming, a marina with access to the Intracoastal Waterway and a host of other amenities, plus a community environment so well suited for people, it actually attracts employees.

And the weather couldn't be nicer.

PalmC ast ℠

Fulfilling The Promise For Florida.

- -

Learn more about the Palm Coast business climate. Write: Ernest Maddock, ITT Community Development Corporation, Executive Offices, Palm Coast, Florida 32051.

Name _____ Title _____

Company _____

Address _____

City _____ State _____ Zip _____

Phone _____

- "Red-tape" facilitation—guidance through the "bureaucracy" that follows any corporate real estate activity, such as acquiring needed licenses or legal assistance;
- Modern public services—recognizing and correcting local services' weaknesses, such as increasing water, electricity, or park capacity through new construction.

In terms of financial packages and capital improvements, the city may or may not have its local financing plan, one financed by the community alone. On the other hand, the competitive city needs to be able to utilize every state and federal program available to its advantage. For example, in its prospect literature, the Industrial Development Commission of Mid-Florida, Inc. notes that it has assisted 103 companies to secure industrial revenue bond financing (state) totaling $199 million, and McAllen (Texas) indicates 15 firms are utilizing Mexico's Border Industrialization Program (a twin-city McAllen/Reynosa relationship). Federal programs would include those of the Small Business Administration (SBA) and Housing and Urban Development (HUD) (such as HUD Urban Development Action Grants), whereas states have a number of especially developed grant and loan programs. The cities may only need to assist firms in applying or accessing the financial assistance, while with other forms of financing the cities may direct the funds' use or become active through their own financing mechanisms.

Of particular interest in terms of financing, there is an increased number of programs designed specifically to allow for local-firm expansion or local start-ups. As with the states, cities are now recognizing that in their enthusiasm to bring in new industrial development, they tended to ignore the needs of existing local companies and local prospective entrepreneurs. Various types of funding and assistance, including incubators and venture capital, for such firms or prospective firms are now being included in many city programs.

Beyond these seven frequently offered features, there are several others that are often included in city programs. For example, port cities may have special features in their program related to port utilization, such as free-trade zones or low-cost public warehouses, while those with prime rail locations may provide special railroad-related or storage-related features. Another example of a special feature would be the enterprise zones that have become a popular part of many cities' offerings. Equally important in many communities has been the development of university research parks. An increasing number of cities have worked closely with nearby public and private universities and their states or private developers, or both, in the establishment of these research and development centers.

ILLUSTRATION 4.4

Zeroing in on a small but compelling list of attributes the city has to offer.

In this university city you'll find:

- a 296-acre corporate research park
- a university Center of Excellence in Bioanalytical Research
- a productive, highly educated workforce in a Right-to-Work state
- Enterprise Zones, IRB financing, and a pro-business environment
- More culture per capita than New York City.*

LAWRENCE
Kansas

Community Profile? Contact John A. Myers, Box 581, Lawrence KS 66044, (913) 843-4411

*Rand McNally, 1985 Places Rated Almanac

Advertisement reprinted with the permission of the Lawrence Chamber of Commerce.

MARKETING CITY PROGRAMS

How do cities go about marketing their economic development programs? Even when cities have developed competitive economic development programs, their success in attracting industry is often directly related to their peculiar marketing skills.

The traditional marketing-mix elements available to manufacturers of consumer and industrial products and services include (1) the product; (2) the channel of distribution (wholesalers, retailers, industrial distributors, etc.); (3) the price; and (4) promotion (personal selling, advertising, and public relations). Further, the marketer employs marketing research to better match the firm's offer—its product— to the consumer or buyer's needs. In Exhibit 4.1, a comparison is made between the marketing elements, including marketing research, as they may be optimally employed by an automobile manufacturer and a city economic development office.

ILLUSTRATION 4.5

Using existing "name" businesses as magnets.

Advertisement reprinted with the permission of James A. Covell, Executive Vice President, Albuquerque Industrial Development Service—State of New Mexico.

Of special interest to us in discussing the cities' marketing activities are their efforts to stimulate interest from their target market, in particular, the cities' promotional efforts and the types of materials they provide to companies making inquiries in response to their advertising. Promotion offers the main communication link between the city and the potential new investor; it is the most visible evidence of a city's marketing effort.

What the cities feature in their advertising today, whether it is a quarter-page advertisement in *Plants Sites & Parks* or *Fortune,* generally reflects (1) the city's target audience, (2) the *benefit* the city perceives the target audience is seeking in a new location, and (3) the city's strengths relating to that benefit. In recent advertisements, the benefit employed by the following cities was often quite specific.

- Fall River (Massachusetts). Labor quality/training; "No Labor Shortage." *(New England Business,* June 4, 1984);
- Topeka (Kansas). Quality of life; "Remember when your favorite fishing spot was only 20 minutes away?" *(Plants Sites & Parks,* January-February, 1983);
- Jacksonville (Florida). High-tech skills/employee retention testimonial; "Why Florida's Business City was first choice for AT&T's American Transtech." *(Fortune,* September 3, 1984);
- Tulsa (Oklahoma). Higher productivity for high-tech testimonial; "Bragg on Tulsa." *(New England Business,* November 5, 1984);
- Richmond (Virginia). Results of quality of life study; "Two Opinions on Living in Richmond." *(Inc.,* March 1984).

On the other hand, perhaps nonselective benefitwise, but still targeted, was a San Antonio, Texas, advertisement that highlighted recent industrial expansion planning. In less than five lines of copy, this advertisement touched on numerous benefits, benefits that were perceived by the San Antonio Economic Development Foundation as being significant to a broad range of executives. Although nonselective in terms of benefits, this advertisement still illustrates careful targeting, because of the audience of the medium (*Inc.*). This publication (*Inc.*), unlike a *Business Week,* is directed specifically to executives in all sorts of medium and small fast-track companies. Although the variety of these companies is so great that it would be difficult to employ a *single benefit,* the number of size and success factors makes these companies a target group, one that is a prime candidate for future expansion of some type or possibly even a headquarters move.

TWO LEVELS OF RESPONSE

Increasingly, city economic development efforts occur at two levels—general and company- or industry-specific. Most initial inquiries to city economic development organizations provide little information regarding the company seeking the information. The economic development personnel can readily obtain some secondary information on the company using such sources as Moody's or Standard and Poor's. However, they cannot be too company-specific at this stage, since they really do not know if the company is interested in setting up a regional office, a plant, a warehouse facility, or is possibly considering a home-office relocation.

Therefore, city economic development groups typically provide rather general information in response to an initial inquiry. In addition, they will normally either ask the inquirer to indicate to them what other

EXHIBIT 4.1

**Comparison of City and Automobile Manufacturing
Optimal Use of Marketing Elements**

Marketing Element	Marketing Objective	Automobile Manufacturer	City Economic Development Office
Product	Compete for each desired niche	Individual model(s)	Economic development program
Price	Compete in relation to relative product quality	Model(s) price (including various margins)	Financial portion of the package including tax incentives, loans, etc.)
Channel	Reach target market most effectively	Automobile dealers (regional distributors)	Direct contact or assistance from or cooperation with industrial realtors, states, etc.
Promotion	Communicate desired message, build image, create awareness, complete transactions or desired goal	National advertising, local advertising, national sales force, dealer's sales force, public relations	National advertising, inquiry response, sales teams, (state and/or local) brochures
Marketing Research	Provide better understanding of potential customers or clients and measure effectiveness	Targeting specific consumers or niches (identify needs/ company image, etc.)	Targeting specific industries and companies (identify needs/city image, etc.)

information might be useful to his or her company *or* include a questionnaire that asks for details on the prospective move so that the city can provide the prospect with appropriate detailed data. In either instance, it is a frequent practice by city economic development personnel to follow up the written response to an inquiry with a telephone contact. Such calls are designed to stimulate the inquiring company to provide the information the city development group needs in order to create a company-specific response and to qualify the

ILLUSTRATION 4.6

Focusing on a single strength.

WITH 5% DOWN YOU CAN BE UP AND RUNNING IN CRANSTON, R.I.

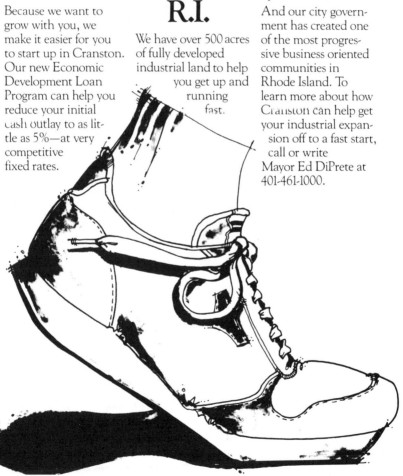

Because we want to grow with you, we make it easier for you to start up in Cranston. Our new Economic Development Loan Program can help you reduce your initial cash outlay to as little as 5%—at very competitive fixed rates.

We have over 500 acres of fully developed industrial land to help you get up and running fast.

And our city government has created one of the most progressive business oriented communities in Rhode Island. To learn more about how Cranston can help get your industrial expansion off to a fast start, call or write Mayor Ed DiPrete at 401-461-1000.

City of Cranston, RI, Department of Economic Development
869 Park Avenue, Cranston, RI 02910, 401-461-1000

Advertisement reprinted with the permission of Ken Willette, Director, Economic Development, Cranston Department of Economic Development.

prospect. In terms of the latter, city development officials often receive information requests that are not from bona fide prospects, that is, requests from companies that are planning to make some kind of location decision now or in the near future. Such a problem most often occurs from the responses the city economic developers receive from magazine "bingo cards."* To help alleviate this bingo card problem, a few magazines have begun to assist the advertiser in qualifying prospects. For example, *Plants Sites & Parks* telephones those individuals who have completed their bingo cards and who are questionable, in order to prequalify them.

CITY TARGETING EFFORTS

Few cities today have focused their efforts on a single industry or industry category. Even the cities that were identified historically with particular industries were actually more diversified than they were perceived or stereotyped to be. Thus, Detroit (automobiles), Akron (rubber), Hartford (insurance), and Hershey (chocolate) produced other goods and services beyond their basic industries, even though there was considerable truth to their images.

Recent articles, announcements, or advertisements have indicated that Ottawa intends to remain Canada's microelectronics technology center, while San Diego and San Antonio have set their sights on taking the lead role in biotechnology. With all the attention now being given to high technology, more and more often we see cities (as well as states) turning their attention to high-tech industries. And we often find a voiced concern for planned economic development that maintains the environment. To illustrate, a brochure on Orlando published by the Industrial Development Commission of Mid-Florida, Inc., says the Commission "... will always continue to strive for its original goals: To plan for and control the influx of clean industrial growth, while sustaining the high-quality lifestyle and environmental balance that makes the Orlando area so desirable."

Even when centering their promotional activities and recruiting forays on particular industries, however, a relatively small number of cities would ignore the possibility of obtaining a "low-tech" company, especially if it was one that employed a large number of workers. While each company undoubtedly uses its share of high-technology in its particular activities, one would not generally refer to a Greyhound

---

*Trade and business publications have tear-out cards with precoded numbers that refer to particular advertisers. To receive more information, the reader simply completes the address information, circles the appropriate number(s), and mails the postage-paid card to the magazine's reader service department. Often the publication will ask the reader (prospect) to complete several background questions, as a form of prequalification. The magazine service then sends each advertiser the names and addresses of the companies or those readers (prospects) requesting more data on them. These cards are called "bingo cards" in the trade.

Lines' accounting headquarters or an Armstrong Rubber Company's manufacturing subsidiary as a "high-tech" acquisition. Still, Des Moines was proud (and rightly so) to advertise these two recent acquisitions in *Plants Sites & Parks*. After all, the two represented 1,200 new jobs for the Des Moines area. Similarly, Greenville (South Carolina) and Fort Wayne (Indiana) were among many cities eager to obtain Mazda's automobile and GM's truck plant, respectively.[1] Neither of these, of course, would be producing high-tech products or be nonsmokestack in production. Further, local efforts, such as enterprise zones, incubators, and financial packages and assistance for existing companies, are generally designed to encourage a variety of industry segments, not just narrow targeted groups.

What are we suggesting then? Are we saying that cities are not typically targeting their economic development efforts or that cities are inconsistent—saying one thing and doing another? Not really, as we have noted recruiting efforts and trade missions often are very directed. We are actually talking in terms of emphasis. Seemingly countless cities and states have developed, or are in the process of developing, university research parks or special technology centers, or both. (The latter refers to the traditional private or public industrial/business parks that are limited to high-tech companies.) Such efforts strongly suggest that these cities are "going for broke," that is placing all their attention on one or more specific technologies. These efforts are highlighted in their public and private actions, which may even involve ongoing contact with top executives or real estate executives in all the companies in one or more specific industries. Further, these cities may have developed special financial packages for these companies or may have conducted marketing research, to better learn about these companies' needs.

Thus, what these cities emphasize is clear and consistent, for whatever reason, be it the desire to be on the "cutting edge," to enhance their image, or to provide a balance with their current lower-tech industrial base. They have all chosen a special focus to their economic development efforts. Still, the desirability of other investment is rarely completely ignored in their marketing efforts. A classic advertisement that demonstrates this consistency and central focus on the one hand, and this latter flexibility on the other, is provided by the Montgomery County (Maryland) Office of Economic Development. This advertisement features the Shady Grove Life Sciences Center and its recent selection by a Japanese company for a biotechnology research facility site. And it also discusses other high-tech companies' selection of Montgomery County. The copy concludes with the statement, "... Whether you're developing computer chips or chocolate chips, if *your* company wants to grow, Montgomery County's Office of Economic Development knows more ways to help you make that

ILLUSTRATION 4.7

Excellent attention-attracting qualities.

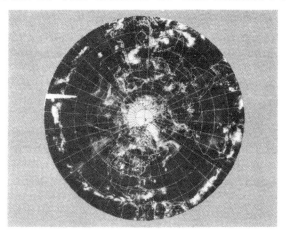
Advertisement reprinted with the permission of William F. Heins, C.I.D. Commissioner, Town of Hempstead, Department of Industry and Commerce, State of New York.

happen than anyone else."[2] The brief comment on "chocolate chips" artfully leaves the door open for non-high-tech companies and demonstrates the economic development group's flexibility.

CITY PROGRAM CONTENT ANALYSIS

The many articles that have been written on the economic development programs that have recently been established by cities and states suggest a high degree of program sameness. To a great extent, one comes to believe that all cities have (1) local financing for construction/ site construction; (2) tax incentives (deferrals and write-offs, for example); (3) university research parks; (4) incubators; and (5) a host of other offerings to provide new industry (relocations, start-ups, and so forth). This, of course, is *not* correct. So much attention has been focused on the premier city programs, and these often do include many of the above state-of-the-art features that are now in vogue, that we fail to recognize that the bulk of the cities are grappling with questions such as what type of financial package they *can* offer and how they can put together an effective promotional program that will attract the interest of "potential new industry."

In late 1982, we contacted 25 city economic development organizations and asked them to send us the package of materials they send to companies making inquiries about their communities. We then employed content analysis to allow us to take an in-depth look at these materials. We were concerned with analyzing the type of information being provided, as well as the quality of the data (currency, relevancy, and so forth) and the marketing attractiveness of its presentation. To provide a basis for our analysis, we chose to compare each city's information materials with an extensive list of factors that had been traditionally seen as potentially important to firms interested in relocation. For example, we could determine if city A commented on local employment conditions, such as the availability of labor in particular employment categories, the extent of unionization, and the provision of training programs. Further, we could rate the city in terms of the general relevance of the labor information provided and the overall marketing of its labor presentation.

The eight major categories of location factors that we felt should be included for the purposes of the content analysis were:

- site-specific
- financing
- economic
- tax base
- cultural
- employment
- special incentives
- area company data

Although the list of the subcategories for each location factor is shown in Chapter 3 as Exhibit 3.1, it might be useful to briefly comment on these eight major categories. In particular, we will note what we considered to be important when we rated each category for the 25

ILLUSTRATION 4.8

Using a local tradition to attract attention and encourage readership of an advertisement packed with pertinent location-specifics.

If You're Looking For The Ideal Place To Relocate, Chew On This For Awhile.

Just send us your name and title on your company stationery and we'll send you not just one piece of salt water taffy, but a whole box full of strawberry, orange, lemon, lime, vanilla and chocolate.

While you are chewing on the taffy, you can study our full color booklet of facts and information about the Virginia Peninsula. You'll learn about our Port of Hampton Roads, our right-to-work law, our institutions of higher learning, our labor force, our abundance of inexpensive locations, and our quality of life.

You'll quickly realize that when we say "If you knew about us, you'd already be here," we mean it. Relocating to the Virginia Peninsula is an easy decision to make. We'll provide you with the knowledge to make that decision. Just write Bud Denton, Executive Director, Virginia Peninsula Economic Development Council, Dept. T, P.O. Box 6000, Newport News, Virginia 23606, (804)873-0000.

VIRGINIA PENINSULA
If You Knew About Us, You'd Already Be Here.

cities.

Site specific: Since the initial print materials sent to a company making an inquiry tend to be general, that is, this mailing often occurs prior to a *needs assessment,* information regarding various industrial parks and sites, and so forth may be inappropriate. However, it must be remembered that an advantage cities have is that they can be much more specific even in their initial inquiry response materials—brochures, data books, and so forth—than can states. Take Washington state, for example, where Pullman and Seattle are quite different. Thus, general information regarding area transportation facilities, topography, climate, utlities, local development services, and other site-specific considerations can and should be included. Further, we subjectively rated each city in terms of whether the site-specific information had relevance to business—any business—or was merely "boilerplate" to make the package larger and more impressive.

Financing: Again, at the initial inquiry stage, we felt it inappropriate to send the inquiring company detailed information about each form of financing available. Rather, we felt that a company should be given a concise presentation that outlines the alternatives and perhaps the local considerations relating to each. For example, city A may have access to state industrial-revenue bonds, but the availability of loan guarantees and private financing may have certain local tax or other advantages which could be noted. One of our major considerations when rating this factor was whether or not the information was presented with the corporate executive reader in mind. Very often, the material is presented from the city's perspective and is designed to enhance the mayor or council's image.

Economic: In the United States, there seems to be a virtual limitless amount of economic data. Therefore, it is quite easy for any city to offer a virtual potpourri of statistics and still provide the inquiring company no data of any real relevance. Retail sales data for every possible classification of goods can be provided for the past 50 years, as well as population data for a comparable period. But, is this the type of information companies need? Again, at the initial inquiry stage, the emphasis should not be on the bulk of data that can be pieced together, but rather on giving a clear, concise market-oriented economic picture of the community. Such a market-oriented economic brief is shown in the McAllen, Texas example. (Vignette, Chapter 10).

Tax base: While considerable detail may be offered in any discussion of taxes, our major focus in this category concerned whether or not the materials were presented from the corporate inquirer's perspective or the taxing body's perspective. And again, the emphasis should be on conciseness rather than detail.

Cultural environment: Just as some cities tend to pad their package of promotional materials sent to inquirers with economic trivia, there is a tendency to perform a similar cultural overkill. Because we are increasingly finding that quality of life plays an important role in many location decisions, a city needs to be quite concerned about the way that it presents its cultural environment. In our content analysis of this critical factor, we were concerned with whether the city had developed special cultural materials for the prospective business or had merely thrown together every local brochure available. The latter may even include library handouts giving hours of opening or miscellaneous historic-site pamphlets.

One New England city that we analyzed featured a historic statue as its cultural centerpiece and enclosed a brochure describing it. Granted, the city had no symphony, zoo, or art museum. However, it was relatively close to Boston and could have stressed those cultural opportunities, combined with its own unique New England life-style. In other words, a selling point would have been the cultural opportunities of Boston, without its accompanying "hassle." Since the life-style could also be found in many similar communities, this would likely not be the reason the community would be selected by a relocating firm. However, it would place the community on an equal life-style base with the other New England towns and use another factor, possibly a site-specific one, as its plus. As it was, the use of the statue as its central cultural attraction made the community appear to have no understanding of what "cultural environment" means to an executive.

Often when analyzing city promotional packets, it is difficult to determine just what culturally-related activities and facilities are available. It seems that those preparing the materials hope that the business executives reading the booklets or brochures will be swayed by "glittering generalities" and will ignore specifics. After all, you can overuse words such as "sunshine," "outdoor living," "rugged landscape," "urban," and "skiing." It might be added that companies are becoming increasingly concerned about the availability of continuing educational opportunities and about the quality of primary and secondary education, each of which is important to retaining their best people in any relocation move.

Employment: Whereas the employment category can best be discussed in terms of company specifics and is better handled after the economic development group knows a company's needs, there are several concerns that are common to relocating firms. These include the extent of unionization (right-to-work state or not), the training programs available, the employment statistics *by job classification,* and examples to support claims of good labor relations. Often, of course, key support personnel, such as secretaries and other office workers, will not make the move to a new location. What is the pool of available workers in these areas?

Incentives: Although some of the industrial development incentives may have been referred to or alluded to elsewhere in the city's promotional package, we feel that it is extremely helpful to the relocation decision makers to itemize them in a separate category. In this way, industrial-revenue bonds, tax-exempt financing, job-incentive programs, and periods of corporate tax deferrals or exemptions, or both, can be highlighted, without offering detail. If a city, county, or state has taken the critical steps necessary to have such incentives available, it should certainly wish to make this availability easily known, not by merely mentioning it in some lengthy and technically written financial treatise.

Companies: Relocating firms are often quite interested in the types and characteristics of existing local industry. Of course, their reasons for this interest can vary widely. Some need to draw on the services of particular types of suppliers, while others may be looking for potential customers or complementary industry. A firm involved in heavy industry may be seeking an area that is already familiar with companies of its type, one that is not surprised by its side effects of noise, some pollution, or blue-collar workers.

On the other hand, high-technology firms may wish to know if existing firms have already helped develop the research and development and educational base that they need. Through the efforts of their predecessor firms, the local university may have already instituted a new computer science or robotics advanced degree program, for example. Thus, background on the existing companies becomes an essential ingredient in the relocating firm's decision, even for no other reason than their effect in establishing a hospitable business environment.

CONTENT ANALYSIS RESULTS

Given the fact that we wished to take an extremely critical and candid look at the 25 cities' promotional packages, we have chosen *not* to refer to the cities by name, but rather to use a geographical reference. Exhibit 4.2 contains the list of factor categories (and subfactors) that we employed as the basis for the content analysis. Exhibit 4.3 lists the cities on the horizontal axis of the chart and the factor categories on the vertical axis.

Each city was rated on all eight factor categories as either A (superior), B (strong), C (adequate), or D (weak). If the city did not mention the factor at all, it was assigned an E (not mentioned). Such a matrix approach makes it easy to compare cities and, in fact, is a useful technique that is employed in some form by corporate-location specialists. While it makes the process a bit more complex, the approach we followed in the content analysis goes an extra step. It highlights or identifies particular subfactors that deserve special attention. For example, city WC 11 (West Coast) is shown in Exhibit 4.3 as receiving an overall rating of A (superior) for its site-specific presentation. In particular, it received an A for its information on transportation and water.

Category IX (overall quality) reflects our overall subjective evaluation of the city's promotional package. This assessment, to some extent, reflects the overall attractiveness and appropriateness of the economic development package the city offers to prospective industry, but also includes an evaluation of how well it has been tailored to a *business audience*. Further, a city's failure to include critical factors, such as financing, as part of its economic development program lowered its overall rating. (Naturally, companies considering relocation would wish to assign greater weight to some of the factors than to others.)

Based on our in-depth content analysis of the materials that the 25 cities provide to inquiring firms, there are certain overall general conclusions we reached, which in turn offer suggestions or reminders to city economic development groups. These are:

Conclusions	Suggestions
(1) Cities often fail to offer (or if offered, to effectively communicate) financing or financial incentives in their economic development package.	(1) Build on federal or state financial programs. Consider a city or private financial-incentive program. Temporary tax relief or deferral may be the most direct (and simplest). Clearly and concisely articulate this package to inquiring companies. For newer firms, venture capital may be essential.
(2) Cities often provide inquiring companies "boilerplate" economic and cultural data—a potpourri of materials that often have little relevance to company officials, but are easily prepared by the city economic development committee. Unfortunately, the objective of this initial contact is often lost in the quest for speed and convenience.	(2) City economic development planners need to ask the question, What economic information is relevant to the executives involved in corporate location or relocation decisions? Then they need to ask a similar question regarding culture. It is important that the answers be specifically designed for the business executive and presented in a form that will offer a complete and concise picture of the community in his or her terms.

(3) The bulk of the response (size of the mail package) to the inquiry will not "outweigh" substance and message targeting. Too often a city's primary concern seems to be making the package appear large and impressive.

(3) The types of information executives need and want are discussed in later chapters. The city's presentation should be concise and targeted to the needs of corporate-location decision makers. The size of the package is *not* the first concern of the executive. Perhaps the economic officials should ask a company that recently moved to their area, "What information did you receive that was useful in making your decision?"

(4) No single region included in the content analysis appeared to be consistently strong (or weak) in terms of their overall quality of city programs. The West Coast and Northeast seemed to have an edge regarding incentives, and the West Coast cities were consistently strong in providing site-specific data.

(4) City economic development professionals should trade industrial development materials with counterparts in other areas of the country and with others in their region. No area has all *good* or *bad* programs, so new ideas would be useful to all.

(5) A surprising amount of city materials are either mimeographed or poorly printed. Appearance often seems to be a minor concern to many economic development officials.

(5) Quality of presentation and professionalism in economic development go hand in hand. It would be better imagewise to offer a smaller, carefully targeted, attractively printed package—even a single brochure—than one poorly printed. Remember the types of materials a business executive is accustomed to receiving.

(6) Site-specific really means city-specific to a great extent. However, many cities seemed to fail to recognize the difference between being city-

(6) The city should be as city-specific as possible. It should draw on the whole state or area for its pluses only when it has nothing special to offer

specific and area- or state-specific. Having a good harbor, for example, gives a "city edge," not merely a plus for the whole state.

itself. The state may have several harbors, but in describing its own pluses a city should put its emphasis on its harbor.

(7) From their perspective, none of the 25 cities would seem to have any image problems. Yet in reality, several do. Cities appear to believe that by ignoring problems, the location decision makers in prospect companies will do the same.

(7) Corporate location decision makers are likely to be more aware of the perceived negative factors about a city than are the general public. City economic developers should address these concerns in this initial contact, because it may be their only opportunity to do so. If the Southwest is perceived to have water problems, a Southwest city needs to take this concern on directly.

EXHIBIT 4.2

Category-Specific Location Factors

I. Site Specific
  1. Transportation
    a. Rail
    b. Highway
    c. Trucking
    d. Air
    e. Bus
    f. Port
    g. Rapid Transit
  2. Water
  3. Soil
  4. Space
  5. Zoning
  6. Buildings
  7. Utilities
  8. Price
  9. Topography
  10. Climate
  11. Drainage/Flood Control
  12. Housing
  13. Communications
  14. Security
  15. Advice/Development Services
  16. Natural Resources/Raw Material
  17. Ethnic Breakdown

II. Financing
  1. Industrial Revenue Bonds/
    Tax Exempt Bonds
  2. Lease Agreements
  3. Grants
  4. Low Interest Loans
  5. Loan Guarantees
  6. Private Financing
  7. Municipal Bonds

III. Economic Factors
  1. Diversification of Industry
  2. Banking
  3. Income
  4. Infrastructure
  5. Location in Terms of Markets
  6. Demographics
  7. Retail Sales
  8. Economic Indicators
  9. Growth
  10. Wage Rates
  11. Stability
  12. Building Permits

IV. Tax Base
  1. Rates
  2. Gross Receipts
  3. Foreign Trade Zone
  4. Tax Exempt Financing
  5. Target Job Tax Credit
  6. Real Property Net Taxable Value
  7. Business Fees

EXHIBIT 4.2 (Cont'd)

8. Employment Tax Credits
9. Valuations
10. No State Income Tax
11. No Local Income Tax
12. Periods of Exemption
13. Investment Tax Credits
14. Tax Advantages for Renovation

V. Cultural Environment
   1. Religious
   2. Educational
   3. Recreational
   4. Arts
   5. Museums
   6. Media
   7. Historical
   8. Quality of Life
   9. Parks
   10. Libraries

VI. Employment
   1. Availability
   2. Training
   3. Extent of Unionization
   4. Employment/Unemployment Statistics
   5. Employment by Category/ Distribution
   6. Work Stoppages
   7. Labor Relations
   8. Work Ethic
   9. Labor-Force Participation Rates
   10. Referral Service/Job Placement

VII. Incentives
   1. Tax Exempt Industrial

Revenue Bonds
2. Foreign-Trade Zone
3. Tax Exempt Financing
4. Port of Entry
5. Period of Tax Exemption
6. Job Incentive Programs
7. Free Services
8. Freeport Status
9. Grants

VIII. Companies
   1. Large Industries
   2. Listing of Employers, Numbers Employed
   3. Targeted Companies
   4. Dollar Sales by Business Categories
   5. Distribution/Types of Industries
   6. Number of Companies Located in Vicinity

EXHIBIT 4.3

City Assessment of Key Economic Development Factors
(Competitive Matrix)

	EC 2	EC 3	EC 4	EC 5	EC 6	EC 7	S 1	WC 2	WC 3	WC 4	WC 5	WC 6	WC 7	WC 8	WC 9	WC 10	WC 11	SW 8
I. Site specific	B	B	C	B	D	C	B	A	C	C	B	B	B	B	B	A	A	C
II. Financing	C	A	C	D	B	E	E	B	B	E	E	E	E	E	E	E	A	E
III. Economic factors	B	B	C	B	C	C	C	A	C	B	A	B	C	D	C	C	B	E
IV. Tax base	C	A	C	D	C	D	C	C	C	C	C	A	D	E	C	C	C	C
V. Cultural Environment	C	B	E	C	C	B	C	B	C	B	B	E	C	C	C	C	B	E
VI. Employment	D	B	E	C	D	C	C	A	C	A	A	A	C	C	C	A	A	E
VII. Incentives	B	A	C	E	B	E	B	A	B	E	E	B	E	E	E	C	B	B
VIII. Companies	E	C	D	C	C	D	C	B	E	C	C	C	C	D	C	C	D	D
IX. Overall quality	C	A	D	D	D	D	C	A	C	C	C	C	D	D	D	C	A	D

Assessment rating scale (emphasis):
A = Superior; B = Strong; C = Adequate; D = Weak; E = Not Mentioned or Poor

City Code: SW = Southwest; S = South; EC = East Coast; WC = West Coast and numbers = specific city in the region.

EXHIBIT 4.3 (Cont'd)

**City Assessment of Key Economic Development Factors
(Competitive Matrix)**

	SW 7	SW 6	SW 5	SW 4	SW 3	SW 2	EC 1	SW 1	WC 1
I. Site specific	C	D	B	C	D	C	D	D	C
II. Financing	E	E	E	E	E	A	B	E	E
III. Economic factors	B	C	C	C	D	A	B	B	B
IV. Tax base	C	C	C	C	D	C	B	B	A
V. Cultural Environment	C	C	C	C	C	C	B	C	B
VI. Employment	C	C	A	E	C	B	B	C	C
VII. Incentives	E	E	C	E	E	B	B	B	B
VIII. Companies	E	B	C	C	C	C	C	B	C
IX. Overall quality	D	D	C	D	D	B	B	C	C

Although the content analysis research we have just discussed only included 25 cities, it was conducted among cities in the higher-growth areas and did include representation from some of the most rapidly growing cities in terms of industrial development. For these latter cities, the omissions or program weaknesses we noted in our in-depth analyses are often offset to a great extent by these cities' overwhelming pluses, such as weather, proximity to leading universities, or research centers. This is a luxury that most cities in the United States do not have, however. Clearly, cities located in less advantageous areas must be particularly concerned about the overall quality of their economic development programs, as well as the initial promotional package they send to industrial prospects. Thus, the content analysis—pointing out the strengths and weaknesses of the 25 city programs and packages— should be most useful in a city's self-analysis of its own programs.

CITY DILEMMA: GETTING ITS ACT TOGETHER

Cities (and their counties) are often their own worst enemy! While we would like to end this chapter on a positive note, we feel that this is the best time to point out the nature of the albatross (one or several) that so often sinks even the best conceived city economic development program.

Many, if not most, cities seem characterized by problems created by political infighting, special interests (industrial or groups), and multiple economic development organizations. Some, of course, have been able to resolve, or at least subordinate, these problems much more effectively than have others. To be a bit more specific, let us highlight some of the typical problems and conflicts that may arise.

- City and county governments may each have economic development units that compete, rather than cooperate.
- Major cities are often surrounded by suburban communities, and each may have separate and competing economic development units.
- Dissatisfied with local governmental efforts, private-sector organizations may become actively involved in economic development efforts.
- State efforts may overlap or compete with any, or all, local governmental efforts.
- Egos of the involved public officials, for example, mayors, county commissioners, aldermen or city councilmen, and even the governor, may result in conflicts, such as who contacts, and who receives credit when dealing with prospects (or announcing successes).
- Local special-interest groups, such as public utilities, real estate brokers, land development organizations, and banks and lending institutions, often place undue pressure on the involved governments or "take over" the private-sector organizations.

Naturally, there are many other possible problem areas, but these suggest a few that must be recognized and resolved.

How dysfunctional can these conflicts be? Recently, *USA Today* reported that Colorado's intrastate rivalry was "... stifling."[3] For example, Colorado Springs and the state (on behalf of Denver-Boulder) presented separate proposals to Microelectronics and Computer Technology Corporation (MCC), which subsequently chose Austin, Texas, for its high-tech research consortium location. As one Colorado Springs executive put it, "... We really attempt to put feathers in our own hat."[4] While this illustration reflects a city/state/private-sector cooperation problem, a similar conflict can occur within an immediate area. Cleveland is one of the cities that is tightly bound by smaller, incorporated cities and, further, has an extremely aggressive county government (Cuyahoga County). In summer 1984, the city and county officials found themselves on separate sides of a plan to build a domed stadium in Cleveland; a tax proposal to fund the project was placed on the ballot by the county commissioners, while the mayor, being "left out," did not support the issue. Tied to the proposal were promises by outside industrial leaders that they would invest in hotels and so forth if the issue were passed. Such a conflict over "who got credit or whose idea was this" should not be surprising in Cleveland, which had been famous for earlier squabbles ranging from the responsibility for a burning river to a vote over a proposal to assist a potential bar-mill investor (new industry).

While it is easy to pick on Cleveland where in the past the public and private sectors have so often appeared to have little in common, the same conflicts occur elsewhere as well. As one city official from the South recently told us, ".. you can never tell someone from the governor's office that you have a new industry acquisition to announce. They will break the story first and claim credit for it." As a result of one such premature announcement, a major firm decided it was best to go elsewhere.

Another type of conflict may occur when developers, banks, and so forth, work to promote a single location within the city rather than within the community itself. This kind of aggressive effort may be expected, of course, and it is natural for a developer to advertise its particular sites and industrial parks in national media. The problem occurs when these self-interest efforts occur within a supposed community-wide representative body such as a committee of 100, the local chamber of commerce, or even the local public-sector economic development commission. This could lead to a city of private organization funding efforts that were beneficial to a single party or group.

Is it possible to organize a community-wide effort, one that transcends the types of conflicts that we have described? The answer is yes. However, it requires a heavy dose of community spirit; a spirit that is willing to put aside immediate self-interest for the general success of the city. It may be difficult for a politician or politicians to give up the opportunity to announce a new factory, because such announcements by a mayor or councilman can be translated directly into votes. But it may not be necessary for the affected politician to give up the opportunity; perhaps a shared announcement involving the county commissioners, the mayor, and other involved parties could be a compromise. And frankly, where cities have been successful in offering a unified front, a great deal of compromise has often occurred.

What we feel to be essential is a recognition on the part of the community's development officials and groups that such conflicts are commonplace. And the sooner they are recognized, and addressed, the more effective the community's efforts will be. A mechanism for ensuring that the city presents a similar or at least complementary (and cooperative) face to the outside is essential. Frequently, this will take the organizational form of an umbrella body whose mission is to coordinate the efforts of the multi-economic development organization. Although the "umbrella" is perhaps better than nothing, too often it has very limited authority. To be effective, such an overseer body needs to be able to redirect the various groups' activities when necessary or even halt certain efforts. In other words, such an overseer body needs to have control.

An even more effective alternative for conflict resolution is suggested by the organizational structure of the Industrial Development Commission of Mid-Florida, Inc. (This structure is detailed on page 155.) In effect, the many local economic development units in Orange and Seminole counties were merged into a single, private-sector company to represent the entire area. Such an effort, of course, was not easily accomplished and represents a major step that few cities are likely to take.

CONCLUDING COMMENT—ATTITUDE

The assumption in our previous section on conflict was that the city (and its citizens) views industrial development as positive, so positive, in fact, that many wish to take credit for any successes. But, what about those locales where the public is truly ambivalent or where a heavy percentage of the community is actually negative toward industrial development?

It is quite likely that a majority of communities have pockets of negativism regarding new industry and, most certainly, towards certain types of new industry. If however, this pocket is large and vocal (or is perceived as large), this will be a strong deterrent to the attraction of companies planning to expand or relocate. In some instances, the public officials may even be divided on the question. Such a negative business environment is one reason often cited for firms choosing to leave an area to relocate and, therefore, will obviously hinder the attraction of other industry. Further, once a community develops an image of being negative or nonsupportive of business, it becomes difficult for it to later alter what can be a widely held perception among the business community.

We recently learned of a community that had received an inquir from a very large company that was planning to build a new plant. While this community had been eager to attract new industry, it had not expected to be the location for a facility that would virtually double its current labor force. After much public discussion the city council voted six to five in favor of "allowing" the company to build there. As one would guess, the company was hardly impressed by the community's favorable "mandate" and chose to go where it was truly wanted.

What we want to stress here is that we do *not* find fault with a city's desire to remain small or environmentally clean, or whatever. What we do find fault with is its failure to clearly send the appropriate signals to industry, as it promotes itself and, of course, its failure to decide in advance just what its industrial development parameters are. For example, will the community warmly welcome foreign workers? It is one thing to talk about foreign investment and to send task forces on overseas jaunts. However, if successful, this would mean the city may have foreign business people at the top of the community's pay scale and it could even mean offering courses in Japanese in the local school system. One local resident in Smyrna (Tennessee) has been quoted as saying, "Before Nissan, Smyrna was a small, nice, quiet community. Now it's a bigger, nice, not-so-quiet community."[5] While generally favorable, it reflects the adjustments a community must be prepared to make. Since there has been considerable attention given to the problems of uncontrolled growth,[6] it behooves a city to establish its economic development parameters before embarking on its programs. Otherwise, future changes can have very negative image results.

Vignettes

MENTOR, OHIO, FIGHTS BACK:
A REAL SUCCESS STORY*

Mentor is a city of 43,000 people located near Lake Erie just northeast of Cleveland. Mentor's traditional industrial base has been heavy manufacturing. But with the recession of the early 1980s, this foundation cracked. Catepillar announced it would close its Mentor plant and shift the production of lift trucks to Korea; plant closings or layoffs by the C.E. Tyler Company, Lindsay Wire Weaving, Fluid Controls, and others exacerbated the problem. Mentor's prompt and effective reaction to this downturn in its fortunes is a story worth telling.

In 1982, with funding from the city, an economic development program was planned and implemented. The major part of the budget still goes into advertising, participation in trade shows, mass mailings, and related promotions. Mentor also assists in getting financing for new business through industrial-revenue bonds and the Mentor Economic Assistance Corporation, which administers SBA 500 loans through the Small Business Administration. Mentor constructs roads, sewers, and water lines, and finances businesses via municipal bonds. It later pays off the bonds by assessing the businesses that purchase the land.

Mentor sends out a probusiness signal. Its mayor, Donald Krueger, says, "Our community is very anxious for industry. Companies that want to locate here won't meet any resistance." In addition to this spirit of cooperation, Mentor has many economic and quality-of-life amenities. It is geographically situated such that one-half of the population of the United States and Canada and 24 of the top 50 industrial markets are within a 500-mile radius. Mentor is easily accessible by good highways, rail, air, and water. Moreover, it offers a good school system, cultural and recreational opportunities, affordable housing, reasonable taxes, 3,000 acres zoned for industrial use, and seven industrial parks. The city will even assist small companies in developing their business plans and the chamber of commerce provides a variety of ongoing programs and information to small enterprises.

The result of Mentor's efforts have been truly remarkable. Since 1981, there has been a plethora of industrial development based primarily on scores of small- and medium-sized light-industrial, high-tech, and medical companies. Mentor has done an exemplary job of targeting industry that makes the best sense for a city of its size and strengths. Most of all, the community did not quit on itself when the plant closings and layoffs hit so hard in 1980-1981. And already, its growth strategy has nearly offset the loss of the blue-collar, heavy-industry jobs. Mentor's ability to blend savvy industrial development marketing strategy with a pervasice upbeat community posture toward business is making for a winning combination. Elaine Lane is the Administrative Assistant for Economic Development for the city of Mentor.

---

*Information for this vignette is based on "Focus on Mentor's Business Boom," *Crain's Cleveland Business*, October 22, 1984, F1-F8, and on a visit to Mentor.

ECONOMIC DEVELOPMENT: BROWARD STYLE

The Sunbelt may be getting the lion's share of economic development lately, but the attention is justified. Among the golf courses and palms, James Garver, president of the Broward County Economic Development Board, is actively sifting through mailing lists and SIC codes to identify just the right companies that could benefit from locating in Broward County.

One new addition to the Broward business listings is a British-based telecommunications firm located in Deerfield Beach, Florida.

THE INITIAL CONTACT.

Before selecting a site for their new facility, ABC Telecommunications prepared a specific list of attributes the location of their new facility would need to possess. After narrowing their location choice to Florida, they began to investigate specific regions in the southern part of the state.

Both the manager of the international division from the London office and the president of the U.S. division from the New York office requested information from the Broward Development Board. In response, a special information packet was prepared and forwarded to the headquarters in New York.

LOCATION SELECTION CRITERIA.

Because of the international nature of ABC, it was in need of a location that provided quick access to an international airport with regular flights to London and New York. Additional charateristics desired included proximity to an upscale residential area to accommodate those employees transferred from the East and immediate access to an interstate highway.

Given these and other selection criteria, the Broward Economic Development Board isolated feasible locations from its list of about 80 industrial parks that could support the described facility. Consideration was given to zoning regulations, construction possibilities, and building styles. A representative from New York was then given a "windshield tour" of the potential sites.

Deerfield Beach was selected following approval from the board of directors in England and a visit from the president of the UK division. However, the final vote was not held until after Florida repealed the unitary tax. The company expressly stated that if the unitary tax bill was not repealed, the location of the facility would be changed to another state.

GROWTH AND ASSISTANCE PROGRAM.

Even after the final papers have been signed, the Broward Economic Development Board continues to support the company. Usually three press releases are prepared, one to announce the intentions of the firm to locate in Broward, the next to commemorate the ground-breaking, and finally an announcement to celebrate the ribbon-cutting.

After the ceremonies are over, the development board still acts as an information service to aid the companies with everything from customs problems to removal of palm trees to facilitating the filming of a new movie.

Vignette prepared by Lori Mitchell, a doctoral student at Kent State University.

SOLON, OHIO; NOT BY RUST ALONE

Principally due to Cleveland's unfortunate image, Northeast Ohio has been unflatteringly referred to as being part of the "Rust Belt." Without debating the accuracy of Cleveland's image, we can say that the entire region does not deserve being painted with the same broad brush. Solon, Ohio, is a case in point.

Under virtually any economic development success measure, Solon would fare extremely well. Its growth had been steady—but perhaps not spectacular or headline-grabbing—until the recent announcement that it had been selected as Nestle's U.S. headquarters site. However, when the world food giant from Vevey, Switzerland, chose Solon over such cities as San Francisco and White Plains (New York),[6] economic development experts began taking a second look at this Cleveland suburb. As Exhibit 4.4 indicates, Solon has developed an interesting blend of high-tech and lower-tech companies, diversified industries, and foreign-subsidiaries and U.S. home offices. (Some 35 of the U.S.'s *Fortune 500* industrials are represented in Solon, as are five of the *Fortune 100* service companies.) In other words, Solon is clearly not a single-industry community, the type that is most vulnerable to shifting market needs.

There are some other revealing statistics regarding Solon. For example, Solon has a current population of 17,000, but a daytime-only population of 38,000, an important signal of the economic vitality of the area. Further, a suggestion of Solon's steady growth is illustrated by the number and amount of industrial-revenue bonds (IRBs) issued between 1968 and 1985. During that period, there were only 4 years in which no IRBs were awarded.

There have been several reasons given for Solon's growth in the face of Ohio's general industrial workforce decline. (A recent *New York Times* article ranked Ohio sixth in terms of factory jobs lost between March 1979 and March 1985.[7]) One is the community's selective policy regarding industry; Solon's Planning and Zoning Code developed in the 1950s was designed to prevent what Mayor Charles J. Smercina has reportedly called "... dirty industry ... noisy industry ... pollution."[8] Others have cited such reasons as low taxes and good services.

To put things in perspective, we asked Mr. Donald Lannoch, AICP, Director of Planning & Development for Solon, to comment on the city's economic development. He told us:

> The successful economic and physical development of Solon has been the result of a great many factors working together. With little or no growth pressure until relatively late in this region's development, Solon was in a much better position than most other communities. We had the

EXHIBIT 4.4

Solon Companies with 100 or More Employees (June, 1985)

Company	Employees
Technicare Corp.	2,000
Stouffer Foods Corp.	1,700
Tecmar, Inc.	600
Keithley Instruments, Inc.	500
Erickson Tool Co./Kennametal	495
Erico Products	400
AAV Companies	375
AT&T Corp.	350
Crawford Fitting Co.	350
Davies Can Co.	304
Kroger Co.	280
Harshaw Filtrol Partnership	277
Mannesmann Demag Co.	260
Joy Manufacturing Co.	250
Bird Electronic Corp.	240
Advancement Corp.	200
The S-P Manufacturing Corp.	190
Container Corp. Of America	175
Harris Wholesale	175
Tecnicom Corp.	175
Zircoa Products/Corning Glass Works	150
Monroe, Inc.	150
Roach-Reid Co.	141
Kennecott Corp./SOHIO	136
Sandusco, Inc.	135
HPL Ohio, Inc.	130
The Tool-Die Engineering Co.	130
Ardell, Inc.	120
Allied Steel And Tractor Products, Inc.	111
Hunter Manufacturing Co.	110
TRW, Inc. Automotive Worldwide	109
Jerpbak-Bayless Co.	100
Revere Products Corp.	100
	10,918
Approximately 200 Other Smaller Companies	19,000
Total Employees	**29,918**

opportunity to learn from the success and mistakes of others. We had a relatively blank sheet of paper to work with, and a substantial number of legal and planning tools to help implement our plans.

Of equal importance was the good fortune of having far-sighted leaders at the beginning, when our entire future could have been altered by different decisions. At that critical time, they made a conscious decision to make Solon something other than a bedroom community. Over 2000 acres, or one-sixth of the city, was reserved for revenue-producing industrial uses. This industrial area was also well located. It was isolated from the residential area, but with very easy access for industrial traffic (both highway and rail).

The early decision makers also decided that ours would be a quiet, clean and attractive industrial area. They established regulations which, in effect, created a "step-up" environment for businesses which desired a certain public image. These regulations have remained relatively unchanged to this day. They worked so well, the Chamber of Commerce gives annual awards for attractive industrial properties.

Until very recently the original decisions and controls, a naturally ideal geographic location, industrial revenue bond financing, and a very cooperative city hall were sufficient. Industry came to Solon. A general trend in the 60s and 70s toward "suburbanization" of successful companies also helped a great deal.

Within the last five to ten years, however, it became evident to our leaders that even more was needed to continue our successful attraction of industry. Since the beginning it was also apparent that we had, at the same time, made Solon an extremely attractive place to live. That generated dramatic residential growth which made it even more important to maintain an equal growth rate for industry. New industry was constantly necessary to pay the costs of providing city services to the new residents.

For these reasons, Solon entered a new era of aggressive economic development. Promotional materials and community fact sheets were produced. An In-house Planning and Development Director was hired. Audio-visual and visitation programs were developed. Ever-increasing time, effort, and money were devoted to competing with all of the other cities and states which were beginning to promote their own economic growth.

Because of our initial decisions and our natural advantages we were convinced we could successfully compete if more of those we were trying to attract knew what we had to offer. Within the last two or three years, therefore, we have greatly expanded our "outreach" efforts. We now take our promotional material and information to regional and national trade shows with an expensive exhibit. We have also been stressing public relations, with editorial features in business publications and close attention to media relations.

Equally important, we have learned that the City's attitude of coopera-tion is invaluable to our efforts. Not only has it helped us be a leader in attracting new industry, but it has made us much better able to retain existing development.

The one thing we have not done is to become complacent. We recognize our predecessors left us with an extremely valuable legacy which we must protect. With the City only 60% developed, we cannot rely on past accomplishments. So far we have continued to remain flexible, adjusting and expanding our efforts to accommodate our needs, the times, and economic trends. We will only remain successful if we continue to do so.

With such a proactive and noncomplacent attitude, it is quite likely that Solon's past successes will be carried into the remainder of the 1980s and beyond.

ADVANTAGE: CITY (THE OMAHA EXAMPLE)

Community-level economic development programs have the potential of being *far* superior to state economic development efforts in providing hard-hitting, company-specific information. While state programs must take into consideration the multiple interests, strengths, and weaknesses of all their cities, community-level programs can be highly specific. In fact, the better programs are sharp and clearly focused: They speak directly to the benefits they can offer to prospective investors. And, the better programs are carefully targeted toward specific types of industries, not toward corporations and companies in general.

The materials provided to prospects by Omaha is an interesting case in point. The Omaha Economic Development Council (OEDC), like many community development groups, sends prospects a most attractive packet. But, simply sending colorful brochures is hardly the key. What the OEDC has recognized is that most prospects do not really want to read through a plethora of glittering generalities. If they do, one brochure in the Omaha packet provides such information. It describes the city as having "... a sturdy foundation of neighborliness ..." and "... a zesty tang of cosmopolitanism." (The latter, of course, could be used to describe a host of cities.)

Where the OECD captured the particular advantage a city can employ lies in its "Did you know?" list on the packet cover in which *18* specific attributes of Omaha are listed. These 18 attributes are not generalizations; they are 18 varied strengths peculiar to Omaha, Nebraska. Then, the OECD packet features a six-page foldout brochure entitled, "The Case for Omaha: An Executive Summary." In no-nonsense terms, this brochure touches on topics such as energy and taxes, with Omaha-specific data.

We feel that both substance and packaging are important in a city's initial contact with a prospective company. After all, the old saying about first impressions was much more than a simplistic adage; it is one that marketing research has now supported.

EFFECTIVE ORGANIZATION: THE ORLANDO MODEL

When we rated the economic development programs at the local (city or regional) level, we found that there are many good-to-excellent programs and a few *standouts*. One economic development organization that was a standout under all our measures was the Industrial Development Commission of Mid-Florida, Inc., a unique blend of the public and private sectors. Based on its high degree of excellence, we felt that this Orlando-based organization deserved special attention.

As the accompanying advertisement suggests, we could focus on the Mid-Florida group's promotional program. However, what we found in visiting this most successful program was that the key to its effectiveness is organizational structure and management strengths. In fact, this economic development organization, which encompasses a two-county area (Orange and Seminole), has what we have come to feel is an optimal organizational structure. It is a structure that allows it to be lean and flexible; that permits it to explicitly minimize traditionally inhibiting special interests; and that accommodates both supply-side and demand-side planning. Further, we feel that the organization's principles that have driven this successful economic development organization offer direction—a model, if you will—for other such groups.

Call him the Mid-Florida group's program architect or guru or whatever, but the person behind this very special organizational scheme is Mr. Roy L. Harris, Jr., who serves as its president. Mr. Harris was interviewed for this vignette in his Hartford Building office on December 26, 1984, a time when many would still be savoring their holiday leftovers. Providing us with additional assistance and comments was Ms. Holly Bennett-Thatcher, Mid-Florida's vice president.

Before detailing the organizational model developed for Mid-Florida and providing some of Mr. Harris' comments, there are a couple of points that perhaps should be made. First, we have heard some say that anyone could successfully shepherd an economic development program in Florida, that the greater challenge would be Nome, Alaska, or International Falls, Minnesota. Certainly, Orlando is attractive, but the temptation in a location such as this is to be complacent. And, with all due respect to this lovely site of Disney World, Sea World, and Epcot Center, there are many, many other similarly attractive "summary" locations in such states as Florida, California, and Arizona. Further, as a state, Florida offers few contrived incentives to business. Instead, the state and its regional economic development groups depend on the lure of the climate, low-cost labor, varied and affordable housing, location, and other factors to draw new business. This in itself makes the selling job a challenge. Finally, there are some individuals in the Sunshine State and the Orlando locale who have opposed the efforts to industrialize. Members of what might be termed the "shoemaker-should-stick-to-his-last" bunch seem to feel nothing can or should replace the orange or the tourist as the focal point of the region's efforts. Thus, the Mid-Florida economic development assignment offered this IDC many of the same types of challenges that have faced its counterparts throughout the states, and overseas as well.

THE INTERVIEW AND THE PRINCIPLES

During our lengthy interview, Mr. Harris traced the history leading to the establishment of the Mid-Florida organization. In capsule, there were three local development "interest" groups prior to Mid-Florida's formation in 1977, and as has happened so often, they competed with each other rather than Miami or Charlotte or Los Angeles. Egos, political-clout battles, individual private interests, and giving credit for successes to the right group were on the line of every issue. This parochialism impedes development and hampers the probusiness atmosphere most regions spend thousands of dollars in promotion to create. The prospects are then confused, where do they go for information? Must they, too, get caught up in the political hassles evident from the very start? Instead, a cohesive economic development program permits combining resources—advertising budgets, widespread and unified political and business support, and space inventory of land and buildings.

While so many other cities have accepted such fragmentation as a way of life, what occurred in the late 1970s in Orlando is the first evidence that success can occur to a greater degree when the ID program is decidely *different*. Several prominent businesspeople—the most influential businessmen—came forward and said, "Enough is enough." And, they said it with sufficient clout, that the Mid-Florida organization was formed (Exhibit 4.5) and its president could decide how it could be professionally structured, structured, for example, in a way that would permit *minimal* government representation; would discourage special interests such as real estate developers and bankers from comprising the majority of its board; and would permit economic development professionals to be truly in charge.

What you have as a result of this shakeout is one single voice representing the industrial development actions not only for the city of Orlando, but the entire area covered by Seminole and Orange Counties. (And it has Osceola County now waiting in the wings.) There has been an effective use of the monies formerly being channeled into the segmented groups. Now, salaries, office expenses, audiovisual materials, promotional budgets, and publicity efforts are combined under one roof, and the entire region is reaping the benefit. This

EXHIBIT 4.5

Mid-Florida IDC Organizational Chart

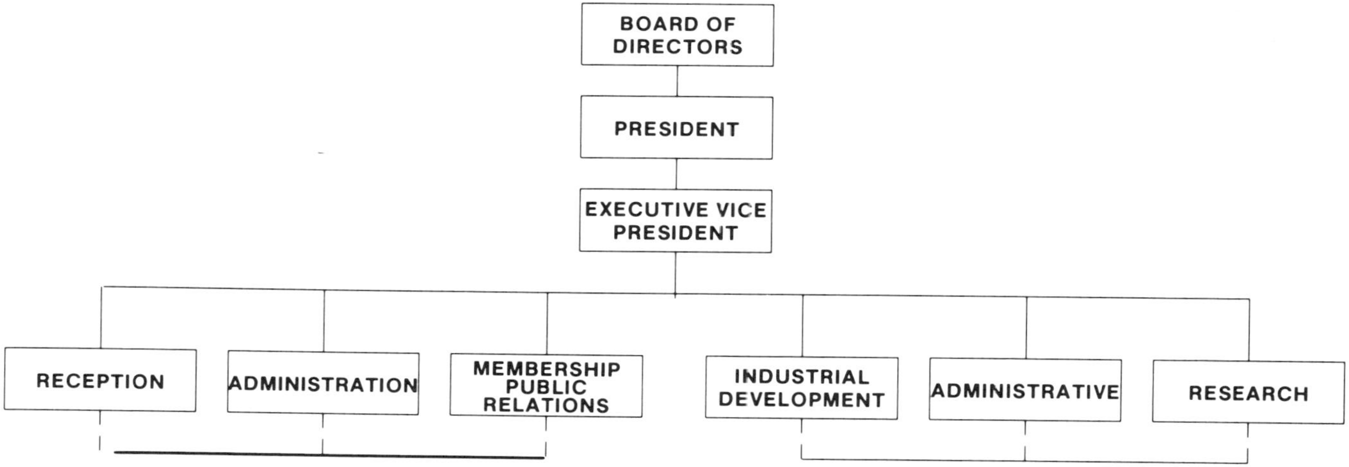

regional group encompasses 14 communities in Orange County and 8 in Seminole County. To illustrate the effectiveness of the industrial development unit, Seminole County had only six industrial projects in the 3 years prior to joining IDC, and 27 during its first 2 years under IDC jurisdiction. More recently, Mid-Florida had 75 new or expanded industrial projects for the region from September 30, 1983 to September 30, 1984, which translated into 6,600 new employees. The IDC publicity promotes the entire region. Outside the area, the IDC promotes the attributes the region offers a burgeoning business; within the community, the IDC creates a probusiness image, positioning the IDC as the influential agency it is in order to be able to move freely throughout the community for the advantage of its "clients."

The current Mid-Florida group now may be characterized as a highly professional body with more than 1,300 members that is a *private corporation.* It is run by a full-time professional staff of seven, headed by the president, and governed by a 12-member volunteer, nonpaid board. Initially, the board membership did not include such special interests as banks, real estate developers, or utilities, but currently there is one representative from each. Further, the public sector's input has been limited from the start to the mayor of Orlando and one commissioner from each county. Though the structure prevents segmentation or parochialism, the structure does allow for keeping key government leaders "in the know" so they can assist new firms with the typical red tape of permitting, zoning, and other government relations. The IDC works closely with area governments to ensure that they are working toward the same goals—a diverse economy while maintaining a high quality of life. The remainder of the board includes such influentials as the president of the University of Central Florida and key business people (See Exhibit 4.6). The level of executives active on the IDC board provides access to information, contacts, and government officials that is many times necessary for the successful completion of a project. Thus, this structure minimizes the sort of political and special interest intrigue that is rampant in many public bodies *and* permits the body of decision making to rest with the staff of professionals. The widespread private-sector support is key. Area business leaders become the eyes and ears of the IDC, providing leads and the crucial "first-hand" testimony many prospects desire when analyzing the area as a business site.

In short, the organization designed by Mr. Harris features:

- centralized control, "one-stop shopping" for prospects;
- high flexibility, that is minimal decision-making approval levels;
- professionalism;
- minimal special interest;
- limited political influence.

EXHIBIT 4.6

Mid-Florida IDC Board of Directors—1984-1985

CHAIRMAN OF THE BOARD	Honorable Tom Dorman
	Orange County Commissioner
William C. Schwartz	
President	Honorable Robert Sturm
Schwartz Electro-Optics	Seminole County Commissioner
	Honorable Bill Frederick
VICE CHAIRMAN	Mayor—City of Orlando
Walter O. Lowrie	Robert Harrell
President	Community Leader
Martin Marietta Aerospace	
	Jerry C. Sibley
	Division Manager
SECRETARY/TREASURER	FMC Corporation
Robert E. White	Selby Sullivan
Regional Senior Vice President	Chairman
Southeast Bank, N.A.	Hubbard Construction Company
	Troy W. Todd
DIRECTORS	President
	United Telephone Company of Florida
Robert C. Allen	
Vice President	
Walt Disney World	
Trevor Colbourn	
President	
University of Central Florida	

Of equal importance is that the organization permits tailoring of programs to corporate needs. Earlier, we indicated that we see this structure as providing a model and cited as one reason the fact that it accommodated both supply-side *and* demand-side planning. By this, we meant that initially, the Mid-Florida industrial group could establish the parameters for the type of industry it wanted to attract, that is, it could be supply-side in its planning, and still tailor its program to *industry needs*—be demand-side in its planning.

This supply-side/demand-side question can best be illustrated by a recent example. According to Mr. Harris, the organization has given special attention to the attraction of high-tech, environmentally clean companies—its supply-side planning. Given this somewhat restricted focus, however, it then turns to aggressively taking whatever steps are necessary, within reason and equity, to attract such firms. That is, it takes a demand-side (or "customer-side") orientation. This means determining what the potential investors they seek are looking for in a

ILLUSTRATION 4.9

**Attracting business in keeping with development objectives
concerning industry types.**

Economy
Industry
Environment
PROPER PLANNING IS THE KEY

There's a delicate balance that must be preserved during a period of growth such as Mid-Florida is experiencing. Growth can be managed, harnessed to work to everyone's benefit. Preserving the delicate balance.

It takes planning and control

The Industrial Development Commission is a group of Mid-Florida business people and industries concerned about the growth and prosperity of Central Florida — and our quality of life.

Careful planning and solicitation of clean, desirable industry for our area supports our commitment to keep Mid-Florida a healthy place to live and work.

A healthy economy benefits everyone

A healthy economy means jobs for all our residents, less inflation and a better quality of living that extends to every area of our lives.

A healthy economy depends on newcomer industries supplying hundreds of new jobs each year, pumping millions of dollars into our community and benefiting us in countless other ways. But growth is not without its problems.

New industry can be the answer

Through the tax dollars generated by clean new industries, we'll resolve any environmental problems that may occur. We know that environmental protection is necessary to maintain our quality of life. But we also realize that environmental perfection in any community is an ideal that is virtually impossible.

An eye to the future

By careful planning and continuing control, industrial growth can be balanced with environmental protection. We're committed to a balanced and commonsense approach to industrial development and environmental protection in Mid-Florida.

We seek a climate where industry blossoms within the environment, not at its expense.

Planning helps us keep our balance

We're committed to maintaining the delicate balance. A balance of industry and environment and progress and quality of life. The solicitation of clean, desirable industry, coupled with careful site planning and preparation, reaffirms that commitment. Our industrial development must be balanced to meet the needs of both life and progress in Mid-Florida. And planning is the key.

**Industrial
Development Commission
of Mid-Florida, Inc.**

P.O. Box 2144, Orlando, FL 32802
Serving Orange and Seminole Counties

Advertisement reprinted with the permission of Mr. Roy Harris, President, Industrial Development Commission of Mid-Florida, Inc.

new location, being as company-specific as possible. In a case Mr. Harris used to illustrate this point, a high-tech company was interested in the area, but was concerned about the lack of a particular type of engineering specialty at the local state university (University of Central Florida). With the immediate cooperation of the university's administration, this void was corrected by establishing the engineering program in question and recruiting the faculty to staff it. Not surprisingly, the company agreed to establish its proposed facility in Orlando. This illustration demonstrates the Mid-Florida group's understanding of the prospect's needs, its power to activate the local community, and the area's cooperative spirit.

Undoubtedly, such a first-rate program is not simply the result of having a particular organization design—a one-voice, private sector with public-sector involvement approach. Essential to its success is having the right people and an overall willingness to put community needs over private interests. But, the lessons this organization offers are dramatic. Would Orlando and its immediate environment have achieved its present development level without the Industrial Development Commission of Mid-Florida, Inc.? Our answer is no and, after all, that is the ultimate bottom line in this game.

REFERENCES

1. Humel, R. (1984, October 5). Cities, states scramble for auto plants. *USA Today*, p. 1B.
2. Montgomery County advertisement, *Plants Sites & Parks*, October 1984, p. 194.
3. Hillkirk, J. (1984, October 23). Colorado weighs hi-tech price tag. *USA Today*, p. 3B.
4. Ibid., p. 3B.
5. Warnick, M. (1984, June 24). Japanese auto plant is a boon to small Tennessee town. *Lexington (Kentucky) Herald-Leader*, p. B10.
6. Hillkirk, J. (1984, October 30). Oregon seeds hi-tech. *USA Today*, p. 3B.
7. Stouffer's Growth Seems to Parallel Solon's, *Crain's Cleveland Business*, February 4, 1985, p. F10.
8. Greenhouse, S. (1985, June 23). The fragile Middle West. *New York Times*, p. F10.
9. Swindell, H. (1985, February 1). City seeks the 'right kind' of neighbor. *Crain's Cleveland Business*, p. F2.

5

"AND A CAST OF THOUSANDS"

EXECUTIVE SUMMARY

The job of economic development stimulation and the whole area of corporate relocation and expansion goes well beyond the work of city and state officials. Generally, the efforts of the private sector are designed to augment public programs in regard to industrial growth stimulation. The primary exception, however, lies with the marketing activities of the industrial realtor. This important business-service category becomes directly involved in the relocating or expanding corporation's final decision phase, the decision stage in which the actual physical site in the community is chosen. As one would expect, the marketing activities of industrial realtors go well beyond attempting to attract companies to their community. They are quite concerned that the "attracted company" employ their particular firm's real estate services. In recent years, the establishment of nationwide industrial realtor organizations (or cooperative groups) has led to their offering countrywide consulting and selection services. For example, they tell the company, "Let us help you choose the state and city locale for your move, as well as help you in the actual physical site selection." Further, other private organizations are involved more specifically in the development of industrial and office parks, site-selection consulting, and other related activities.

What is particularly worth noting is the extent to which the services offered by the various private-sector organizations have blurred. For example, railroads, such as CSX Railroads and Burlington Northern

161

Railroad, are actively involved in site selection and industrial-park development. It has become increasingly difficult to categorize the primary business of many of these private-sector companies. Today's realtor may be tomorrow's developer or the public utility becomes a site consultant. To properly put this blurring in perspective, however, the tendency is for these private firms either to add new services or ventures, or to expand into regional or national entities.

Our research in the private sector was conducted among industrial realtors, a national sample of more than 50. They told us that in their view, the most important factor in terms of a company's headquarters relocation decision is ". . . the availability of a qualified work force." However, this view was not a unanimous one and tended to be cut along geographic lines. Southern industrial realtors, for example, saw companies putting more importance in "lack of red tape" and "can-do spirit." What this and their other views suggested is that the company's final decision criteria have been honed to one or two very important concerns by the time that company has contacted the industrial realtor, and that these are bases for selecting an industrial realtor in the particular area. Thus, it was not surprising that industrial realtors' views were different geographically but, at the same time, revealing in terms of the "whys" for geographic preferences.

∞

The phrase "and a cast of thousands" is a relic of the MGM posters and film credits of the 1930s and 1940s. But, it is an apt description of the number of players in the economic development field. Ed Coene, in fact, in his column in the 1984 Site Selectors Guide issue of *Business Facilities,* points out that some 5,000 contact listings were included in that particular publication[1] and, in many instances, only an officer, not the complete membership of an organization was listed.

So far, we have concentrated on the economic development efforts of the public sector—cities, counties, states, and foreign governments. Although the public sector's economic development efforts are sometimes vertically integrated (for example, they include everything from the initial creation of a conducive environment for business to making available, and selling, local sites), they generally avoid direct involvement in the corporate location decision maker's final decision stage or stages, which involves site-specific decisions. For example, Solon (Ohio) recently reinterpreted its planning and zoning code to allow Murphy Oil Soap Company, a "clean" soap manufacturer, to build a plant in its city.[2] Solon's goal was obtaining a new industry that would employ 80 people and be compatible with local environmental restrictions, not with obtaining new industry for a specific site in the community.

On the other hand, the cast of thousands includes a number of important private-sector players. And while a city or state government may be concerned only with attracting business or industry to its area or locale, these private-sector players most often wish to attract the new industry to their particular industrial park or high-rise office building or to a site they are selling or leasing for a client.

If, however, there have been problems in generalizing about public-sector economic development efforts, these are nothing when compared to discussing the private sector. Few private-sector firms or organizations are easily classified or categorized. Although some appear to be concerned mainly with office building construction, or sale or rental or both, a closer look often indicates that they represent other site developments as well or are involved in financing or site-selection consulting. Clearly, it is beyond the scope of this book or our intention to provide such a definitive classification system or to even identify and discuss all of the types of private-sector participants in the economic development field. Rather, it is our intention in this chapter to:

- consider the businesses or organizations that directly complement (or attempt to complement) the economic development efforts of the public sector. These organizations include public utility companies, banks, transportation companies, and so forth;
- offer a brief overview of the role that private-sector site consultants and office- and industrial-facility developers play in city and state economic development;

- identify a number of the principal trade or industry associations that are involved in economic development and indicate how their services may be accessed;
- explore in somewhat greater detail the efforts of the industrial realtor in the corporate site-selection process.

Further, in addition to looking at the industrial realtor's role in economic development, we will present the *key* findings of a survey that we completed among a sample of industrial realtors. With this group, we explored questions ranging from the factors that they feel are most important to corporate location and relocation decisions to their views on the practices of public-sector economic development bodies. Their attitudes, views, and insights offer a particularly interesting conclusion to our "a cast of thousands" chapter.

PROACTIVE SUPPORT FOR PUBLIC SECTOR

Currently, public utilities, transportation companies, and banks are stepping up their efforts to complement the programs of city, state, and foreign economic development groups. Not only is this support on the increase, however, but the level and nature of this complementary work is changing. Take, for example, the *Wisconsin Economy Scan* that the Federal Reserve Bank of Chicago prepared for the Wisconsin Strategic Development Commission in mid-1984,[3] or Ameritrust Corporation's (Cleveland) commission of Stanford Research Institute to conduct a research project, *Choosing A Future: Steps to Revitalize the Mid-American Economy Over the Next Decade,* designed to identify new ways to add vigor to its area.[4] These represent activities that go beyond "the norm" in attempting to support governmental efforts. In fact, it may well be that the Chicago Federal Reserve Bank will prepare a similar scan for other states in its geographic area.

What had been more the norm for banks had been the preparation of materials to include in a state or city mailing packet; the packet mailed in response to inquiries, or to be included among the advertisers in its state's or city's advertising supplement in national or regional magazines. (For an example of the latter, see the Special Advertising Section on St. Paul in the December 1984 issue of *Business Facilities,* or the French Special Advertising Section in the December 3, 1984 issue of *Forbes.*) Or, the bank may develop a separate information service. Valley National Bank of Arizona's packet of materials is just one example of such a local or regional bank complementary activity. While participation of banks in special advertising sections has become quite commonplace, bank campaigns that feature a bank promoting its own services and community and regional advantages are relatively new and are on the increase.

Similarly, public utilities are also becoming more proactive. For example, the November 1984 issue of *Business Facilities* had 16 display advertisements by public utilities. A sample of these 16 public utilities and their advertising themes include:

- American Electric Power. "Available buildings ...," "All the answers ...," "One phone call";
- Lone Star Gas and Electric. "Looking for a plant site? (Ask us about 580 cities and towns in Texas and Southern Oklahoma)";
- Baltimore Gas and Electric. "Professional decisions demand professional information ...";
- Iowa Public Service Company. "In Iowa, we have the energy to take your company well into the future ...";
- Northern Illinois Gas. "In the land of Lincoln, a little goes a long, long way."

Some, of course, such as the East Ohio Gas Company and the Illinois Power Company, featured specific utility-company services such as site recommendations, while others like the one sponsored by Southern Colorado Power were more local-environment and public-support oriented.

Obviously, not all utility companies advertise (or advertise in every publication or issue of a specific publication). In fact, some are too small to do national or even regional advertising, while others are prohibited from advertising by state law. However, one national source does suggest that there are well over 200 economic development specialists now being employed by electric utilities alone. Like the banks and the local and regional transportation companies, the public utilites have much to gain from new industrial development, as well as retaining existing companies. As Lanham and Hockensmith point out, "... there is clearly an identity of interest between firms in a region and the local electric utility."[5] With the high competition in the economic development arena today, it is small wonder that the utilities have become highly aggressive in their development efforts.

Many examples of the current aggressive efforts of the public utilities can be offered. Particularly noteworthy are the information materials offered by the Portland General Electric Company and the Mountain Fuel Supply Company. Mountain Fuel, for example, provides a packet that includes information on the company and its natural gas rates, as well as data on Utah and Wyoming. In particular, Mountain Fuel indicates that it is prepared to provide an inquiring company with any needed data on *any* site location within its geographic area.

On a much-less-active scale, regional airlines are beginning to promote economic development in their areas, as are the large international (country) carriers. While to-date most of these efforts have been confined to the carrier's own in-service publications, a few are using major publications. Often in the case of the international carriers, their efforts amount to public- rather than private-sector support, however.

THE RAILROADS
As the primary intercity and interstate link for many years, the railroad has long played a key economic development role in the United States (and overseas). Simply having access to rail service was

a primary requirement for a city and state's development prior to the interstate highway system, and still is a major determinant for many types of industry.

However, it is not the railway as a transport mode that causes us to single it out for special mention. Rather, it is the new role that the railroad is playing in economic development matters that has attracted our attention and that of the broad-based economic development community. We feel that trade-publication headlines often tell an important story about industry trends and, if so, consider the following:

- "The Railroads Will Change the Face of Real Estate Development," (*Business Facilities*, December 1984, cover);
- "Railroads Diversifying Land Development," (*Plants Sites & Parks*, July-August 1984, p. 5).

Today's railroads, in fact, do find themselves heavily engaged in every phase of industrial development. In 1982, Southern Pacific (SP) reported that it "... can provide valuable assistance in every phase of site selection."[6] The company's brochures indicate that it owns 70 industrial parks over its 14-state region and that it offers professional consultation on all types of locational matters. Further, to demonstrate its objectivity, Southern Pacific noted in its brochure that "... we locate most of our customers on land *owned by others*...." Now merged with the Sante Fe (SF) railroad, the combined SF/SP land holdings include 65,000 acres of land zoned for commercial and industrial uses.[7]

But is SF/SP unique? No, it appears that SF/SP represents a competitive position that many of the major railroads are taking today. Take, for example, the advertisement by CSX Corporation (Chessie System Railroads, Seaboard System Railroad, Texas Gas Resources) that appeared in the November 1984 issue of *Dun's Business Month.* CSX Corporation states "... We offer you construction costs on a representative cross section of industrial buildings, the facts on more than 5,000 different sites, plus the latest data on transportation, labor, water, taxes, you name it."[8] Stated quite simply, Upland Industries, a Union Pacific Corporation subsidiary, calls itself "The Resource."[9]

Clearly, the railroads seem to have identified a niche for themselves in the site-selection field, one built upon key real-property holdings.

MANAGEMENT CONSULTING FIRMS

Another area of private-sector competition in economic development involves the management consulting firm that specializes in location-related problems. Many companies, such as public accounting firms, include site selection among their consulting offerings, while others tend to focus on site selection and related location concerns. In fact, *Business Facilities* mentions over 50 such examples of the latter in its *1984 Annual Site Selectors Guide.*

The Fantus Company and Arthur D. Little, Inc. illustrate two firms that are actively engaged in site-selection activity. In its advertising,

Little stresses a century of experience. Similarly, The Fantus Company describes itself as "... the oldest and largest management consulting firm specializing in location related problems."[10] Each, of course, emphasizes its competitive advantages and indicates services well beyond the selection of a site, for example, the strategies involved in relocation (Fantus) and the strengths and weaknesses of competitors' facilities configurations (Little).

PRIVATE LAND DEVELOPERS (OFFICES AND INDUSTRIAL PARKS)

The National Association of Industrial and Office Parks (NAIOP) has a membership of some 4,000 firms involved in industrial and office-park development. As the organization points out in its literature, it is the private developer that often takes the lead in providing the industrial facility that attracts the relocating company or the company adding a new plant or office to its existing locations.

Interestingly, Ira C. Magaziner, president of Telesis and the principal architect of Rhode Island's Green House Compact (an economic plan defeated by Rhode Island voters), recently chided the public (and public sector) for its unwillingness to accept economic development funding risks.[11] While states and cities have developed or helped finance (or both) industrial parks, plants, and so forth, much of the final location-specific land improvements (plants, office buildings, etc.) have remained private-sector efforts in the United States. As might be expected, some industrial parks and other developmental efforts by the private sector have been speculative and have proven unsuccessful, as have publically funded ones. However, the important role of the land developer in economic and industrial development must not be minimized. Often working in close concert with local community leaders and government officials, the private-sector's response via industrial parks, office complexes, plant-site developments and the like to company needs is essential to a city or state's economic development efforts.

NATIONAL AND REGIONAL ASSOCIATIONS IN ECONOMIC DEVELOPMENT

Real estate executives, city economic development officials, building contractors, and architects all have much in common with their "competitors," and have mutual issues and problems that can best be addressed working together. Just as hardware producers, public accountants, and robotics manufacturers have formed associations to represent them in Washington, or to help establish industry standards, the same has been true in the economic development arena.

Previously, we have singled out the Society of Industrial Realtors (SIR) and the NAIOP. In addition, as shown in Exhibit 5.1, there are a number of other organizations that are involved in representing their particular constituencies. Most provide their members with up-to-date

ILLUSTRATION 5.1

Example of a developer emphasizing a locale's strengths.

EXHIBIT 5.1

Key Business and Professional Organizations

American Association of Port Authorities
American Economic Development Council
American Federation of Small Business
American Institute of Architects
American Industrial Real Estate Association
American Institute of Real Estate Appraisers
American Marketing Association
American Planning Association
American Public Works Association
American Railway Development Association
American Society of Appraisers
Associated General Contractors of America
Building Owners and Managers Association
Chamber of Commerce of the U.S.A.
Industrial Development Research Council
Institute of Real Estate Management of the National Association of Realtors
International City Management Association
Mid America Economic Development Council
Mortgage Bankers Association of America
National Association of Counties
National Association of Development Organizations
National Association of Industrial and Office Parks
National Association of Real Estate Appraisers
National Association of Real Estate Investment Trusts
National Association of Realtors
National Association of State Development Agencies
National Association of Towns and Townships
National Community Development Association
National Council for Urban Economic Development
National Development Council
National (International) Association of Corporate Real Estate Executives
Sales and Marketing Executives
Society of Industrial Realtors
Southern Industrial Development Council
Urban Land Institute

---

information and news, trade and professional statistics, educational services, and, in addition, conduct research in their particular areas of problems, concerns, and interests. For example, the Building Owners and Managers Association (BOMA) includes among its offerings to members "... 'how to' guides on building operating systems, leasing procedures, standard methods of floor measurement, lighting, energy management, feasibility analyses, and more."[12] Such industry-specific kinds of research that companies need can often only be found via an association in its field. Further, most are engaged in what might loosely be described as lobbying or, perhaps more correctly, ensuring that their body has a representative voice in federal and state or regional matters and in related legislative actions.

ILLUSTRATION 5.2

Developer calls attention to location specifics.

Room to Grow in the Garden State

McBRIDE ENTERPRISES

For more than 40 years, McBride Enterprises has successfully helped companies, both large and small, find -- as well as build, the perfect corporate space in the Garden State. Convenient location and accessibility are the prime requirements of any business, so McBride Enterprises has selected only the finest corporate sites in New Jersey -- sites that offer easy access to major highways, urban centers and all the necessary resources your company will need.

After sampling the facilities on this page, it's easy to understand why companies like IBM, KODAK, NABISCO BRANDS, PAN AM, VOLVO, UNION CAMP, FUJI AMERICA, UNITED AIRLINES and CYANAMID have turned to McBride Enterprises to satisfy their space requirements.

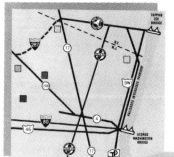

■ FAIRLAWN-McBRIDE OFFICE & RESEARCH CENTER, Fair Lawn: a 250,000 sq. ft. facility with construction scheduled to begin this Fall. Occupancy is planned for late 1985.

☐ ROCKLEIGH-McBRIDE OFFICE & TECHNICAL CENTER, Rockleigh: offers 50,000 sq. ft. of office space on schedule to be completed by mid 1985

In addition to the planned buildings in the following corporate sites, a COMPLETE "TURNKEY PACKAGE" is available and includes site selection, building design, engineering, construction, construction management, and sale, lease and/or lease back financing, specifically designed to meet your individual corporate requirements.

☐ RAMAPO RIDGE-McBRIDE OFFICE & RESEARCH CENTER, Mahwah: 200 acres. Sites available from 5 to 100 acres. 84,000 sq. ft., 3-story facility scheduled to be complete in time for Fall 1985 occupancy.

■ OAKLAND-McBRIDE OFFICE & TECHNICAL CENTER, Oakland: 200 acres. Join the 25 companies who have already chosen this center for their individually designed corporate facilities.

■ WAYNE-McBRIDE OFFICE & RESEARCH CENTER, Wayne: 550 acres. Perfect site for corporate offices and research center. 65,000 sq. ft. building complete and ready for immediate occupancy.

For further information about these corporate facilities, with the necessary room to grow in the Garden State, contact:

FRANK HEILMANN, Vice President

Executive Offices
McBRIDE ENTERPRISES
808 High Mountain Road
Franklin Lakes, N.J. 07417
(201) 891-3900

Circle Reader Service Card No. 222

DEVELOPERS OF: Fair Lawn Industrial Park,* Fair Lawn, N.J.; Glen Rock Industrial Park, Glen Rock, N.J.; Glynco-McBride Jet Park, Brunswick, Georgia; Oakland-McBride Office & Technical Center, Oakland, N.J.; Ramapo Ridge-McBride Office & Research Center, Mahwah, N.J.; Ridge Realty, Mahwah, N.J.; Rockleigh Office & Technical Center, Rockleigh, N.J.; Urban Farms, Franklin Lakes & Wayne, N.J.; Wayne-McBride Office & Research Center, Wayne, N.J.

naiop
National Association of
Industrial & Office Parks

ASSOCIATE MEMBER

Advertisement reprinted with the permission of Frank Heilmann, Vice President, McBride Enterprises. Advertisement created by Allen London Advertising.

Of particular importance to most members of such organizations is their periodic newsletter. One illustration is provided by *The NASDA Letter,* a publication of the National Association of State Development Agencies (NASDA). The topics covered in the December 4, 1984 issue of the publication included a discussion of recent changes in the economic development programs offered by the Department of Housing and Urban Development (HUD) and another on ways to market enterprise zones. Similarly, The *REIT Report* is informative for the members of the National Association of Real Estate Investment Trusts, Inc. (NAREIT). In its January/February 1985 issue, this publication covers a congressman's presentation on the strategy the organization might follow in getting a REIT modernization bill through Congress, and provides a host of industry statistics and an industry review. As with NASDA, one of the primary roles this association plays is providing its membership with an interface with Congress.

INDUSTRIAL REALTORS

While developers, public utilities, banks, consultants, and railroads are active participants in the economic development game, a key role in the private sector is undoubtedly played by the industrial realtor. Virtually every new corporate move or initial location decision involves, or is affected by, the industrial realtor.

In some instances, the industrial realtor is contacted at the outset by companies seeking to move their headquarters or to construct some type of facility (warehouse, factory, sales office, etc.). In other instances, the industrial realtor becomes involved at a later stage, if only in the critical final site-selection or choice decision. In their role, industrial realtors are in a unique position to work with local and state officials in attracting new industry or to deal directly with corporate decision makers, or both. These industrial realtors perspectives' on the economic development process are, therefore, especially useful.

Industrial realtors are represented by SIR, an organization that to a great extent epitomizes the activities of a private-sector professional organization. The organization numbers in its membership the principal industrial realtors in the country and includes among its objectives two critical goals:

1. To unite those REALTORS who are engaged in buying, selling, renting or leasing for others and for compensation the lands, buildings, factories, warehouses, research facilities, offices and other real estate used in the processes of industry and manufacturing.

6. The cooperation with all governmental, national, state and city departments and civic organizations, public utilities, financial and insurance companies, by proper contact.[13]

These objectives suggest that this 1,600-member group may, in fact, be the private-sector counterpart to the public side—the governmental and civic economic development champions. In order to complete any picture relating to the economic development process and to determine how the use of marketing might be (or is) employed in such efforts, an understanding of this body's views on the process is essential.

To be more specific, the industrial real estate broker's functions cover such areas as financing, real property valuation, acting as a principal in a real estate development, and providing brokerage and related services.[14] In terms of the latter, the industrial real estate broker is becoming more and more involved in advice and counseling for either the purchaser (lease-holder or renter) or the owner. Recently, we have seen the growth of some important national and regional industrial real estate companies.

INDUSTRIAL REALTORS CORPORATE LOCATION SURVEY

The industrial realtor is able to provide a unique perspective on economic development due to his or her special vantage point in the site determination process. As we have just shown, the industrial realtor may be involved in a company's location decision making from the very outset of its quest for a new headquarters or plant site. Or, the industrial realtor may become involved in the firm's search efforts at any stage along the way; for example, it may even have its first contact with the company when a site within a city needs to be chosen. Further, the industrial realtor frequently interfaces with the public sector (governor's office down to the local council or commissioners level), sharing a mutual interest in attracting new development to the state and city.

From its vantage point, the industrial realtor can offer insight on both the corporate location decision process and the performance of state and local economic development organizations. In particular, the industrial realtor's views on questions such as, What factors do company's consider when making their location decisions? and How often do they (companies) seek information from state or city economic development groups as they make their location decisions? are useful as we examine the role marketing can best play in economic development.

SURVEY

To obtain the industrial realtors' views, we conducted a mail survey among a stratified sample of some 175 corporate realtors. We were particularly concerned with having a broad, geographic representation of this group and, therefore, we made certain that each state and major city was represented in our original sample. The company and individual names were drawn from the 1984-1985 directory of the membership of the Society of Industrial Realtors. Only full and active members were selected; the organization has associate members from a variety of related industries, such as railroads, utilities, and businesses.

Further, in order to avoid a company bias, we made certain that we did not have a disproportionate share, that is, multiple responses, from the large national and regional industrial real estate organizations. In most instances, the mail questionnaire employed in the survey was sent to the CEO or president who heads the firm. We received usable responses from some 51 industrial realtors for roughly a 30 percent response rate.*

And, did the industrial realtors take the survey seriously? A few select comments to several of the open-end questions suggest the candor and forthrightness of the industrial realtors to our survey. For example, consider what they said about state development agencies:

- "Far more contacts are (made) through utilities than the state";
- "State (development) agencies should disseminate information and stay out of brokerage areas";
- "EDO's are usually of little value in my experience."

Or, what they said about the likelihood of a continued trend of business movement toward the Sunbelt:

- "Already diminishing, many plants vacated. Climate doesn't affect labor efficiency";
- "Yes, most definitely. Climate, less unionization, better work ethic";
- "No, out of the mainstream of business."

In virtually all of the more than 50 responses, we were impressed by the level and quality of the response.

WHAT DID THE INDUSTRIAL REALTORS TELL US?

The industrial realtors identified the headquarters and plant location factors that they feel are *most important to companies today.* They told us their opinions regarding key economic development issues, such as the trend to Sunbelt location and the impact of state unitary tax laws. They indicated the steps and personalities that occur in the site-specific decision stage. And, they commented on the efforts played by their state and city economic development organizations.

Headquarters location factors: The number of location factors that might have some degree of importance to companies seeking to relocate their headquarters is, of course, finite, but judging from those mentioned in the popular press, academic journals, trade, and pro-

---

*Most direct mail organizations expect to receive only a 2% (or less) response to their sales materials; the typical mail survey response rate is likely to be in the 20% range. Therefore, this response rate is quite acceptable and is sufficiently representative to permit us to generalize about the findings.

fessional books, one would think them infinite. Some, as in the case of GM's Saturn headquarters and plant location, are quite company- or industry-specific, while other factors such as climate, tax structure, and cost of living have broader applicability.

We provided the industrial realtors with a list of the 31 factors that we had found from our research to be most often mentioned by the location literature, and then provided them with additional space on the survey form to add to their own. Then we asked them to rate* the importance of each of these factors to companies making a head-quarters move. We asked them to base this rating on their experience with executives in relocating companies, not on their own preference.

Rated most important by the corporate realtors was the *availability of a qualified work force*. Their complete ranking of the top 10 factors in terms of headquarters location decisions is as follows:

1. the availability of a qualified work force;
2. labor relations;
3. "can-do" spirit;
4. quality college;
5. work ethic;
6. level of government red tape;
7. tax rate/business;
8. business travel;
9. housing availability;
10. proximity to markets.

Next, in order to determine if there were regional differences in terms of the respondents, we divided the industrial realtors into four groups (Northeast, North Central, South, and West.) Three of the subgroups were relatively equal in number, but the fourth group—the South— accounted for 40% of the respondents. Because the South is seen as having received an inordinate share of headquarters moves over the last decade or so, this slightly disproportionate response rate might be viewed as a plus, that is, this group may have had more experience with relocating firms. This division of realtors into groups produced a few rather startling differences. In particular, the southern respondents placed "lack of red tape" in the number one slot and also rated "can-do spirit" and a "quality school system" much higher than did the industrial realtors from the other geographic areas. In contrast, the industrial realtors in the Northeast gave a significantly higher rating to "incentives" and the western respondents gave the highest score to "availability of workforce," followed closely by "quality college." Because the different areas of the country rely on their own special

---

*We employed a standard even-point Likert-like scale that ranged from *no importance* to *very important* (0 to +6). The higher the score assigned to a particular factor, the more important it was felt to be to the corporate decision makers responsible for the selection of a new headquarters site.

pluses, such differing views could be expected. Possibly the biggest surprise was that none of the four regions gave a particularly strong rating to "warm climate," as being a factor in headquarter's location decisions. It was only surprising, however, due to the many references to sun in the popular press.

What these ratings suggest is that each region's new relocators have based their decisions on somewhat different factors. On the one hand, those industrial realtors from the South see companies they deal with focusing first on such qualitative concerns as "lack of red tape" and "can-do spirit," followed by more measurable factors such as "labor relations," "availability of a workforce," and "the quality of the school system." In contrast, the other areas see more quantitative factors, for example, "incentives" in the Northeast and "availability of a workforce" in the North Central and West, as most important for headquarters move decision makers. Assuming their assessment to be correct, such findings have important implications for city and state site-selection program planners.

Plant/subsidiary locations: Next, the industrial realtors were asked to rate a similar set of factors in terms of their importance to companies that were making a site selection for a subsidiary or a new or additional plant, or were relocating an existing plant. As might be expected, the industrial realtors again chose "availability of workforce" as number one, but this time it was tied with "labor relations." Further, several of the other top 10 factors are quite different than those they picked for a headquarters move. The top 10 plant location (relocation) factors, according to the industrial realtors, are:

1. availability of the workforce;
2. labor relations;
3. work ethic;
4. low unionization;
5. transportation;
6. incentives;
7. proximity to company's markets;
8. lack of government red tape;
9. tax rate/business;
10. adequacy of water systems;

The first four factors in importance are personnel-related, either availability of trained workers or performance- or productivity-related. Further, in most cases, the factors are quantitatively measurable.

Again, we looked for possible regional differences. A few are apparent, but not to the extent they are in regard to headquarters moves. In particular, the western industrial realtors feel that "proximity to a company's markets" is a bit more important in plant or subsidiary locations in their area, while the Northeast industrial realtors gave "housing availability," "tax rates for individuals," and "incentives" greater importance than did their counterparts in other locales. In the main, however, the industrial realtors were quite consistent overall with one another, and generally favored the most pragmatic considerations.

Corporate decision makers: Another prime concern for marketers is the decision process itself. Questions such as, Who (in the company) initiates the contact with the industrial realtors? and Is the president of the company involved in the final location decision? are very crucial to marketing planners, for example.

According to the industrial realtors, their initial contact from a company generally comes from its real estate director or a vice president who is responsible for real property decisions. (One of these two initial contact points is cited by over three-fourths of the industrial realtors.) The company's president was mentioned as the individual most likely to make the initial corporate realtor contact by only 16% of the respondents.

Regarding the question of the president's (or CEO's) active involvement in location decisions, the industrial realtors indicated that it depends on whether you are talking about a headquarters move or a plant or subsidiary location decision. The industrial realtors were virtually unanimous in their view that the company president or CEO plays a most active role in the headquarters relocation decision. In fact, 94% reported that in their experience the chief corporate executive becomes actively involved before any final decision is made on the headquarters site.

In contrast, the industrial realtors feel that fewer chief executives tend to be involved in the selection of plant or subsidiary locations or relocations. Some 71% of the industrial realtors said that the president or CEO typically is actively involved in the plant- or subsidiary-location decisions, while nearly 30% (28.6%) disagreed. The key judgement here, of course, concerns the word active. In a headquarters move, the president or CEO is likely to make his or her presence directly felt and this individual may even be in direct contact with the industrial realtors. (As one industrial realtor put it, "... Many corporate [headquarters] locations are chosen because the CEO has a particular reason to be there.") In a plant or subsidiary location decision, especially in a very large corporation, the president may simply be involved more indirectly in the process or behind the scenes. Further, the chief executive's participation in plant- or subsidiary-location decisions may depend more on the size of the particular investment than on other considerations. General Motors' Saturn location decision certainly involved the company's president William E. Hoglund along with everyone else. Whether one should view this location decision as a headquarters-type move or as merely a plant/subsidiary location decision could be debated. In any case, however, it was the magnitude of the investment and its importance to the company's future that apparently made it a priority for top management involvement.

More operationally, we asked the industrial realtors how many *specific* alternative sites typically are considered before a final decision is made by the firm. Although the average response was six, nearly 40% of the industrial realtors said that the firm considers at least three or four sites. The number is apparently a bit higher in the South, where the industrial realtors indicated the firms they work with consider at least four or five site alternatives and in the Northeast, where six or seven is the number. As one western industrial realtor pointed out, however, the number of alternatives considered depends on such considerations as "... land availability, costs, building costs and the quality of the sites."

State Involvement: *Are state economic development organizations generally involved in assisting companies in their site-selection decisions? How do the industrial realtors see the state's overall performance?* The industrial realtors see the state's primary involvement as being one of attracting the corporation to the state. This view is not unanimous, however, but the majority seem openly critical if the state's economic development group goes too far beyond this role. As one industrial realtor in the South put it, "... [State] agencies should disseminate information and stay out of the brokerage area." Or, according to another southern industrial realtor, the "... most effective state agencies create/stimulate interest (and) then turn the prospect over to qualified S.I.R.'s utility reps to achieve the final city and site selection." This negative view is perhaps best stated by one western industrial realtor: "... EDO's are usually of little value in my experience." Overall, some 56% of the industrial realtors indicated that their state's economic development organization is generally involved in assisting in the site-selection process.

Naturally, how proactive the states are in the site-selection process does vary and, of course, most of the industrial realtors are speaking from just their own state's perspective. Further, many industrial realtors, though not a majority, would like to see their states *more* involved in the process. These industrial realtors feel their states are not being as active as other states. One industrial realtor from the West says, "... The ---- government needs to be more aggressive in these matters," while one from the North Central area indicates that the utilities are doing "far more" than the state.

Thus, where the state's involvement should end and, in fact, its overall role in economic development, beyond simply company attraction, are areas in which the industrial realtors lack clear agreement. State governmental skeptics are likely to say this appears to be a bit of a "damned if you do, damned if you don't" situation. They would say complaints of "too little" come from industrial realtors in states where state involvement is low and complaints of "too much" come from the states with high levels of activity. To some extent this is correct, but not entirely. Rather, it tends to be a turf issue. The appropriate level of support to be offered by the government—whether local, state, or national—has long been an issue in business-government relations, so it is not surprising to see it surface here. What is important for both the state and the industrial realtors is that any conflict that may occur over turf is not seen by the corporate location decision makers. This would lead to images of a "poor business climate," which would be counterproductive to all concerned.

Several industrial realtors indicated a strong partnership between their state and the real estate community with each partner's appropriate tasks agreed upon in advance. Such a working relationship would seem optimal based on the majority of views expressed in our research and, as one southern industrial realtor indicates, often gives an area with this type of cooperation "...an edge."

Other concerns: *How do the industrial realtors feel about the oft-mentioned trend toward the Sunbelt? How concerned are they about state unitary tax law?* Both the "trend toward the Sunbelt" and the "inequalities of state unitary tax laws" are issues that have received considerable attention in the business press. For years, one could hardly read a major business publication, such as the *Wall Street Journal* or *Business Week,* without finding some reference to one or both of these issues. States and industrial realtors outside the Sunbelt found themselves contending with an image problem and sought to counter what many of them felt to be a Sunbelt myth.

We asked the industrial realtors, who represent all geographic areas, if they saw the trend toward the Sunbelt continuing in the future. Most of them said yes, but few cited quality of life and the sun as their reason and many saw the rate of movement to the Sunbelt diminishing in the future. The factors most often cited for the perceived slowdown in the Sunbelt trend were labor- and energy-related. As one Northeast industrial realtor put it, "...Labor costs are catching up with the more industrialized states." A North Central industrial realtor added, "... Improved energy conservation has reduced the costs of operating in the northern areas...." The southern industrial realtors were quite vocal, however, in seeing the trend continuing, and possibly even increasing. "Yes, climate is an important consideration...salary levels generally lower, large workforce availability and less unionization," says one deep South respondent.

The industrial realtors responded equally strongly regarding unitary taxation, which has been a major issue until quite recently when several states repealed their legislation. As an industrial realtor in one state with the tax views it, unitary taxation has a "very negative impact. There is a great deal of competition for industries to locate in various states and those without a unitary tax have a great deal of advantage." Speaking from a state without a unitary tax, another says,

If it is in addition to the usual taxes, real estate payroll, inventory, etc., it will have a very negative effect. A firm seeking a new location will certainly study the total tax structure.

Finally, speaking of taxes in general, a southern industrial realtor adds "... Any state seeking any form of unfair taxing advantage over business or its employees will learn over time that business will endure only so much abuse, then it (the business) will be gone!" This, of course, is a lesson that many state legislatures, city councils, and so forth, have learned and others will learn the hard way.

Summary: Given the amount of information provided by the industrial realtors, a summary seems in order. Among the principal findings from this research are the following:

- The industrial realtors see different sets of site-selection factors as being important in the headquarters and plant/subsidiary moves;
- The headquarters move considerations are more qualitative in nature;
- The relative importance of various factors changes by geographic region;
- The president or CEO is more directly involved in headquarters relocation decisions;
- The company's real estate director tends to be the first contact point with the industrial realtor;
- The industrial realtors tend to feel that the state economic development organizations should *not* become involved at the site-specific level.

In addition, we found that the industrial realtors have very strong feelings on two recent topical concerns or issues in the economic development industry: the Sunbelt trend and unitary taxation. From their *aggregate perspective,* the former seems to have lost a bit of its earlier momentum, while still important, and the latter is a difficult barrier to overcome and may be seen as a reflection of a state's business climate.

Finally, we conclude that the industrial realtors' responses demonstrate considerable site-specific insight and experience on the factors that influence the relocating or expanding companies, particularly those firms that moved to their area. To complete the picture, of course, we as marketers now need to look at the reasons offered by the companies themselves. Rarely do companies follow the GM Saturn approach of taking bids from all over. Rather, they take some delimiting steps themselves (or via consultants, national industrial realtors, etc.) prior to contacting specific states and the local industrial realtors. The factors we found important to the companies will be considered in chapters 8, 9 and 10.

Vignettes

TAMPA: A CITY ON THE MOVE*

The best-seller *Megatrends* wrote glowingly of Tampa, Florida. And the favorable publicity sent land prices soaring as speculators went into action. Tampa, indeed, is a city on the move.

Tampa's Committee of 100 (local business executives), its chamber of commerce, and its mayor, Robert Martinez, have cooperated in stimulating and promoting economic development. This private- and public-sector cooperation has not always been the case in Tampa, but it is now. In making Tampa more economically attractive, Mayor Martinez has reduced property tax rates for 5 consecutive years.

Located near the University of South Florida in Tampa are an industrial park and a new research park oriented to high technology. Both of these are privately-owned and run with the hope, however, that there will be a symbiosis between firms located in the parks and the state-owned University of South Florida. Indicative of Tampa's ambitions is the Harbour Island project, which is being developed by the private sector. It is to be a downtown community of offices and condominiums, complete with its own people mover.

Tampa generally tries to sell itself to prospective businesses by calling attention to its average or below average costs of doing business, its strategic location, a quality of life that is seeing the city's inherent recreational and weather amenities being augmented with cultural events, a progressive probusiness attitude in city government, close public- and private-sector cooperation, and a dynamic business community. Tampa wants to be perceived as "a place to be."

Even with all the advantages going for Tampa, it is not without its problems. But, all in all, even though Tampa is experiencing some growing pains, it is no doubt a city of tomorrow.

---

*Information based on published reports and on an interview with Vicki F. Wagner of Merrill Lynch Realty/Florida, Inc.

SATURN RISK: DOES CORPORATE
BALLYHOO BACKLASH?

Did your state and city participate in the 1984-1985 GM lotto? How much did it spend to "win"? Were there actually *no* losers, as state leaders were quoted as saying?[15] How many economic development (and possibly governor-level) heads will ultimately roll as a result of GM's selection of Tennessee? Will irate Youngstown losers now vow to buy anything but Saturns?

Undoubtedly, the great Saturn race attracted more attention than did the 1985 running of the Preakness stakes and may even have matched turn-for-turn with the Indy 500. The *New York Times* reports that "...25 state governors came courting to the northern suburbs of Detroit..."[16] during the 7-month-long Saturn sweepstakes. Early reports that suggested the winner would be Michigan proved false and, therefore, the credibility of the race was preserved. However, there has been no estimate of the overall dollar cost of the battle to the states.

From our perspective, any post mortem of the Saturn plant location decision should probably focus on several nagging questions that remain after the smoke has cleared away and Tennessee begins to fulfill the promises it made to GM. These questions are:

- Did GM intentionally or unintentionally create excessive media hype in its search process? (And a corollary: Did it hurt its overall image in the process?)
- What lessons might future "GMs" learn from the Saturn search process? (And a corollary: What lessons did economic development officials learn?)

Columnists and cartoonists took advantage of the media hype associated with the Saturn search process to make tongue-in-cheek attacks on GM and their local state and city officials. Although space does not permit offering too many examples, Stuart Warner, *Akron Beacon Journal* columnist, offers an excellent case in point. In his column *(Warner's Corner)* of March 11, 1985, he raised the intriguing question, "Are we willing to sell our souls for Saturn?"[17] After noting that Davenport, Iowa, was reported willing to jump as high as GM wanted it to and that Kansas City had promised $260 million in economic incentives, Warner suggests, "...Let's give Cleveland to GM...."[18]

Thus, having captured the full spirit of that "preposterous" suggestion, Warner recommended (1) renaming the city (Cleveland) Saturn, (2) renaming its baseball team the "Engines," (3) renaming Terminal Tower (a Cleveland landmark), the Transmission Tower, (4) renaming the *Plain Dealer,* the *Wheeler Dealer;* and (5) a host of other renamings. The column was a classic in satire and was extremely humorous. But, the point it made was undoubtedly not lost on the readers: How far should a state or community go in its industry-attracting efforts? And, to what extent were the "excesses" inflamed by comments such as Saturn Executive Vice President C. Reid Rundell's reported quote, "...Every state has a chance...," while GM Chairman Roger Smith only ruled out Florida and Wyoming.[19] This led to everything from kids writing to GM in behalf of their communities to seven governors appearing on Phil Donahue.[20] Setting aside what GM officials must think about America's state and city public officials, one wonders what many Americans must now think about GM.

Are there lessons to be learned from the Saturn site search? First, the evidence suggests that GM followed a decision process that kept it close to the criteria it had long emphasized. It simply ignored or, in some instances, "played along with" but was not "swayed by," the carnival atmosphere surrounding the decision. Tennessee appears to have taken a *professional approach* and avoided the TV host or children's crusade approach. Second, despite GM's protestations that everyone had an equal chance, a careful analysis of the product (an automobile) and its primary markets seemed to strongly suggest that a Utah or a New Mexico or a Maine had little chance in winning. (And, the latter did not enter the competition, according to reports.)[21] Possibly some states figured they had nothing to lose in trying; the governors could at least demonstrate their resolve to support economic development. However, their efforts may have been better spent in seeking industry they could win. Or, the need is to prioritize your efforts.

The bottom line to all this is a question we cannot avoid. Would we have recommended to GM (or any leading company) that they embark on such a high-visibility site search? Our answer is no and there are several reasons for our answer. In the first instance, the risk is too high. The company was already being criticized in some quarters for its linking with Toyota to produce the Nova; a copout some have termed it. While GM may argue that this put Saturn on the tip of everyone's tongue, it does not tell us about the taste it could have left in many mouths. Just as Detroit underestimated the demand for the small car in the 1970s, it gave the appearance of having ignored the concern for employment in the 1980s. Second, GM embarrassed too many public officials, some of whom are destined for the Congress, Senate, and possibly even the White House. Such open disregard for so many officials' public careers is unlikely to create a ground swell of support for GM if it ever needs a Chrysler-like bailout. We admit that the results are still out, but the real point is that GM could have achieved the exact same deal, same increased product awareness, and so forth, in a far less risky fashion.

THE FANTUS COMPANY

Playing a key role in the economic and industrial development field are a number of consulting firms. High on anyone's list of such organizations would be the Fantus Company. Fantus works with its client companies to develop a location strategy that is consistent with these firms' overall objectives.

Perhaps the most basic question that one might ask a firm such as Fantus is, Why should companies seek Fantus assistance in 'location problems'? According to a Fantus promotional brochure, the answer is:

> They should engage the best available "hands on" specialists to provide practical solutions to their complex tactical and strategic problems.
>
> Fantus finds that less than 2% of the *Fortune 1000* companies have developed even a rudimentary management system to determine *what* facilities they will require in *which* locations to achieve their overall strategic plan. Even fewer companies engage in a regular asset management audit of every significant corporate facility, with recommendations on its most appropriate short-term and long-term utility for the company.
>
> Whether in a $5 billion or $25 million company, rarely does a senior manager have specific responsibility for "location planning." Rather, the issues are fragmented between various departments, and any action is likely to be ad hoc rather than comprehensive.

This response is based on the experience the company has acquired in handling over 6,000 location assignments since its inception in 1919.

Carrying our inquiry further, we asked Phillip D. Phillips, a vice president in the Fantus Company's Chicago office, to indicate what a typical site-selection assignment for a new production facility involves. He identified a 17-step process which begins with the decision to build a new facility and concludes with the production start-up from the new plant. Phillips sees the complete process involving the following:

Steps in the site selection process
1. Decision to build a new facility
2. Definition of the facility
3. Geographic analysis of the market
4. Geographic analysis of suppliers
5. Freight analysis
6. Definition of a search area
7. Initial community screening
8. Detailed community screening

9. Field investigation
10. Ranking of alternatives
11. Engineering/legal analysis
12. Site options/inducements
13. Approval and site purchase
14. Construction/modification of facility
15. Transfer/hiring of personnel
16. Purchase and set up of machinery and equipment
17. Production start-up

To him, "site selection" is all-encompassing. In fact, in one of his recent articles, Phillips pointed out that the

> charter of a corporate site selection team considering locations for a new plant typically includes analysis of markets, suppliers and transportation costs, as well as variations in labour costs and labour-management relations climate, utility availability and cost, and living conditions for transferees. All this is in addition to the selection of a specific physical site, assuming that a green-field facility is planned.*

Fantus, of course, is able to assist clients in all phases of the site-selection or plant-location process and, more broadly, in strategic location planning. Further, as a comprehensive consultant in the field, the company is also involved in providing development advisory assistance to public-sector agencies at all levels.

---

*Taken from Phillips, P.D. (1984, Special Edition). Selecting the right site—Will you make the wrong decision. *Area Development*, p. 22.

188

REFERENCES

1. Coene, E. (1984, March-April). 14th annual site selection guide: The biggest ever. *Business Facilities*, p. 6.
2. Swindle, H. (1985, February 4). City seeks the 'right kind' of neighbor. *Crain's Cleveland Business*, p. F2, F8.
3. Federal Reserve Bank of Chicago. (1984, June 12). *Wisconsin economy scan*, Chicago, Illinois.
4. SEI International. (1984, March). *Choosing a future*. Menlo Park, California.
5. Latham, W. R., III, & Hockensmith, P. (1984, March/April). Investor-owned utilities as information sources. *Industrial Development*, p. 36.
6. Letter from C.F. Penna, Vice President and General Manager of Southern Pacific Industrial Development Organization, dated October 29, 1982.
7. The railroads: Real estate development will feel their increasing impact. (1984, December). *Business Facilities*, p. 23.
8. CSX Corporation advertisement. (1984, November). *Dun's Business Month*, p. 112.
9. Upland Industries advertisement. (1984, March-April). *Business Facilities*, pp. 24-25.
10. The Fantus Company advertisement. (1984, September-October). *Plants Sites & Parks*, p. 15.
11. Simon, J. (1984, August 6). Poor image problems blamed in defeat of R.I. greenhouse. *New England Business*, pp. 36-37.
12. BOMA brochure obtained from BOMA International, 1250 Eye Street, NW, Suite 200, Washington, DC 20005.
13. Society of Industrial Realtors of the National Association of Realtors. (1984). *Industrial real estate* (4th ed.) p. 23. Washington, DC.
14. Society of Industrial Realtors of the National Association of Realtors, pp. 20-21.
15. Chan, M. (1985, March 4). Saturn race heads into final stretch. *USA Today*, p. 1B.
16. Holusha, J. (1985, August 4). Saturn Division finds a home in the heartland. *New York Times*, p. E5.
17. Warner, S. (1985, March 11). Promising the moon in trade for Saturn. *Akron Beacon Journal*, p. C1.
18. Ibid, p. C1.
19. Chan, p. 1B.
20. Chan, p. 2B.
21. Chan, p. 1B.

6

THE RAGING BATTLE FOR HIGH TECHNOLOGY

EXECUTIVE SUMMARY

High technology is dramatically changing the United States. It is both creating and obsoleting jobs, and is rapidly bringing labor-saving devices and processes to bear on American's lives and work. Yet, the capacity of high technology for generating new jobs for communities hard hit by problems in the basic industries has too often been embellished. Most states, communities, and even nations do not have the ingredients necessary to attract high-tech industry. In addition, high technology is not a substitute for lower-tech forms of enterprise; rather it is a means to make other forms of endeavor more productive. High-tech and smokestack industries, for example, are complementary to one another, not adverse.

If a nation, state, or community is to foster high-tech development, entrepreneurship must be viewed by the relevant government and the salient population as a worthwhile, productive activity. Ideally, entrepreneurs should be viewed as growth-creating, jobs-producing heroes of sort. Moreover, entrepreneurship per se, not solely high-tech entrepreneurship, must be encouraged. In the first place, high-tech entrepreneurs are but a small fraction of all entrepreneurs and, further, account for only a small fraction of net new-job growth in the U.S. economy. Second, it is not feasible nor advisable to target high-tech entrepreneurship and ignore lower-tech entrepreneurs. High-tech entrepreneurship is subsumed by a larger entrepreneurial process, not the other way around. And low-tech and middle-tech businesses not only account for far more jobs than high-tech firms, but their profits usually finance high-tech ventures.

Nevertheless, states and communities, as part of more comprehensive programs to foster entrepreneurial economic development and to encourage existing businesses to relocate or expand, can increase their chances of high-tech development through various initiatives. Similarly, the private sector can undertake their own initiatives, often in conjunction with the public sector. Even nations, particularly in Europe but also in the Third World, are competing in the high-tech sweepstakes. So a state or community might conceivably find itself up against a foreign nation for a new high-tech facility. What form do high-tech development initiatives typically take at the state and community levels and in the private sector? What is going on across the United States in these respects?

Finally, are high-tech personnel unique in what they want a community to provide in the way of quality of life? Or can they be attracted to a geographic area in much the same way that any other business people might be attracted? The answer is a little of both.

∞

HIGH TECH, HIGH ATTRACTIVENESS, HIGH HYPE

Definitions of high technology are numerous and diverse. The terminology has been grossly overused and misapplied to products and processes that in no way justify the nomenclature of high technology.

According to the U.S. Department of Commerce, high technology differs from pure science in that the former is technology developed for commercial application. Pure science focuses on knowledge irrespective of any relationship it may bear to commercial applications. A Department of Commerce publication also states:

> High-technology industries are identified by the simultaneous presence of two characteristics: (1) an above average level of scientific and engineering skills and capabilities, compared to other industries (alternatively, research and development effort relative to sales can be used); and (2) a rapid rate of technological development.[1]

In our book, *Marketing High Technology,* we suggested that a truly high-tech company and its relevant market have three characteristics:

- The business requires a strong scientific/technical basis;
- New technology can obsolete existing technology rapidly;
- As new technologies come on stream their applications create or revolutionize markets and demands.[2]

Businesses and markets that are inarguably high technology include computers and software, industrial robotics, biotechnology, pharmaceuticals, fiber optics, guided missiles and spacecraft, and other such obviously technology-intensive commercial endeavors. At the other extreme are consensus low-tech businesses and markets. In between, of course, are many arguably high-tech, arguably low-tech industries. Therefore, no definition of high technology is so exact as to allow one to really categorize all businesses and markets as high-tech or low-tech.

Although there are no universally accepted definitions of high technology, there is a consensus that high technology has and is changing Americans' ways of living and working. Some people go so far as to assert that high technology has engendered a second industrial revolution. Just as the first industrial revolution changed an agrarian and small town America to a factory and city society, so too is high technology having a widespread economic and social impact. Job skills are shifting even more from blue-collar to white-collar technical and professional. The still-powerful basic industries have lost much of their political and economic clout to the relatively newer knowledge-based industries. And the power of the unions that has grown up around the basic industries has ebbed noticeably.

These trends have promoted an industrial class war of sorts between the basic industries, the so-called smokestackers, and the far more glamorous high-tech businesses. As a result, a geographic war has emerged between the Frostbelt, where the basic industries were generally founded and nurtured, and the Sunbelt, home to a plethora of start-up high-tech companies and to manufacturing facilities of smokestacks that have fled to perceived greener pastures of lighter taxes, fewer regulations, and less unionization.

In response to the declining fortunes of both the basic industries in the United States and to the traditional industrial heartland where they grew up, calls have been heard from some vested interests in business, government, and labor for proposed remedies along the lines of domestic content legislation, further restrictions on international trade, targeting of government financial help to industries selected by Washington, and a sweeping industrial policy. We will consider some of these proposals and how they might affect economic development in the United States.

One conclusion regarding the hopes, promises, and fears of high technology is certain: No more hype, misleading assertions, and unrealistic expectations have been more associated with any economic evolution (or, if you prefer, revolution) in memory. To some observers and participants, high technology is an economic and social panacea that will create interesting jobs, raise our standard of living (for example, by improving education), and free us from mundane and sometimes dangerous tasks—already, robots can be used in fire-fighting. To others, high technology has and is promoting economic and social tribulations. In this view, high technology replaces workers with machines, makes for permanent structural unemployment of untrainable older workers, substitutes low-paying technical-type and clerical jobs for high-paying factory jobs, and leads to further urban decay in the once dominant Frostbelt. A few critics even predict and fear the demise of the American middle class as we know it. In this scenario, there will be a dichotomy between a very well-paid high-tech cadre of professionals and very low-paid technical functionaries.

Like most anything, high technology has its pros and cons. We think it useful to devote some attention to the issues we have just raised. How much, for example, will high technology affect the number of jobs available in the United States and are high-tech companies and smoke-stackers really adversaries?

DOSE OF REALISM

Almost every state and city of any size has hopes of getting a piece of the high-tech action. The well-publicized Silicon Valley, Research Triangle, and Route 128 success stories have served to heighten interest in attracting high-tech industry, especially in those places so

EXHIBIT 6.1

A Cross-Section of Major Existing and Aspiring High-Tech Areas in the United States

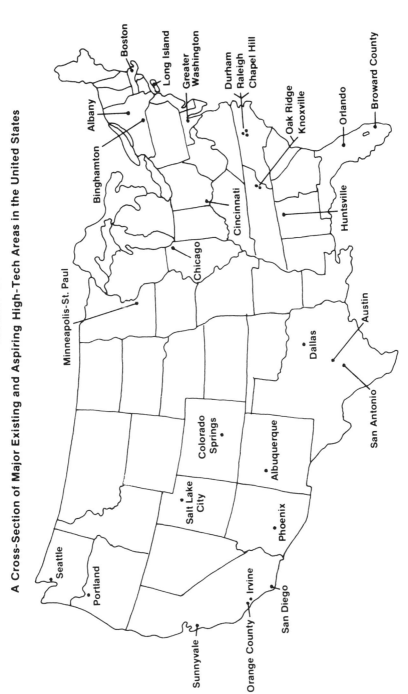

hard hit by erosion of their traditional industrial bases and concomitant structural unemployment. Exhibit 6.1 depicts a cross-section of major existing and aspiring high-tech areas in the United States.

The glamour and lure of high technology stem mainly from three perceived benefits—jobs, clean industry, and recession resistance. In combination, the thinking goes, these benefits create a superior quality of life. But this line of thought is debatable.

Take quality of life. It is no foregone conclusion that high-technology industry necessarily leads to a better quality of life, because quality of life criteria are a matter of individual taste. Given the choice between a cleaner environment and lower average wages, a high-tech scenario, versus a more polluted environment and higher wages, a basic industry-manufacturing scenario, there could be debate about which scenario yields a superior quality of life. Whenever Akron, Ohio's, air quality was criticized during the city's heyday in rubber manufacturing, many people were quick to point out that what one smelled burning was high-paying jobs.

Recently, an executive with a premier computer company told one of us that his firm regretted the choice it had made in locating one of its plants. The city housing the facility had many amenities—warm weather, low pollution, and modern structures in its downtown. It was only after the company located there, however, that its technical and professional employees found that, in their opinion, the city was intellectually and culturally sterile. Quality of life is a matter of personal taste and thus varies from person to person.

The job-generating capacity of high technology has been discussed and argued more than any economic or social issue attendant to high technology. The *Wall Street Journal* wrote in 1983:

> A recent study by the Congressional Budget Office estimates that between now and 1990, a combination of automation and capacity cutbacks in basic industry will eliminate three million manufacturing jobs. Some robotics experts believe that by the year 2000, factory robots will be doing what seven million human beings do now. The question thus becomes: How many jobs will technology save or create—and where?[3]

David Birch is director of the Program on Neighborhood and Regional Change at the Massachusetts Institute of Technology, which conducted a study on high technology and its economic and social effects. In a 1984 speech at Bentley College, Birch reported that high technology employs about 2.5% to 3% of the U.S. labor force. Moreover, although high tech is more resilient in recessions, and thus fewer jobs become at risk, high technology is not necessarily a *net* job creator. Low-technology enterprises create more jobs, because high technology often *replaces* jobs in other sectors of the economy. And, as Birch said, high-technology companies tend to be concentrated; therefore, the jobs they generate are also geographically concentrated.

ILLUSTRATION 6.1

Accompaniment of persuasive factual information to high-tech companies with attention-grabbing creativity.

What an opportunity for your high technology firm. A flourishing valley with room to grow. A place with a sense of adventure and optimism as bright as our famous sunshine.

That's the opportunity of Phoenix. A city poised for a leap into the Twenty-First Century.

No matter what size your business is—big, small, just getting started, or looking to expand—there's a place for you in the Phoenix area. Prime industrial land is still available within minutes of the airport. And, there's still plenty of office space and affordable housing.

The area's commitment to high technology is represented by Arizona State University's $32 million engineering research center and 320 acre research park. In fact, 49% of our manufacturing employment is already in high-tech. So support firms and facilities abound.

Arizona's leadership has put a premium on maintaining a favorable business climate and as the results from a recent national study indicate, they have been successful. Arizona ranks number one in the nation in government-controlled business factors.

There's an abundance of electric power, too, and a ready supply of water. At Salt River Project, we've seen to that since 1903, and have planned for decades of growth to come.

To find out more, send for our free report, "Economic Assets of Metropolitan Phoenix," by writing to Larry Evans, Manager, Commercial and Industrial Division, Salt River Project, P.O. Box 52025, Phoenix, Arizona 85072-2025.

You'll find you won't have to invent any reasons to move here.

Salt River Project
WATER ◆ POWER

COME TO PHOENIX AND INVENT THE FUTURE.

Advertisement reprinted with the permission of Larry Evans, Manager, Commercial and Industrial Division, Salt River Project, Phoenix, Arizona.

Business Week examined the jobs potential of high technology in an excellent article titled, "America Rushes to High Tech for Growth." Their conclusion was, "Many call it [high tech] a panacea, but hopes for new jobs are overly optimistic...not enough jobs are there."[4]

THE EITHER/OR FALLACY

Much of the misleading assertions and dialogue about high technology have come from a mistaken either/or mentality on too many people's parts. High-technology innovation is encompassed by entrepreneurship per se, but is not a substitute for it. Similarly, high technology is not a replacement and threat to basic industry—the two are natural allies.

According to MIT's Birch, "high tech is neither the economic savior of America's economy nor its over-touted false hope." The MIT study, coauthored by him and Susan MacCracken, confirmed that high tech creates relatively few jobs in and of itself, again about 2.8% of the jobs and only 5% of the employment growth in the 1980s. In Birch's view, innovation of any kind is the key, not just high-tech innovation. And high tech is a small, but integral, part of a larger system of innovation Birch suggested that innovative industries to watch include several relatively low-tech ones—motorcycles and bicycles, railroads, household appliances, dried and frozen fruits and vegetables, and steel and steel products. Surprisingly, according to the study, these are among 15 of the most innovative sectors of the American economy. The MIT study also noted that it is large companies with their considerable human and financial resources that play a significant role in developing innovation, even though small firms continue to produce most new jobs overall. Importantly, the study stated that "one form of innovation is not inherently superior to another."[5] In short, in terms of creating jobs it is innovation and entrepreneurship of all kinds that need to be fostered, not solely the high-tech variety.

Like high-tech innovation versus innovation per se, the high-tech/-smokestack dichotomy is a false one. It is true that various kinds of high technology have eliminated jobs in the basic manufacturing industries, most notably in computer-assisted design/computer-assisted manufacturing (CAD/CAM) and robotics. However, it is the synergy derived by applying high technology to basic industry manufacturing that is the one best hope for revitalizing steel, automobiles, rubber, and the others. Productivity gains will make for a stronger defense against foreign competition. High technology is not an end in itself; it is a means to improve something else, whether it be a society's leisure time, educational progress, or productivity in the workplace. As Isaac Asimov remarked about robots, "There was a time when mankind faced the universe without a friend. Now he has creatures to help him; stronger creatures than himself, more faithful, more useful, and absolutely devoted to him."[6]

Yet, what about all the people put out of work by this marriage between high technology and manufacturing and other forms of economic activity? What about the kind of concern voiced by the late United Auto Workers head Walter Reuther when he reacted to a partially robotized auto plant: "And tell me, these wonderful new robots, will they go out and buy cars from your company?"[7] We know these concerns to be natural, but think them unfounded. As MIT's David Birch pointed out in his 1984 speech at Bentley College, not a single (net) new manufacturing job has been created in the United States since 1966, yet 30 to 40 million new jobs have been added to the American economy. The processes of innovation and entrepreneurship have served their societal role. We would not be surprised if 10 to 15 years hence, maybe less, labor scarcity will be a major and pervasive problem facing the United States. Indeed, we expect it.

Even though innovation per se has and is generating far more jobs than high-tech innovation by itself, and even though high technology and the basic industries should be viewed as natural allies rather than adversaries, there are still influential people from business, government, and labor who want to see the United States adopt an industrial policy and target aid to certain industries.

For example, Murray Seeger, director of information for the American Federation of Labor and Congress of Industrial Organizations (AFL-CIO), has said:

> We know that high technology by itself does not create jobs. And it's a dead end for us to compete with lower wages abroad, because there are so many more of them than us... We're advocates of a very heavy investment program in basic American industries, plus a period of protection against imports so they can get back on their feet and American workers can maintain their high standard of living.[8]

Similarly, consider the rather startling results of a 1984 Louis Harris poll, commissioned by *Business Week,* of more than 600 executives, many of them chief executive officers, of 1,200 large U.S. corporations. The principal conclusion of the opinion poll was:

> American Business executives are on the brink of a profound change in their view of the future of U.S. industry. What appears to be happening is this: Top corporate managers are becoming so concerned about the viability of large segments of American's productive capacity that they are more willing than ever before to consider radical measures—including a major role for government in some form of centralized planning of a national 'industrial policy.'[9]

A 1984 *Wall Street Journal* article titled, "Congress is Debating Federal Role in Setting Technological Priorities," reported:

> Four years ago, Congress authorized $285 million to help American industry explore the potential of high technology. But the Reagan administration, committed to keeping the government out of industrial

planning, has spent only a fraction of that money. Now several bills that would fund research for industrial technology are slowly moving through Congress, reviving the debate over who should be getting the nation's technological priorities. The debate is between those who think the government should use tax and other incentives to encourage private technological development and those who think the government itself should plan and fund that development.[10]

Our own view on this important question is that government should not attempt to "target" winners and losers in the market-place. If targeting had been a long-time role of American government, it is highly doubtful that many of the Apple Computers of the industrial scene would have been targeted. Moreover, the British efforts with central planning have been failures and, for central planning performance at its worst, one need only to look at the Russian experience and that country's woeful shortage of consumer goods and services.

The "market" is a much better targeter of goods, services, and industries than government bureaucrats or tripartite boards of business, government, and labor. Any industrial policy unavoidably would involve targeting, and the wrong industries, in terms of America's future worldwide, might well be selected because of (1) sheer miscalculation and (2) political pressure by various industries and geographic areas of the country. The politics of industry advocacy are a poor substitute for impartial and nonpolitical market forces.

Interestingly, Japan, the country most often citied as the exemplar of industrial policy and the so-called targeting of winning industries, is moving away from this policy at the very same time industrial policy advocates in the United States are becoming more vocal . Jiro Tokuyama, dean of Tokyo's Nomura School of Advanced Management, and a close friend of Prime Minister Yasuhiro Nakasone, has observed:

> [Government] coordination is all right if you're building a steel and car industry on the model of other people. But now we're in an era of rapid change, of integrated circuits and microprocessors. I don't think our large organizations can move quickly enough to make the changes. We must find our model among the entrepreneurs like those in...Silicon Valley.[11]

Even the bureaucrats at Japan's Ministry of International Trade and Industry (frequently cited by enthusiasts of industrial policy in the United States as the prototype for a planning agency) now advocate wide-scale deregulation of the economy and they devote heavy resources to fostering small start-up companies. Peter Brooke, a Boston venture capitalist who was asked by both European countries and Japan to assist them in instilling entrepreneurial vigor, has stated the obvious irony:

> It's incredible that some Americans are going for heavy state planning when I'm being asked to go to Europe [and Japan] to help them disband theirs. We shouldn't follow their mistakes. Hell, we're the ones with the answers.[12]

We concur with MIT's David Birch and numerous others that it is innovation that creates jobs. And a government policy that encourages innovation is the best recipe for the economic future of the United States. Congressmen Ed Zschau (himself an entrepreneur) and Don Ritter have proposed measures that they believe can "help to revitalize America's 'smokestack' industries and stimulate new 'sunrise' enterprises." For instance, in addition to reducing federal budget deficits substantially, they recommend:

- increasing government-sponsored basic research;
- modifying antitrust laws to permit research-and-development joint ventures among corporations;
- making the 25% R & D tax credit permanent;
- strengthening patent laws;
- offering tax incentives for corporate contributions to educational institutions;
- focusing and streamlining export controls to eliminate unnecessary obstacles to trade;
- negotiating away trade barriers.[13]

These are the types of initiatives that can make for an attractive climate for economic development—entrepreurship, innovation, and business expansion.

In closing our discussion of industrial policy, we refer to Peter F. Drucker's article, "Europe's High-Tech Delusion."[14] Drucker gives an incisive critique of "high-tech targeting" in Europe, an analysis that should be on the reading list of all proponents of a U.S. industrial policy. He demonstrates why "the European belief that high-tech entrepreneurs can flourish alone without being embedded in a larger entrepreneural economy is a total misunderstanding." For example:

To provide the new jobs needed to employ a growing work force a country needs 'low-tech' or 'no-tech' entrepreneurs in large numbers— and the Europeans do not want these. In the U.S. employment in the *Fortune* 1000 companies and in government agencies has fallen by six million people in the past 15 to 20 years. Total employment, however, has risen to 106 million now [1984] from 71 million in 1965. Yet high-tech during this period has provided only about six million new jobs—that is, no more than smokestack industry and government have lost. All the additional jobs in the U.S. economy, in other words, have been provided by middle-tech, low-tech, and no-tech entrepreneurs;

If entrepreneurial activity is confined to high-tech—and this is what the Europeans are trying to do—unemployment will continue to go up as 'smokestack' industries either cut back production or automate;

High-tech entrepreneurship is the mountaintop. It must rest on a massive mountain—middle-tech, low-tech, no-tech entrepreneurship pervading the economy and society. In the U.S., 600,000 businesses are now being founded each year. ... But no more than 1.5% of those—about 10,000 a year are high-tech companies and

No-tech, low-tech, and middle-tech provide the profits to finance high-tech. Contrary to what most people think, high-tech is distinctly unprofitable for a long time. The world's computer industry ran at a heavy overall loss every year for 30 years; it did not break even until the early 1970s.[15]

Drucker goes on to say that unless European governments change dramatically in their attitude toward entrepreneurship, their infatuation with high-tech entrepreneurship will neither revive the rather stagnant European economies nor supply much high technology. In Europe, there is still much government hostility toward entrepreneurs, other than high tech, and the French government is contemptuous of entrepreneurship.

In capsule, the process and results of entrepreneurship are better left to an impartial marketplace than to the preferences of a targeting board, no matter how supposedly representative the board's members are of society. Jobs and economic development derive from innovation of all kinds, not just high-tech innovation.

The Europeans are likely to end up disappointed with exclusive targeting of entrepreneurship on high technology. A similar fate will befall most state governments and local communities that push high-tech development to the detriment of less technologically intensive forms of entrepreneurial enterprise.

BEING REALISTIC

Kokomo, Indiana, was a Silicon Valley of the early 1900s. The automobile, the carburetor, and the pneumatic were reportedly all developed there. Kokomo is no longer the high-tech hub it once was, nor is the Midwest of which it is part any longer the force it once was in American industry. As we saw in our discussion of industrial policy, what to do about the Kokomos of the world is the subject of considerable debate. In the context of this chapter on high technology, it is reasonable to ask, "Should a Kokomo attempt to go high tech?"

SRI International developed and prepared an extensive 1984 report commissioned by Ameritrust Corporation (Cleveland) called *Choosing A Future: Steps to Revitalize the MidAmerican Economy Over the Next Decade.* One caveat in this report is especially germane to answering the question, "Should Kokomo attempt to go high tech?"

There are pitfalls still ahead, however. The increasing fascination with high technology means that what was once smokestack chasing [offering tax rebates and industrial revenue bonds to all comers] could become 'silicon chip chasing.' Without a *balanced* revitalization strategy, the dependence on a 'quick fix,' high-tech explosion could prove to be a mistake. Not every state has the ingredients for another Silicon Valley or Route 128. Each state can, however, apply new technologies to its own auto plants, foundries, and mills to make them more competitive. Similarly, each state can make a difference in the growth of new business, the education of its people, the quality of its infrastructure, and the development of emerging technologies that build on the unique resources and strengths of the state.[16]

In a *New York Times* article titled "Everyone's Trying to Start the New 'Silicon Valley,'" the paper quoted Michigan State Senator Lara Pollock, as follows:

How many 'Silicon Valleys' or Route 128's can this country sustain? Most of the high-tech industry is smaller businesses working in the service of heavy manufacturing. But there's no harm in trying for a 'Silicon Valley.' If the state will make a heavy investment in education—kindergarten through college—to see how far it can go, it's worth it.[17]

We agree with Senator Pollock, but only up to a point. As the SRI/Ameritrust Corporation report indicates, there may be a great deal of "harm in trying" if a city, state, or region's attempt to attract high-tech business diverts resources from the "balanced" revitalization strategy needed. A "no-harm-in-trying" approach can quickly lead to "silicon-chip-chasing" economic development. In brief, what is needed is balance and realism (can we really compete in the high-tech sweepstakes?) when it comes to revitalization.

IN PURSUIT OF THE HIGH-TECH ACTION

Most places—states, cities, and even regions—simply do not have the ingredients to attract and foster high-tech enterprises. At a meeting of the National Conference of State Legislatures, James M. Howell, a senior vice president of the First National Bank of Boston, remarked, "I go to 100 cities a year, and the one question I hear is 'How can I get it [high technology industry]?'" Howell believes that only Massachusetts and California will be good parents to high-tech companies; that is, they will be states where start-up high-tech firms originate. In Howell's opinion, Texas might join these two states, as oil money gradually shifts to high-tech investment. A second group of states consisting of North Carolina, Minnesota, and Arizona can become reasonably good foster parents to high-tech firms. These three states will not be laden with start-ups, but they will be attractive to high-tech companies looking to expand. According to Howell, "For the rest of them [the states], the ballgame's over. They should not even enter. They are not going to be a participant."

Most speakers at this National Conference of State Legislatures shared Howell's assessment that the educational and financial ingredients which produced Route 128 in Massachusetts and Silicon Valley in California cannot be even closely replicated in most states.

ILLUSTRATION 6.2

**Appeal based on educational resources available
in support of high-tech industry.**

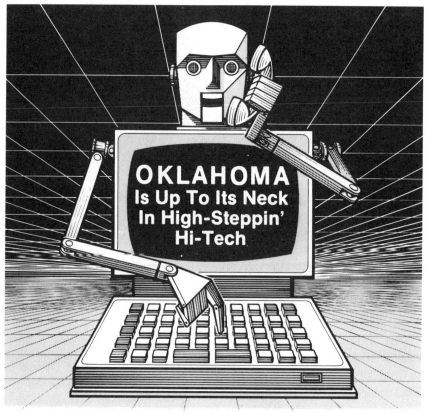

Long Before There Was A Silicon Valley Or Route 128
Oklahoma Was Deep Into Advanced Technologies

Oklahoma led the way in energy industry Hi-Tech through companies like **Phillips Petroleum, Conoco, Halliburton** and **AMOCO.** Now advanced research at Oklahoma State University and the University of Oklahoma, plus Oklahoma's superior Vo-Tech Training For Industry Program, are attracting industries involved in everything from biogenetic agriculture to space rockets.

AT&T has chosen Oklahoma to produce its large multi-use computers, aided by **Magnetic Peripherals, Inc. (Control Data). Fife Corporation** here is world leader in computerized measuring equipment. Components for rockets that propelled man to the moon were produced by a skilled Oklahoma work force. **Hertz** and **American Airlines** placed their world-wide reservations centers in Oklahoma. **Dyna Turn** and others are producing rigid computer discs, on-line data processing facilities, sophisticated medical equipment and much more.

Oklahoma is right on top of Texas. Next time you head this way, stop off in Oklahoma. We've got high-steppin' High-Tech operations to open your eyes.

The Profitable Place To Be

WRITE TO:
Director, Industrial Division, Oklahoma Department of Economic Development, Suite 204 , **P.O. Box 53424, State Capitol Station, Oklahoma City, OK 73152 (Phone 405-521-2401).**

Advertisement reprinted with the permission of Stephen P. Matthews, Executive Director, Department of Economic Development.

For example, J. Herbert Hollomon, a professor of engineering at the Massachusetts Institute of Technology, observed that a key ingredient is "world class" engineering departments at local colleges to supply skilled workers. By definition alone, how many world-class engineering departments can there be? Time and again, we have heard well-meaning individuals say that the engineering or medical school at a "local" university can lead the community into high-tech endeavors. Realistically, however, most of these schools have neither the research-oriented faculty or staff nor the necessary physical and laboratory facilities to do so.

A 1983 report by the National Governors' Association Committee on technological innovation has specified four basic prerequisites that a locale needs if it is to spawn and attract high-tech enterprises. They are:

- reasonably priced investment capital or seed money;
- a sufficient research base generating scientific and technical advances;
- a managerial structure with the vision, experience, and know-how to transform good ideas into marketable products and services;
- a well-trained labor pool of scientists, engineers, technicians, and skilled workers.

The report was quite specific that the centers of high-tech innovativeness in the United States are close to the "finest research universities." Yet, some of the states with undistinguished colleges and universities, low per capita spending for elementary and secondary education, and consequently a relatively poor technically skilled work force, are aggressively seeking high-tech industry. They appear to be undaunted by the long odds facing them. One can not only question the wisdom of allocating scarce dollar resources this way, but also can readily see that some low-tech states have the cart before the horse. Upgrading educational quality and technical skills of the labor force surely must precede any realistic hope of attracting high-tech industry.

Most cities and states that make a concerted effort to foster high-tech development will likely have a few successes to showcase. However, from a cost-benefit standpoint, the successes will often not have been worth the city's or state's efforts. Even so, the battle to foster and attract high-technology industry goes on unabated. Some efforts will succeed, but most will fail because the necessary ingredients will not be there.

HIGH-TECHNOLOGY DEVELOPMENT INITIATIVES IN THE UNITED STATES

It is our view that the most comprehensive and informative research to date concerning high-tech development has been conducted and reported by the U.S. Office of Technology Assessment (OTA) in a 1984 report entitled *Technology, Innovation, and Regional Economic Development: Encouraging High-Technology Development.*[18] Thus, we have used it here as our primary reference tool regarding high-tech development, and draw extensively upon its findings.

In the last one to two decades, several regions of the United States have developed buoyant local economies founded on high-growth technology-intensive industries. Because of these successes, public- and private-sector groups in other regions are launching initiatives to develop high-tech industrial bases of their own. These initiatives can be classified into six general categories:

• Research, development, and technology transfer. Perhaps the most fundamental initiatives are those that aim to quicken the flow of innovation itself. Because most basic research is still performed by universities, many of these initiatives focus on improving linkages between universities and industry. Some, such as joint research ventures and research consortia, involve formal, long-term collaboration between a university and one or more companies. Others, such as research centers and technical extension services, provide technical assistance or perform short-term research for local firms in exchange for fees or other support. In other cases, alumni groups have become active in patenting and commercializing the results of university research.

• Human capital. Other initiatives focus on developing the human capital needed to exploit innovations. University/industry collaborations include continuing education for people already employed and improving science and engineering training. State governments and local employers sometimes offer training or retraining programs for technical workers. A number of state colleges have developed magnet high schools or technology-based curricula in their vocational education programs. And high-tech firms sometimes offer student internships. These examples are fairly typical of human-capital initiatives.

• Entrepreneurship training and assistance. A special subset of human capital is entrepreneurship, and many initiatives by both universities and private-sector groups are designed to provide training, technical and management assistance, and other support needed by those who create new technology-based companies. As many as 400 colleges and universities now offer courses in the creation and management of small businesses, often with financial support from local firms or major corporations, as well as state governments. Some of them also conduct seminars and conferences or provide evaluation, consulting, and referral services for local inventors and entrepreneurs. In many cases, they offer this assistance in connection with an innovation center or incubator facility dedicated to nurturing new ventures by students and local entrepreneurs.

- Financial capital. Many universities have also begun to invest in technology-based spin-offs, either directly or through seed capital funds and venture-capital partnerships. In addition, almost half of the state government initiatives identified by the U.S. Office of Technology Assessment provide some form of financial assistance to high-technology firms. Most of this assistance is indirect, taking the form of tax credits, industrial-revenue bonds, or loan guarantees. Whereas many state programs help firms to locate seed or venture capital, very few actually provide risk capital themselves. Venture-capital investing is still dominated by independent firms and corporate subsidiaries, whose investments tend to go where the returns are expected to be greatest. In recent years, this has meant that California and Massachusetts have received the most support. Several universities and local governments have tried to attract these investments to their areas by holding venture-capital conferences. In addition, several state and local governments, in cooperation with local business groups and foundations, have established venture-capital funds with explicit geographic requirements. Seed capital, invested at the earlier and riskier stages of a new venture, does tend to stay local, and several initiatives attempt to increase the level of local seed-capital investments, often in connection with entrepreneurship services and incubator facilities.
- Physical capital. Local governments often seek to encourage high-technology development through changes in land use and zoning, as well as the provision of public services and facilities. Incubator facilities, which provide low-cost office and laboratory space for entrepreneurs and struggling firms, are one form that this type of initiative can take. Far more common, however, are research and science parks—parcels of land set aside for research-intensive firms and facilities, with varying tax incentives and eligibility requirements. Both types of initiatives have also been undertaken by universities on sites adjacent to the campus, often in conjunction with entrepreneurship programs or technical centers.
- Information gathering and dissemination. The first step in almost any state or local high-technology strategy is the creation of a task force or commission, usually with university and private-sector participation. Task forces serve to focus local attention and often have a pronounced networking effect. They also perform a valuable service in gathering information about the needs and problems that can be addressed through high-tech development; the institutional and economic resources that can be brought to bear; and the kinds of actions that might be undertaken (initiatives). The complement to these activities is information dissemination, usually in the form of government marketing programs aimed at target firms and industries. Business groups also undertake promotional campaigns, usually advocating desired changes in public policy but occasionally aimed at increasing the development of member firms.

ILLUSTRATION 6.3

Exploiting a federal advantage.

In 1950, Huntsville, Alabama became the launching pad for Mankind's exploration of space. Today, many of America's fastest growing high technology research and manufacturing firms thrive on the heritage of the nation's space and missile program. Huntsville is a place where the only limit to progress is imagination. Like a child contemplating the wonders of the universe, the possibilities seem endless. The success of those who prosper here proves that in Huntsville, the sky is not the limit.

Contact the Huntsville/Madison County Chamber of Commerce (205) 533-4141.

The OTA correctly states that no one factor explains why some communities and regions have been more successful than others in nurturing and benefiting from high-technology development. Some locales, for example, appear to have all the necessary ingredients, but have so far been unsuccessful. In addition to a strong research university, skilled labor pool, readily available financing, cultural amenities, and so forth, other factors increase the chances of success for state and local high-tech initiatives. According to the OTA study, the other important factors are these:

- Identifying local needs and resources. Different regions have different needs and different resources with which to address them; no simple, all-purpose approach or program design will work in all settings. Success requires a detailed knowledge of local conditions and a clear recognition of the local attributes, both strengths and weaknesses, that influence a region's ability to attract or spawn high-tech industry. These analyses are typically conducted by task forces representing government, university, and industry, or by outside consultants.

- Adapting to external constraints. What works in one area may not work in another, and there are many factors over which a community has little control, such as climate, terrain, and proximity to existing high-tech centers. Successful states and communities recognize these external constraints and adjust their objectives and strategies accordingly. Those without an existing high-technology base, for example, typically focus their initial marketing efforts on branch plants rather than on research— or technology-intensive establishments. Over time, as these branch plants create a skilled labor force and technical infrastructure, the communities will be able to attract more sophisticated operations and encourage local spin-offs.

- Linkage with broader development efforts. High-tech initiatives that form part of a broader development strategy often appear to produce the most substantial results. Most state officials, in fact, consider their high-technology initiatives to be a logical and perhaps unavoidable extension of more traditional economic development efforts. This attitude is apparently correct. Similarly, most local strategies involve not only incubator and technical centers but also more traditional initiatives to make the community more attractive to technology-based firms.

- Local initiative and partnership. High-technology development efforts generally will be most successful if they are initiated and implemented locally. Some communities receive substantial help from state governments in developing university resources and complementing the local marketing program; others use funding and a number of development tools made available by the U.S. government. But, in most cases, the objectives and strategies are developed locally, and local representatives play a major role in the design and implementation of the initiatives. In addition, government cooperation with local entrepreneurs and business groups plays an important role in successful programs. Stable political climate and local government with an efficient, probusiness image are positive influences.

- Sustained effort. Based on the few initiatives that have been in place for a significant period, a minimum of 10 or even 20 years may be a realistic period to develop to the stage where a significant number of local jobs can be credited to products produced by local entrepreneurs or research establishments. As a result, success will depend in part on sustained effort and commitment, including stable long-term funding.

Initiatives designed to encourage high-tech development are several. Notably, there are initiatives of states, universities, local communities, and the private sector.

STATE INITIATIVES

In mid-1983, the U.S. Office of Technology Assessment identified over 150 programs of state governments with at least a few features directed toward developing high-tech industry. Of these, 38 programs in 22 states were initiatives specifically meant to create, attract, or retain high-technology companies. Specific initiatives focus solely on the creation and expansion of high-tech enterprises. States, for example, could provide financial services, conduct research, and disseminate information. The OTA called such specific programs "dedicated" high-technology initiatives and designated them by the acronym HTD. Other types of less-dedicated state initiatives that nevertheless encourage high-tech development were identified as:

- a high-technology task force (TF), usually initiated by the governor's office, for the purpose of identifying needs and formulating policy recommendations;
- labor/technical assistance (LTA). Most labor-training programs have linkages with federal programs. Universities are often involved in technical assistance to high-tech entrepreneurs;
- high-technology education (HTE) programs typically operating from a university and involving assistance with the creation of high-tech start-ups;
- Capital provision/assistance programs (CPA) that attempt to assist high-tech entrepreneurs in finding venture capital; some offer long-term loans or loan guarantees;
- General industrial development programs (GID) that endeavor to encourage high-technology industry as part of a broader state effort to promote industry of any and all kinds.

These various types of high-technology programs are shown state by state in Exhibit 6.2. The numbers corresponding to each state indicate how many programs of a given type a state had in 1983. For instance, Connecticut had three "dedicated" high-technology development programs but no high-tech education programs. Minnesota had no exclusively high-tech development program, but did have programs of high-tech education and general economic development.

In an effort to gain more insight into state government high-technology initiatives, the OTA contracted with the Research Triangle Institute (RTI) to carry out a survey and comparative analysis of high-tech initiatives in 16 states. Of these, half had dedicated (specific) programs to encourage high-tech development before 1981 and half initiated dedicated programs in 1981-1982. The surveyed states and the kinds of high-technology industries they tended to target for development are depicted in Exhibit 6.3.

The RTI study found that high-tech development programs look to be initiated in one of four different ways:

- To alleviate specific needs identified by state task forces or commissions;
- Through the evolution of traditional economic development organizations;
- To alleviate localized problems or needs (e.g., the Center for Industrial Cooperation at University of New York at Stony Brook, formed in 1978 to link the resources of the university with the needs of local industry);
- To take advantage of federal initiatives and funding.

Although the governor's office and state legislature can be the main impetus to high-tech development, the private sector can also play an important role. The RTI study revealed that the role of the private sector was most often that of providing advice and consultation. Still, the private sector was cited as the primary initiator of 10% of the programs in the surveyed states and as significant contributors to most programs. University officials also were identified as the primary initiator of 16% of the programs and as having provided extensive advice and consultation.

UNIVERSITY INITIATIVES

Institutions of higher education can and do promote high-technology development by training technical personnel, expanding the base of scientific and technical knowledge, and transferring this talent and information to the private sector. And several state governments help their public universities to create and run programs that stimulate high-tech industry. Take West Virginia and Kansas, which have both provided state funding for their respective flagship state universities to run centers of entrepreneurship. These centers are there to give students and local entrepreneurs technical and management expertise. University initiatives for high-tech development are fivefold.

EXHIBIT 6.2

State High-Technology Programs by Type[a]

State	HTD	TF	HTE	LTA	CPA	GID
Alabama	—	—	—	—	—	1
Alaska	—	—	—	—	2	—
Arkansas	—	—	—	2	1	—
Arizona	—	—	1	1	1	1
California	1	—	1	1	—	—
Colorado	1	1	—	1	—	1
Connecticut	3	—	—	1	1	1
Delaware	—	—	—	—	—	1
Florida	3	—	1	—	—	3
Georgia	1	—	2	—	—	—
Hawaii	1	—	—	—	—	—
Idaho	—	—	—	2	—	1
Illinois	2	1	—	2	1	—
Indiana	1	—	1	—	—	—
Iowa	—	1	—	—	—	—
Kansas	—	1	—	—	—	1
Kentucky	—	—	—	1	1	1
Louisiana	—	1	—	—	1	—
Maine	—	—	—	—	2	2
Maryland	—	1	—	2	3	—
Massachusetts	1	—	1	1	1	1
Michigan	8	—	—	1	1	—
Minnesota	—	—	1	—	—	1
Mississippi	1	—	—	1	1	1
Missouri	1	—	1	2	2	2
Montana	—	—	—	—	—	1
Nebraska	—	—	—	1	—	1
Nevada	—	—	—	—	—	1
New Hampshire	—	—	—	—	—	1
New Jersey	—	1	—	—	—	—
New Mexico	2	—	1	—	—	—
New York	2	—	—	1	2	—
North Carolina	1	—	2	—	—	1
North Dakota	—	—	—	—	1	1
Ohio	1	—	—	—	2	1
Oklahoma	—	—	—	—	—	1
Oregon	—	—	—	—	—	1
Pennsylvania	2	—	1	1	1	—
Puerto Rico	—	—	—	2	1	—
Rhode Island	1	—	—	1	1	—
South Carolina	—	1	—	1	—	—
South Dakota	—	—	—	—	—	1
Tennessee	2	—	1	—	—	—
Texas	1	—	—	1	—	2
Utah	—	—	—	—	—	1
Vermont	—	—	—	—	1	—
Virginia	1	1	—	—	—	1
Washington	1	—	1	—	—	—

West Virginia	—	—	—	1	—	1
Wisconsin	—	—	—	—	—	3
Wyoming	—	—	—	—	—	1
Totals	38	9	14	28	27	37

[a]HTD-high-technology development; TF-task force; HTE-high-technology education; LTA-labor/technical assistance; CPA-capital provision/assistance; GID-general industrial development.

Source: Office of Technology Assessment.

Research and Science Parks: These are clusters of research-intensive companies and facilities on a site near a university or universities. This arrangement results in a number of benefits. For instance, information and knowledge transfer between business and education is facilitated and business gains access to human and physical resources, students, faculty, computers, laboratories, libraries, and so on. Opportunities and ideas for starting new businesses are promoted by business/university interaction. The Stanford Research Park in California is the oldest university-based science park, but similar efforts are under way in numerous states.

Research and technical centers: These university-based centers conduct applied research for fees and other support. Examples are the Microelectronics Center of North Carolina, a similar center at the University of Wisconsin, and California's MICRO Research Center.

University/industry research partnerships: Many of these have been set up to blend the special technical needs of high-tech industry and particular resources of the educational sector. One form of this kind of collaboration is the cooperative venture between a single firm and one university. For example, agreements are operative between such universities and companies as Harvard and Monsanto, Massachusetts Institute of Technology and Exxon, and Carnegie-Mellon and Westinghouse. Another form of university/industry collaboration is research consortia involving more complex organizational arrangements. Collaboration might be between several corporations and one university (Pennsylvania State University has 20 sponsors for a cooperative program in recombinant-DNA technology), several universities and several corporations (The Center for Biotechnology Research, which is sponsored by seven companies and three universities), or several universities and one corporation (Standard Oil of Ohio and a number of universities).

Entrepreneurship training and assistance: This is another increasingly popular type of university high-tech initiative. Several universities have developed "incubator" facilities. These incubators provide services to new businesses or aspiring entrepreneurs, ranging from low-cost office space to technical and management counseling. The

EXHIBIT 6.3

Targeted High-Technology Industries and Business Activities in the Survey States

	Pre-1981 States							1981-1982 States									Total
	CA	CT	GA	MA	NY	NC	PA[a]	TN	IL	IN	MI	MN	MO	NM	OH	RI	
Targeted high-technology industries:																	
Space/avionics	X	—	X	—	—	—	—	—	—	—	—	—	X	—	—	—	3
Transportation	—	—	—	—	—	—	—	X	—	—	—	—	—	—	—	—	1
Communications	X	—	X	—	—	X	—	X	—	—	X	—	X	—	—	—	5
Electronics	X	X	—	X	—	X	—	—	—	—	X	—	X	X	—	—	5
Microelectronics	—	X	—	X	—	X	—	—	X	X	X	—	—	—	—	—	4
Robotics	—	—	—	—	—	—	—	—	X	—	X	—	—	—	—	—	1
Computer hardware	X	—	X	X	X	X	—	—	X	—	X	—	—	—	—	—	6
Computer software	—	—	X	X	X	—	—	—	X	—	—	—	—	—	—	—	3
Lasers	—	—	X	—	—	—	—	X	—	—	—	—	—	X	—	—	2
Energy	—	—	X	—	—	—	—	X	X	—	X	—	—	—	—	—	2
Biotechnology	—	—	X	X	X	X	—	X	X	—	X	—	X	X	—	—	7
Biomedical	—	X	—	—	X	—	—	—	—	—	X	X	X	X	—	X	7
Pharmaceutical	—	X	—	—	X	X	—	—	X	—	X	—	—	—	—	—	4
None targeted	—	—	—	—	—	—	—	—	—	—	—	—	—	—	X	—	1
Targeted business activities:																	
Manufacturing	X	X	—	X	—	X	—	X	—	X	X	—	X	X	X	—	10
R&D	X	X	—	X	—	X	—	X	—	—	X	—	X	X	—	—	8
Services	—	—	—	—	—	—	—	—	—	—	X	—	X	—	X	—	3

[a] Pennsylvania has targeted 27 specific industries.

Source: Research Triangle Institute, reprinted by Office of Technology Assessment.

oldest of these facilities is the University City Science Center in Philadelphia, founded in 1967 by 23 colleges and universities.

Direct and indirect investment: Finally, this is still another form of university initiative. For instance, Brown University has acquired a major stake in a spin-off in return for the university's contribution of technology. More direct infusions of cash are sometimes made by universities from their endowment or alumni funds. Thus, even state-supported universities can become involved, since no taxpayer monies are involved. Moreover, state governments often work with their universities to foster high-tech business development. The Florida Research and Development Commission is working with Florida's state universities to establish several research parks on campuses, and two universities (West Virginia and Kansas) received state funding for entrepreneurial centers.

In concluding our discussion of university initiatives, we think it useful to excerpt from a U.S. General Accounting Office document called *The Federal Role in Fostering University/Industry Cooperation:*[19]

> Research parks work best at first-tier research universities where a significant proportion of administrators and faculty favor interaction with industry. Industrial participants most likely to benefit from this arrangement are high-technology firms that depend strongly on technological innovation for their success.
>
> Cooperative research centers require a university with strong departments in areas relevant to the focus of the center. Industrial participation is most successful with medium- to large-sized firms which have their own research and development capacities adequate to translate the research results into commercial technological applications.
>
> Industrial extension services are best performed by a university with a strong commitment to community service and a technology focus to assist local, fragmented industrial clients.

LOCAL INITIATIVES

In order to look at and evaluate local high-technology initiatives, the U.S. Office of Technology Assessment investigated 54 high-tech initiatives in 22 communities. Using California's Silicon Valley and Boston's Route 128 as reference points, OTA was able to identify five types of communities, as determined by how much they vary from the Silicon Valley-Route 128 models.

High-technology centers: These already have a foundation of high-technology companies, research universities, and venture capital. These companies and universities continually spin off new firms which are usually founded by former employees of the companies or universities. A problem for high-tech centers is that they are likely to export many of the jobs generated by local companies. This exportation results from land and labor costs increasing as a high-tech center grows rapidly. In a way, high-tech hubs become victims of their own success, as resident companies export their production to lower-cost areas. The upshot is that a community that exports its technologies must continually develop new ones to maintain its healthy economy.

Diluted high-technology centers: Centers such as those in New York City and Chicago also possess a foundation of high-tech firms, skilled work forces, research universities, and venture capital. But this high-tech orientation is diluted in the larger, broader, and more mature economies. The OTA reports that this dilution seems to reduce the innovative and entrepreneurial flavor of the area. As a result, a major thrust of high-tech initiatives in those kinds of locales has been to improve communication among the relevant universities and companies.

Spillover communities: A Naperville, Illinois, or Montgomery County, Maryland, is located adjacent to a high-tech hub or to diluted centers. They usually lack most or all of the ingredients comprising a high-tech center, but they are close enough to exploit a center or centers' resources, amenities, and technology base. Lowell, Massachusetts, through land-use planning, was able to persuade Wang Laboratories to locate a plant there. Later, with aggressive initiatives, Lowell won the competition to become Wang's corporate headquarters. Immediately, a former "mill-town" took on a strong high-tech flavor.

Technology installation centers: These communities also lack most of the ingredients of a high-tech center, but are home to a major research- or technology-based institution. The facility creates a local base of research and skilled workers that can possibly result in high-tech spin-off activities in the local economy. Noteworthy are the high-tech spin-offs emanating from layoffs at the Kennedy Space Center in Florida and the Redstone Arsenal in Alabama.

During the 1960s and 1970s, many subcontractors, including Martin Marietta Corporation, Pratt and Whitney, and Harris Corporation, built plants in Central Florida to supply NASA. When NASA budgets were cut back, those plants became the nucleus of an "electronics belt" of Central Florida. High-technology development in Huntsville, Alabama, home to the George C. Marshall Space Flight Center, grew in a similar fashion. Today, a Huntsville company called SCI Systems makes IBM's personal computers.[20]

Local development efforts are frequently initiated after a falloff in the fortunes or funding of the major research installation. Interestingly, before a downturn in fortunes or funding, high-tech development has often been impeded by the major research installation's rules pertaining to the rights to innovations; prohibitive rules have kept the research staff from starting their own companies.

Bootstrap communities: These communities initiated their development efforts with none of the characteristics of high-technology centers. Their goal has been to attract branch plants of expanding high-technology companies by offering low operating costs and high quality of life. These communities gradually were able to attract more sophisticated operations and, in turn, eventually to foster local high-tech spin-offs. Austin, Colorado Springs, Orlando, Phoenix, and San Antonio have followed this bootstrap route.

As OTA points out, not all cities fit neatly into this five-category scheme. However, the value of the categorization is this: By determining which category a city most nearly approximates, the city can launch the initiative strategy most appropriate and effective in developing a more sophisticated technological base. And the most prevalent strategy initiatives by local governments were these:

- Land use, planning, and zoning, with careful concern for high-tech firms' requirements;
- University improvements, such as developing engineering programs at local universities;
- Vocational-technical training;
- Incubator buildings;
- Marketing programs, with special attention to the identification of firms to which the community would have the greatest appeal, community improvements concerning infrastructure and amenities, and a *targeted* promotional campaign;
- High-tech task forces;
- Venture capital seminars, conferences, and counseling.

PRIVATE-SECTOR INITIATIVES

Participation by the private sector is a vital part of successful high-technology development. Private-sector initiatives is an area where plenty of creativity and concern can be and has been brought to bear on high-tech economic development. Consider a sampling of initiatives:

- Digital Equipment Corporation (DEC) located a plant in the Roxbury-South End of Boston, close to a poor and mostly minority neighborhood;
- Control Data Corporation has adopted a business strategy of "addressing society's major unmet needs as profitable business opportunities," rather than relying on philanthropy. This company is a founder and principal investor in City Venture Corporation, a for-profit consortium that plans and invests in inner-city development projects emphasizing better housing, job creation, and vocational training. Rural Venture is a companion venture fund;
- Honeywell is involved with a science and math "magnet" program in a high school in Minnesota;
- In 1982, the Massachusetts High Technology Council estimated that member companies contributed $40 million worth of equipment;

ILLUSTRATION 6.4

Attempting to position a state in a new market niche.

Louisiana is the emerging biotech capital of the South.

A $125 million research center is just one of the reasons why.

The new Pennington Biomedical Research Center is an impressive addition to Louisiana's biotech credentials. But we have a lot more. Like an international reputation in animal embryo research and tropical medicine. And pioneering breakthroughs in hollow-fibre filtration technology and the use of microbes to clean up pollution.

Plus location. Louisiana's abundant marine, wildlife, mineral and agricultural resources, as well as its climate and geographic location, make it the right place for biotech research, testing and product distribution.

And most importantly, we have professional credentials when it comes to helping biotech companies take off, including tax incentives and start-up training.

For details on how Louisiana can help your company call Bill Hackett at (504) 342-5361, or write him at the Louisiana Office of Commerce and Industry, P.O. Box 94185, Dept. HT-4-5, Baton Rouge, LA 70804-9185.

Out of the South comes a new center of technology, research and business achievement.

LOUISIANA

Advertisement reprinted with the permission of Ronald Faucheux, Secretary, Louisiana Office of Commerce and Industry.

- The private sector is contributing $1.7 million to the state-initiated Advanced Technology Development Center at the Georgia Institute of Technology;
- Cleveland Tomorrow, Inc., a business executive association, has three efforts under way: a venture capital firm investing exclusively in Ohio, a research program specializing in applied manufacturing, and a program providing technical assistance to local businesses.

An important question to ask at this point is whether the local communities that have benefited the most from private-sector initiatives have any characteristics in common. The OTA's investigation found three commonalities that appear to underlie success:

- An organizational culture that promotes a *common civic perspective* and a positive attitude about the attributes and prospects of the region;
- An environment that nurtures leaders, both public and private, who combine an established track record for innovation and entrepreneurship with a broader view of their community's resources and promise;
- A network of business and civic advocacy organizations that attracts the membership of top officers of major companies and receives from them the commitment to work on efforts of mutual concern, including cooperation with the public sector.

FOREIGN HIGH-TECHNOLOGY DEVELOPMENT INITIATIVES

The United States and its various political subdivisions and its private sector are by no means the only ones in search of high-technology development. To the contrary, high-tech economic development has become a worldwide hotly-contested competition.

The *Wall Street Journal* and the consulting firm of Booz-Allen commissioned what is probably the most comprehensive survey of European chief executives regarding technology in a pan-European and multi-industry scale.[21] The survey showed that these executives overwhelmingly believe their continent has declined as a source of technology leadership, with the United States still on top and Japan coming on in importance. Further, in the executives' collective opinion, no European country ranks as the leader in any technological area. As for remedies, some of the executives want less government involvement and some want more.

The 10 Common Market countries have 350,000 research workers; these nations also account for 20% of world research and development spending. Yet, the Common Market Commission has indicated a notable decline in European scientific research and has warned that the trend must be revised if millions of new jobs are to be generated to replace lost jobs in the continent's traditional industries.[22]

As a result of these kinds of prognostications, the European Economic Community (EEC) has embarked on a program called the European Strategic Program for Research and Development in Information Technology, or ESPRIT for short. The goal of ESPRIT is to mount a technological push across EEC countries to attain parity with, if not superiority over, American and Japanese competitors within a decade.[23]

Individual countries in Europe are making their own push as well. For example, Great Britain's science corridor, known as M4, has developed near Heathrow International Airport. One of the companies there is Immos, a government-financed venture begun in 1978 when Britain became concerned that it was lagging in basic semiconductor technology.[24]

In Spain, the National Development Plan for Electronics and Informatics (PEIN) is designed to propel Spain within 5 years to technological equivalency with the remainder of the developed West. The plan proposes separate measures for microelectronics, consumer electronics, components, telecommunications, computers, defense electronics, industrial electronics, and electronic medicine. Spain intends to protect infant high-technology industries behind tariff barriers.[25] Even West Germany, where aspiring high-tech entrepreneurs have traditionally been discouraged by the country's entrenched financial, industrial, and social systems, hopes to join the world high-tech wave. Initial steps taken by the conservative government include much discussion about tax relief for small businesses and increasing entrepreneurial incentives. Moreover, West German banks and large companies, which have long avoided financing new high-tech ideas, are beginning to provide venture capital.[26] However, Europe has a long way to go. As discussed earlier, Peter F. Drucker has pointed out that Europe's effort to target high-tech entrepreneurship is ill-fated unless entrepreneurship per se is allowed to prosper there. But European governments still impose considerable economic and regulatory hardships on entrepreneurs. Moreover, entrepreneurs are generally looked down upon by European financial institutions and by the public at large.

Non-European countries likewise are coming forth with high-tech initiatives. For instance, the government of Israel has played a major role in developing high-technology by financing research and development and promoting investment. The bulk of government R & D financing is funneled through the Office of the Chief Scientist. Incentives for investment also include low-interest loans, special tax provisions, and free repatriation of profits to foreign investors. High-

ILLUSTRATION 6.5

**An international high-tech appeal building on
past successes to establish credibility.**

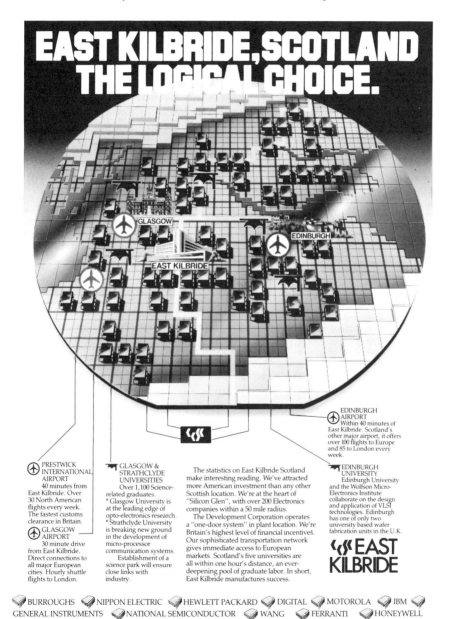

tech development in Israel encompasses electronics, robotics, bio-technology, lasers, medical electronics, and other important areas.[27]

South Korea sees high-technology development as a way to surpass similar developing countries. Four large business groups (Hyundai, Daewod, Samsung, and Lucky-Gold Star) are spearheading the effort, but the South Korean government actively encourages this coopera-tion. In the near term, South Korea realizes it must produce low-cost items that the United States and Japan are ready to abandon. High-tech development, therefore, is viewed as a longer-term economic development strategy. Samsung Semiconductor and Telecommuni-cations Company has its own Silicon Hill. The company has formed a joint venture with Hewlett-Packard to manufacture small computers for South Korean markets.[28]

From looking at these types of efforts, one reality quickly becomes clear: The various states and local communities in the United States must battle more than each other for high-technology development. The economic stakes are great enough that competition for high technology has indeed become global.

ARE HIGH-TECH PEOPLE UNIQUE?

Eccentric, different, flake, and free-spirit are the types of charac-teristics often ascribed to some of the kinds of people working as researchers in high-tech firms. And stories—some no doubt true, some apocryphal, and some embellished—about these people are common. A *New England Business* story, "Corporate Geniuses," says about technological wizards, "They are truly different from most of us ... some executives say the brighter they are, the more bizarre their behavior is likely to be." For instance, a researcher at a company working on artificial intelligence wears a tie and no socks to work because his coworkers wear socks but no ties. One engineer at another company had a religious conversion and tried to build an altar in front of his firm's main elevator. The CEO of a high-tech company reports on a scientist who showed up barefooted at a meeting at which the sale of the company to a conglomerate was completed.[29] The founder of a leading high-tech firm earlier worked as a disc jockey, teacher of transcendental meditation, and mental health counselor.[30]

The *Wall Street Journal* has reported on how a senior engineer for NCR describes his site-selection decision for NCR's chip plant in Colorado Springs (a plant that was the first of more than 20 high-tech companies and some 100 research firms and vendors locating there since 1975):

> He drove up the two-lane blacktop that curls toward the summit of Pikes Peak and had what he now thinks may have been a religious experience. ... 'I stood up there on the mountain and I looked down to the city below. I saw that this place could become a Silicon Mountain. It was like seeing God.'[31]

Everett Rogers and Judith Larsen, authors of the book *Silicon Valley Fever,* observe that Silicon Valley is home to some colorful characters, so much so that it has been dubbed Disneyland North. Rogers and Larsen write that "flamboyant entrepreneurs, men who lost fortunes and then made them again, and competent executives live alongside computer freaks, hackers, and super-specialists from exotic research worlds." However, they add that "Silicon Valley is also home for many more people who are completely normal—and about as exciting as old shoe leather. Engineers, essential to the Valley, are neither flamboyant nor are they anti-social." The common thread running through the flamboyants and nonflamboyants is "being married to one's work."[32]

So the answer to our original question, Are high-tech people unique? is that some are and some are not. Certainly, however, quality of life matters a great deal to these kinds of people, probably much more so than to the average person. And quality of life to them may not readily fit the usual conventional definitions of the term. Like most of us, they prefer to mingle with others of their ilk. Nolan Bushnell, the founder of Atari and Pizza Time Theater, now runs the Lion and Compass restaurant in Sunnyvale, California, which has become a popular gathering place for Silicon Valley high-tech workers. It apparently has the right "culture" in addition to the right food. But, unlike many of us at least, many high-tech employees would not locate in some climes, regardless of the monetary compensation. An engineer with a major high-tech company in the Midwest told us that his company virtually avoids California-based engineers and research personnel when hiring. The company's experience has been that even if they attract California people to the Midwest, they either do not stay long or they stay and are unhappy.

We are convinced that high-tech development need not be confined to a handful of places in the United States. However, we are also convinced that a few locations in the United States will have a disproportinate amount of high-tech development because of not only economic and educational factors, but also because they offer a quality of life that inherently appeals to high-tech employees. Any state or local community needs to keep this in mind before undertaking an economic development program exclusively aimed at high-tech development. The vast majority of states and communities would be far better off focusing on economic development per se and trying to catch what high-tech firms they can in this larger net.

HIGH-TECHNOLOGY—SOME NEGATIVES

For years, Oregon discouraged business investment and population immigration. In the early 1970s, both Data General Corporation and Digital Equipment Corporation rejected Oregon for plants, after the state gave them little support or encouragement. Downturns in Oregon's traditional industries, timber and agriculture, quickly changed Oregon's antigrowth attitude, and the state has been highly successful in luring high-tech companies.[33] But, the high-tech growth will not come painlessly. Take the example of Austin, Texas.

Austin, arguably the fastest-growing city in the United States, has been vigorously pursuing high-tech companies. Yet, the thorns in the high-tech rose have been discovered, as recorded in a feature article in the *Wall Street Journal:*

> ... many people here are left cold by Austin's gain in the nationwide race to attract high-tech companies. They complain of urban sprawl, traffic jams, water pollution, loss of Austin's small-town feeling and say that the rapid changes are even hurting its much-touted music scene. Such quality-of-life issues are taken seriously in this university town, whose gem-like lakes, rolling hills, and amiable atmosphere make it the kind of place where Ph.D's have been known to work as short-order cooks just to stick around after graduation.[34]

So, even if a community is eminently successful in high-technology development, there may be a backlash, at least initially, from a significant or vocal part of the community's residents. Certainly, this kind of social protest will accompany almost any type of economic development. But the "protest factor" needs to be anticipated and addressed by any community with an actual or proposed large-scale high-tech developmental strategy. Looking at citizens' concerns early on, perhaps even in the high-tech task force stage of development, can go a long way toward mitigating problems later on.

Vignettes

THE MASSACHUSETTS PARK TECHNOLOGY CORPORATION (MPTC) BROUHAHA*

MPTC was created by legislation in 1982 to assist Massachusetts to compete even more effectively in microelectronics with California, Texas, and North Carolina. The center's purpose is to train students for electronics jobs and to offer refresher courses to experienced engineers. Twenty-nine sites (communities) were considered for the center, with the final choice boiling down to Westborough, a city close to existing high-tech plants, and Taunton, a city in southeastern Massachusetts with a 1984 unemployment rate of 13%.

After a bitter 5-month debate on the MPTC board, the center was awarded to Westborough. The Massachusetts governor lobbied hard for Taunton. In his opinion, MPTC would have acted as a magnet in attracting industry to the high-unemployment southeastern part of the Bay State. In opposition were most high-tech industry leaders, who favored Westborough.

A number of high-tech executives threatened to withdraw their support for MPTC if it went to Taunton. And several were outraged at the governor's lobbying for and partisanship toward Taunton.

---

*Information for this vignette is drawn from, Geoffrey Rowan, "Tech Center Choice Tilts to Westborough," *Boston Herald*, May 30, 1984, p. 25 and Jane Meredith Adams, "Westborough Picked for High-Tech Center," *Boston Globe*. May 31, 1984, p. 56.

OHIO'S THOMAS ALVA EDISON
PARTNERSHIP PROGRAM

Named after one of Ohio's most illustrious native sons, this program is a plan to bring together public-sector and private-sector monies in an effort to rejuvenate this state's economy. Like other places with heavy stakes in the basic or so-called smokestack industries, Ohio is looking to stimulate economic growth and jobs for displaced workers through more reliance on high technology.

The Ohio Development Department awarded initial grants to seven Ohio universities to create six advanced technology application centers. Each center engages in research and development in its particular high-tech area of expertise. The six general areas designated for research are (1) polymer research; (2) advanced manufacturing, including computer-aided manufacturing and machine vision for automatic inspection; (3) information technology, including computer language and artificial intelligence; (4) high-tech welding; (5) manufacturing automation and robotics, medical and industrial lasers, and other advanced manufacturing processes; and (6) animal biotechnology. Moreover, all Ohio colleges and universities were allocated additional dollars for technical, laboratory and computer equipment.

As for private-sector participation, the Polymer Center is indicative. Fifteen Akron- and Cleveland-based corporations, including Goodyear, Firestone, B.F. Goodrich, GenCorp, and Standard Oil of Ohio, promised to support the Polymer Center with research contracts.

PUBLIC- AND PRIVATE-SECTOR CONTRASTS: VIRGINIA'S CIT AND IRVINE, CALIFORNIA's, SPECTRUM*

Four northern Virginia counties are the home of a plethora of high-tech companies and are also proximate to the many research-sponsoring federal agencies. Yet, there is not a major Virginia university within 100 miles—a gap that Virginia is attempting to bridge by developing the Center for Innovative Technology (CIT) next to Dulles International Airport. In lieu of building a new massive university in northern Virginia at considerable cost to the taxpayer, the idea is for CIT to promote the research capabilities of Virginia's universities and to provide high-tech companies and aspiring entrepreneurs with easy access to technological research output. CIT was the outgrowth of a science and technology task force set up by the governor.

Irvine, California (Orange County), is a marked contrast in funding source; it is a private-sector high-tech initiative. Spectrum is a 2,100-acre project targeted primarily at biotechnology companies. It is the work of the Irvine Company, a privately held, Newport-based land development and real estate firm which owns another 63,000 to 65,000 undeveloped Orange County acres.

Spectrum encompasses a 320-acre Irvine Bioscience Center, which is unusual in that it receives no government assistance. The Irvine experience is not only an excellent example of private-sector technological initiative, it is also an exemplar of realistic target marketing in economic development. The remarks of Ray Catalano, a professor at the University of California's Irvine campus and city of Irvine planning commissioner, show why: "It's too late for us to become a center for basic electronic technology. We realized that and asked, 'What's the next thing?' and realized it's right here, in biotechnology." Small, rapidly growing biotechnology companies are already prevalent in the area and Orange County has the largest concentration of mathematicians, scientists, engineers, and skilled technologists of any place in the United States. In short, Irvine is exploiting its strengths.

---

*Information on Virginia's CIT comes from Eugene Carlson, "Virginia Plans Research Site to serve its High-Tech Firms," *Wall Street Journal*, June 5, 1984, p. 37. Material on Irvine, California is adapted from Susan Antilla, "Irvine, California Goes Biotech," *USA Today*, March 28, 1984, p. 33.

REFERENCES

1. U.S. Department of Commerce, International Trade Administration. (1983). *An assessment of U.S. competitiveness in high technology industries,* Washington, D.C., p. 3.
2. Shanklin, W.L., & Ryans, J.K., Jr. (1984). *Marketing high technology.* Lexington, Massachusetts: Lexington Books, D.C. Heath and Company.
3. Austin, D.W., & Beazley, J.E. (1983, April 4). Struggling industries in nation's heartland speed up automation. *Wall Street Journal,* p. 1.
4. America rushes to high tech for growth. (1983, March 28). *Business Week,* pp. 84-90.
5. Rosenberg, R. (1984, May 30). "Innovation, not high tech, called the big job maker," *The Boston Globe,* p. 31.
6. Halberstam, D. (1983, April 10). Robots enter our lives. *Parade Magazine,* p. 19.
7. Ibid.
8. Hayes, T.C. (1984, March 25). Dealing with overseas job competition. *New York Times,* Section 12, pp. 5, 16.
9. A cautious nod to 'industrial policy.' (1984, March 19). *Business Week,* p. 15.
10. Wynter, L.E. (1984, August 1). Congress is debating federal role in setting technological priorities. *Wall Street Journal,* p. 21.
11. Kotkin, J. (1984, May 13). Will Japan again copy U.S.? *Akron Beacon Journal,* Section C, p. 1.
12. Kotkin, p. 4.
13. Zschau, E., & Ritter, D. (1984, August 1). Encourage innovation instead of industrial lemons. *Wall Street Journal,* p. 18.
14. Drucker, P.F. (1984, September 14). Europe's high-tech delusion. *Wall Street Journal,* p. 24.
15. Ibid.
16. SRI International. (1984). *Choosing a future: Steps to revitalize the midAmerican economy over the next decade,* (p. 153). Menlo Park, California.
17. Saiter, S. (1983, March 27). Everyone's trying to start the new 'Silicon Valley.' *New York Times,* Section 12, p. 67.
18. U.S. Congress, Office of Technology Assessment. (1984, February). *Technology, innovation, and regional economic development: encouraging high-technology development*—Background paper #2 (OTA-BP-STI-25). Washington, DC.
19. General Accounting Office. (1983, May). *The federal role in fostering university/industry cooperation* (PAD 83-22). Washington, DC.
20. Blankenhorn, D. (1984, February). High tech, southern style. *Sky,* pp. 13-14, 20.
21. Huey, J. (1984, February 1). Executives assess Europe's technology decline. *Wall Street Journal,* p. 26.
22. Lewis, P. (1983, April 17). Europe gears up for world class technology. *New York Times,* p. 20E.
23. Carpenter, M. (1984, May-June). Toward a new community. *Europe,* pp. 28-29.

24. Feder, B.J. (1984, April 24). Britain's science corridor. *New York Times,* p. 8F.
25. Brennan, K., & Miller, R. (1984, July 9). Spain outlines ambitious plan for its high-tech industries. *Business America,* pp. 27-28.
26. Thurow, R. (1984, August 28). New vigor is infusing small-business sector of German economy. *Wall Street Journal,* p. 1.
27. Flanagan, J. (1984, March 19). Israel's high-technology growth benefits American manufacturers. *Business America,* pp. 28-29.
28. Browning, E.S. (1984, September 7). Seoul seeks high-tech self-sufficiency. *Wall Street Journal,* p. 24.
29. Jacobs, S. (1984, July 2). Corporate geniuses. *New England Business,* pp. 16, 18.
30. Friedman, J. (1984, August 30). Silicon valley: Hard-won millions. *USA Today,* p. 313.
31. McCoy, C.F. (1984, August 3). High-tech prosperity, basic industry gloom mingle in the Rockies. *Wall Street Journal,* p. 1.
32. Rogers, E.M., & Larsen, J.K. (1984). *Silicon Valley Fever* (p. 155). New York: Basic Books.
33. Tharp, M. (1984, August 28). Oregon turns into a mecca for high tech. *Wall Street Journal,* p. 25.
34. Stipp, D. (1984, September 11). Austin, Texas, keeps courting high tech, irking some residents. *Wall Street Journal,* p. 1.

7

TRADITIONAL LOCATION FACTORS FOR BUSINESS

EXECUTIVE SUMMARY

Top elected officials at all levels of government are under tremendous pressure to foster economic development. The electorate may not be very aware of how many companies a governor lured to a state during his or her term of office, for example, but the voters assuredly know about employment and unemployment rates.

Consequently, as the competition for economic development has intensified, various systems for ranking states on their relative attractiveness to business have emerged. And, without fail, these systems have provoked plenty of controversy. Whether a state ranks 1st, 20th, or whatever, naturally depends on the criteria used in the rankings. For instance, what objective (economic) factors matter most, how much do more subjective (quality-of-life) variables count, and what are the trade-offs involved between these economic and intangible considerations? do the answers depend on the type of location decision (e.g., headquarters vs. a plant) involved? We concern ourselves with more empirical evidence on these questions in chapters 8 and 9. This chapter sets the stage for that discussion by considering some of the state and city ranking systems and how they work, "expert" opinion on key variables in corporate location and site selection, and an overview of some of the location factors that are on everybody's list of important influences. We also provide our views on "special" incentives offered by states and communities to attract business, and the relative desirability of attracting business from elsewhere versus fostering "homegrown" start-ups.

∞

GOVERNOR/MAYOR:
BEG, STEAL, OR BORROW THOSE JOBS

The warfare that states and cities wage for economic development has as its underlying objective the attainment of jobs, jobs, and still more jobs. Most any governor or major-city mayor who comes into office today has incredible pressure for economic development placed upon him or her by the electorate. To be sure, governors and mayors have always been concerned with economic growth for their areas but, due to structural dislocations in the American economy and intensified economic competition among the U.S. states and communities, as well as among the countries of the world, the pressure is far greater in this day and age.

Now it is not enough for a governor or mayor to be an able administrator and politician; he or she is also *expected* to be an effective salesperson for economic development. The governor or mayor had better attract new business and retain and expand existing business or the lack of employment opportunities for the electorate can spell prompt political demise; people do tend to vote their pocketbooks. Voters may not know even approximately how many companies their governor has attracted to the state, or convinced to stay there and expand, during his or her tenure, but they do know what the overall level of economic activity is like when they go to cast their ballots.

Take South Dakota, for example. In describing that state's governor, William J. Janklow, the *Wall Street Journal* said, "luring jobs to South Dakota endears him to voters."[1] In an effort to offset the state's declining agricultural base, Governor Janklow has persuaded about 100 businesses from neighboring Minnesota to relocate in South Dakota—a state with no state tax on corporate and individual incomes. Advertisements by South Dakota in Minnesota newspapers, which urged companies to relocate to South Dakota, touched off a verbal prairie war between the states' governors. Mr. Janklow's state also eliminated its interest ceiling on credit cards; as a result, Citibank's Visa and MasterCard operations moved, along with 1,400 jobs, from New York to Sioux Falls.

Indiana backed the largest economic development package in its history—$26.4 million for improvement of roads and provision of utilities—to ensure the location for a General Motors pickup truck factory in Ft. Wayne. The plant will employ 3,000 people and provide a $100 million annual payroll; but, counting suppliers and related service businesses, the total number of new jobs in Ft. Wayne will be about 10,500. And Greenville, South Carolina, is after a Mazda plant that would employ 2,000 to 3,500 individuals with a $200 to $300 million yearly payroll. Just as Tennessee did for Nissan at a cost of $7.3 million, South Carolina has offered to train Mazda workers, and prior to the time they make the first car for Mazda.[2]

Big-city mayors were once content to attend to local matters and let their governors work to attract industry. No more. Sister cities within the same state often fight it out for business and, in these cases, a "neutral" governor cannot be relied on. Moreover, the task of economic development is often too big to leave to the state. Mayors today are even becoming involved in recruiting new business on an international scale.

Global initiatives are being fostered by both the Conference of Mayors and the National League of Cities. Some cities have established foreign trade offices and others have formed foreign trade zones where goods can be warehoused or worked on under favorable tariff treatment. Foreign trade exhibits sponsored by the Conference of Mayors were rewarded with foreign-owned plants in Nashville, Tennessee, Portland, Oregon, and Macon, Georgia. A number of mayors have been active in traveling abroad and soliciting business for their respective cities. And many of these efforts have been demonstrably productive.[3]

States have also become more savvy and better at economic development. Not only have they become increasingly proficient in attracting new business from other states and nations, but they have learned how to do a better job of helping existing businesses in their communities to grow and generate additional jobs. Many of them have received needed help in this learning process.

The National Development Council (NDC) is a private, nonprofit organization that assists state agencies through what NDC calls "retention strategy," that is, keeping and expanding promising existing businesses (in contrast to attracting businesses from elsewhere) via mostly private investment. It is NDC's philosophy that the best hope for economic growth and new jobs rests with small businesses that would probably not expand rapidly without help from the public sector (the state agencies). The organization trains state agencies to be more knowledgeable in the finer points of creative private-sector financing for home-grown small businesses, and to be catalysts between small businesses and commercial banks. This occurs because NDC is not optimistic about states building jobs through attracting large companies; this strategy has worked in some places in the United States, but has failed in others. The organization is far from enamored with such government efforts as the industrial-revenue bond program, which it considers virtually obsolete. Thus, NDC focuses on private-sector help for already healthy companies (not start-ups or turnarounds) with promising growth potential.[4]

These, then, are the kinds of efforts currently being made as a consequence of the raging war between the states for economic development. The purpose of the remainder of this chapter is to provide a groundwork examination and discussion of the locational factors that ostensibly influence businesses the most whenever they decide to locate a plant or subsidiary facility, and sometimes even a corporate headquarters. By ostensibly, we mean according to the "conventional wisdom." Subsequently, in the next three chapters, we offer more specificity and conclusiveness. We cite empirical evidence, from our studies, on the absolute and relative importance of various location influences, as identified by a cross-section of U.S. corporations of nearly all sizes and lines of endeavor. We suggest what these findings can mean to a given state or community in its formulation and implementation of marketing strategy that is effective in retaining the industry it already has and in attracting industry from elsewhere.

THE BROUHAHA OVER
STATE/CITY RANKING SYSTEMS

Any well-publicized system for ranking states and cities on their desirability for living in or doing business there, or both, is sure to evoke its share of controversy. Several years ago, two authors/researchers published a book with their rankings of some 250 U.S. cities on the criterion of quality of life. This book naturally elicited acerbic rebuttals from representatives of the cities that fared poorly in the rankings. Even a few mayors from cities that did extremely well argued that their cities were better than some ranked slightly higher.

When the Alexander Grant and Company's study[5] ranking state manufacturing climates for 1983 appeared in early 1984, North Carolina's director of industrial development reacted angrily, "How can a state that in 1983 led the nation in new manufacturing plants show up with this kind [number 10] of ranking? It doesn't make a lot of sense." What happened was that in 1983 North Carolina had a small *absolute* increase in union membership, but compared to its also small number of union members, the increase showed up as a deceivingly large percentage rate of change in union membership. And this rate of change penalized North Carolina in Alexander Grant's scoring formula.[6]

A survey conducted for *Business Week* in 1984 among U.S. business executives, found North Carolina to be the preferred site for new manufacturing plants.[7] So, this survey at least lends credence to North Carolina's displeasure with the Alexander Grant ranking. Although the Alexander Grant study comprehensively used 22 "quantitative" factors representing five general categories (e.g., state and local government fiscal policies and labor costs) to rank states on their manufacturing business climates, a very debatable ranking resulted for North Carolina.

Absolutely none of the ranking systems is without deficiencies. Behind the controversy over them lurks two issues: What influences or factors matter most or least to a company when it goes to locate a facility and what are the tradeoffs involved? To what degree will a company trade off labor costs for proximity to markets, for example? If one changes the relative importance of the influences, he or she obviously alters the rankings that result. Additionally, different types of corporate facilities are likely to be located with different kinds of criteria in mind. A manufacturing facility is likely to gravitate to low-cost areas, whereas a corporate research facility might well be put in an area with plenty of scientists and engineers, regardless of the area's cost base. What is more, most of the ranking systems focus almost exclusively on quantitative factors when, in fact, quality-of-life considerations can play key roles in corporation location decision making.

As we indicated, in this chapter we attempt to lay the foundation for our final three chapters that present *actual corporate perspectives* on which locational factors really matter most to them in both head-quarters and plant or subsidiary decisions. For purposes of this chapter, a number of significant locational factors, such as labor climate and financial incentives, are surveyed and discussed, but without regard to quantitatively derived measures of their relative importance.

WHAT "EXPERTS" SAY ABOUT SITE SELECTION

Opinions about what ingredients companies need to look for, or do look for, in site-selection decisions are numerous and sometimes not much in accord. Here is a sampling of "expert" opinion.

Initially, consider some of the advice that the U.S. Department of Commerce (USDOC) has offered to American states and communities about the location factors that foreign direct investors seek in potential U.S. sites for facilities. Its report, *Attracting Foreign Investment to the United States,*[8] counsels that the place for a community to start in its quest for foreign investors is with a self-assessment. (The countries representing the most extensive investment in the United States are the Netherlands, United Kingdom, Canada, West Germany, Japan, Switzerland, and France.) This community assessment should be:

- systematic: a rigorous inventory of strengths and weaknesses in terms of those variables most relevant to the location decision of the foreign investor;
- realistic: an unflinchingly honest enumeration of positive and negative attributes to form the basis for effective marketing and ameliorative strategies;
- comparative: the identification of primary competitors (which may vary with different target audiences) and determination of the community's relative strengths and weaknesses.

The USDOC report goes on to identify five critical categories of variables in foreign location decision making:

- Resources: land, raw materials, natural energy sources, and climate;
- Markets: population, income, industrial purchasers of intermediate manufactured goods, and transportation;
- Labor: wages, unionization, education, and productivity;
- Quality of life: crime, cultural facilities, education, and housing;
- Government: attitudes, regulation, taxation, and stability.

Research cited by the USDOC study proposes that foreign firms decide to establish a U.S. presence for three main reasons: the size of the U.S. market, the U.S. market's potential for growth, and the political and economic stability in the United States. So, the decision by foreign firms to come to the United States might be viewed as level 1. Then, in level 2, a foreign firm decides upon a specific location. A community typically has little or no clout at level 1. However, in level 2, a community's presentation of its assets and strengths can be all-important to a foreign company's decision to locate or not locate in that community. Because over half of all foreign investment is achieved through the acquisition of U.S companies by foreign interests, communities need to keep abreast of firms in their areas that are interested in being acquired or in joint ventures. Key points for communities to keep in mind: The preferred industries for foreign investors have been manufacturing, petroleum (exploration, extraction, and transportation), trade (wholesale and retail), insurance, real estate, and finance. Naturally, the relative importance of the five categories of location-decision variables cited by USDOC (i.e., resources, markets, labor, quality of life, and government) can be expected to vary somewhat across these industries. For instance, manufacturers are likely to place more emphasis than insurance firms on a community's labor situation as it pertains to unionization.

In addition to the aforementioned five categories of location-decision variables, state and local incentives can be important to foreign firms. Business incentives are important, for example, and include low-interest direct loans to business from state financing authorities, industrial-revenue bond financing to assist a firm to raise money to finance construction or expansion of an industrial plant or equipment, and government guarantees on loans made to businesses by private financial institutions. Moreover, foreign firms weigh state and local tax and regulatory burdens and the availability of special concessions such as tax abatement. Oregon abandoned its unitary tax system precisely because the tax was grinding to a virtual halt the state's efforts to attract multinational companies.

The U.S. government sponsors a wide range of incentive programs to help state and local development agencies attract potential foreign investors to their communities. These incentive programs are numerous and diverse, including Business Development Assistance, Water and Wastewater Disposal Systems for Rural Communities, and Technical Assistance and Planning.

A joint committee of the Society of Industrial Realtors (SIR)—of the National Association of Realtors—and the National Association of Industrial and Office Parks (NAIOP) has compiled and written *A Guide to Industrial Site Selection*.[9] In this committee's view, the factors dictating the location of an industrial facility can be classified into six basic categories: market, labor, raw materials, energy, transportation, and government regulations. This list is much like the one provided in the U.S. Department of Commerce study, with one notable exception—quality of life is missing in the SIR/NAIOP list. Even though the report does not purport to be all-inclusive, it is unfathomable that quality of life is not seen to be salient enough to be included in the SIR/NAIOP listing.

Site selection cannot be reduced to a decision based solely on objective or quantifiable factors. Subjective and nebulous factors matter greatly; to ignore them entirely or give them short shrift is to ignore reality. In fairness to the SIR/NAIOP committee, however, they themselves recognize as much. Although they initially identify the six factors dictating the location of an industrial facility, minus quality of life, they later back off by recognizing the importance of quality of life under the heading of community factors. Indeed, the SIR/NAIOP specifically goes on to state: "...many site selection teams currently place great emphasis on the community facilities that will enhance the quality of life for a productive and prosperous group of employees."

The SIR/NAIOP report presents a checklist of regional, community, and site characteristics that may impact upon a company's choice of a region for the location of an industrial facility. For example, the category of regional factors includes availability of types of labor required by a company, proximity to markets, and levels of personal and corporate taxation. Community factors encompasses such items as educational facilities and fire and police protection. And the category of site factors covers zoning, land uses, traffic flow, and the like.

Since 1967, SIR has also published the book *Industrial Real Estate*. Its fourth edition (1984) is a large book that addresses a plethora of industrial real estate topics. One topic is site selection. For example, one chapter identifies what influences matter most in plant locations—abundant labor supply, proximity to markets, abundant water supply, and so forth. These findings are evidently based on various studies and experience. However, there are few attempts to distinguish quantitatively or empirically between and among locational influences in regard to their relative importance, although the book does make some distinctions. For instance: "Relatively few studies describe variations in the importance of site selection factors by type of industry. It is known, however, that technically-oriented industrial firms are anxious to locate near universities with graduate programs for their scientific and professional personnel and in areas with an ample pool of technical employees."[10]

Another listing of locational factors is published in what is called the *Site Selection Handbook*. This publication, which has been added to and revised over several decades, lists more than 1,500 factors for use in expansion planning and site selection. According to the *Site Selection Handbook*, the Checklist of Expansion Planning and Site Selection Factors "portrays a logical sequence of events, taking the expansion planner from determination of need for a facility through establishment of criteria for the specific plant required, to selection of a site, construction of the plant, and, finally, to disposition of the plant as surplus property after it has served its purpose."[11]

None of these foregoing suggested checklists of factors affecting the location of an industrial facility attempts to weigh the relative importance of the criteria. The SIR/NAIOP reports address this point, as follows: "...there has been no attempt in this guide to rate or place relative values upon any of the factors contained here. It would be presumptuous of the authors and misleading to the reader to assign priorities or to weigh individual site selection factors, inasmuch as various industries will have different priorities in their site selection analyses, depending upon company policy, the type of production or distribution facilities involved, economic considerations, etc."[12] We think this statement is too categorial. It is true that the relative weight placed on locational factors depends to some extent on the kind of facility involved. Nonetheless, as we see in chapters 8, 9, and 10, some generalizations about relative value of locational factors can validly be made. We believe that the SIR/NAIOP conclusion begs the question and too readily precludes the possibility of developing not hard-and-fast weights, but rather "guidelines" or proximate weights based on competently conducted research. Surely, empirically-derived guideline weights, although imperfect, are far better than no weights at all. The economic development specialist at least needs some "ballpark" estimates of the relative importance of labor climate versus quality of life, for example.

Take this example of productive and helpful research. The firm of Denmark, Donovan & Oppel, Inc. (DD&O) has come up with some useful findings on a very relevant question: Of those corporate expenditures that vary by location, which five have the greatest impact on a company's operating performance?[13] DD&O sampled 10 site-selection projects that it had conducted in 1981. The projects spanned a wide range of manufacturing activities. The location factors having the greatest influence on corporate profits were hourly labor, financing, energy, transportation, and state and local taxes. These five factors accounted for 98% of geographically variable costs—in other words, costs that vary directly from location to location. Of this 98%, the specifics were as follows:

Factor	Percent of Geographically Variable Costs
Hourly labor	60
Financing	13
Energy	11
Transportation	10
State and local taxes	4
Total	98

Thus, as this DD&O data indicate, it is possible to draw some inferences about the relative importance of the various factors that affect corporate location decisions.

ECONOMIC LOCATION INFLUENCES ON EVERYBODY'S LIST

Irrespective of whose list one looks at, several locational factors always appear. Such considerations as labor, capital, infrastructure, and financial incentives are universally viewed as being important in attracting and retaining business to nations, states, and communities.

LABOR CLIMATE

The subcategories that together comprise labor climate include work ethic, availability of the kinds of workers and employees a company needs for its line of endeavor, extent of unionization, incidence of wildcat strikes and work stoppages, and how government leans in management and labor relations. Perhaps labor climate is the most-often-given reason for a company leaving one area of the country for another. Certainly, a low-cost, low-unionization, right-to-work environment is the Sunbelt's big attraction to Frostbelt-based companies.

In the mid-1970s, George M. Steinbrenner moved American Ship Building Company's (AmShip) headquarters from Lorain, Ohio, to Tampa, Florida. During the remainder of the 1970s and early 1980s, Steinbrenner, AmShip's chairman and also well-known owner of the New York Yankees, gradually relocated other AmShip facilities to Tampa. These were times of turmoil. For instance, both a U.S. senator and U.S. Congressman, as well as local elected officials and union leaders, accused Steinbrenner of reneging on promises to them to have work on a navy contract done at Lorain. The work was carried out in Tampa instead. To these charges, Steinbrenner claimed he made no promises. Moreover, he blamed labor for AmShip's lack of competitiveness in Lorain. In order for AmShip to keep open its Lorain shipyard, the company in 1983 proposed that workers accept either a $2.50-an-hour pay cut (from $10 an hour) or a complete loss of health benefits. Steinbrenner lamented the work situation at the Lorain shipyard: "A carpenter couldn't fit a light bulb—it had to be an electrician. Everyone was worried about their own little bailiwick." At one stormy meeting between Steinbrenner and union leaders, Steinbrenner reportedly said, "I don't know about you boys, but I'll be eating three meals a day." On Steinbrenner's wage-commission package, James Unger, president of the local boilermakers union and chief union negotiator at the shipyard, rebutted: "I laughed at him and said, 'You got to be kidding.'" Unger went on to say, "When I presented that to my members, they wanted to cut my throat. They said they'd rather see the yard close than be ridiculous." What was the result of this impasse? On December 1, 1983, AmShip announced it was closing the Lorain shipyard.[14]

Consider the case of another executive in the Frostbelt, who is moving part of his company's operation to Dallas, Texas, due to problems in dealing with the local labor market. He gave this rationale:

> And then there are the unions. There was a TV show—20/20, I think—that featured some unemployed auto worker from around here. I saw it, called him up, and offered him a job the next day. Not because I felt sorry for him, but because I thought he could help my business. Turned out he didn't *want* the job. He said he could make more on unemployment. Well, hell, I can't afford to compete with my own unemployment bureau. That's screwy.[15]

The executive went on to describe what Texans told him in his initial meeting with them concerning the possibility of his moving some operations to Dallas: "Come on down, but don't bring any of your Northern crap with you. No unions, no polluters, no anti-Southern bias."

Dennis T. Donovan, the aforementioned president of Denmark, Donovan & Oppel, Inc. was asked if, in his judgment, right-to-work legislation is a valid factor for a company to use in the early stages of community selection for a plant or other facility. His answer was no, generally speaking. His firm had found that attitudes of a local labor force are the primary ingredient that companies look for. He elaborated:

> It is true that the level of unionization is lowest in states with right-to-work legislation. However, this legislation reflects the philosophy of the people residing in a particular state. In nonright-to-work states, unions typically exert substantial political influence at the state level. They do

not necessarily have uniform power throughout the state. Several cases in point are central Pennsylvania, southern New Hampshire, and central New York State. In these and other areas it is possible to find communities where the prevailing attitude of local citizens is antagonistic to third-party representation between an employee and employer. Hence, a firm that would have good reason to locate in a region where right-to-work is not in effect (e.g., mid-Atlantic) should avoid automatically discarding entire states because of the absence of such legislation.[16]

Charges and countercharges between prounion and antiunion individuals and groups have flown fast and furious in the United States. On the one hand, it is popular among labor leaders to talk of union-busting. A minister in Pittsburgh, in a predominantly steel-worker-attended church, received national publicity and was eventually removed by his clerical superiors for his sermons on "corporate evil." On the other hand, management talks about union intransigence and arrogance in the face of the need for U.S. companies to meet and beat foreign competition.

Beneath this controversy, actions are speaking louder than words. The realism has sunk in that the U.S. economy has been evolving for years away from a traditional blue-collar-majority work force; the U.S. Steelworkers Union has recognized as much by openly discussing, at their national convention in 1984, the possibility of modifying the union's name to attract new categories of white-collar workers. And there is no turning back from the process whereby U.S. manufacturing must compete with foreign competition by improving productivity, notably through robotics, and by seeking lower-cost labor areas in the United States and elsewhere.

The United States is irrevocably involved in a world economy wherein, for example, General Motors is competing against car companies all over the world instead of against just Ford, Chrysler, and AMC. The same can be said for many, many other American firms and industries. Although most unions and some companies want import protection from the U.S. government, protectionism is not in the cards. American consumers will not stand for it. For instance, the highly respected Brookings Institute has estimated that the cost to Americans of saving one job in the automobile industry, via so-called voluntary quotas on imports, is $160,000 per job in 1984 dollars.

This world economy literally forces "labor climate" to a central place in management's calculation of the competitive equation; management has no choice but to strive for competitive labor costs by robotized manufacturing and the location of plant facilities in low-cost areas. This is not to say that plants and other facilities will inevitably locate or relocate in the lowest-cost areas. Management is also interested in quality of a labor force in terms of the required worker skills that are gained through education, training, and experience. So trade-offs are often involved.

The conclusion concerning labor's effect on economic development is manifest: The states and communities in the United States with the most conducive labor climates (attitudes and relative costs and skills) will continue to attract industry, and those with high-cost, labor-strife, heavily unionized histories will need to change quickly or continue to lose industry. Right-to-work laws may not automatically disqualify a state from consideration for a company's facility or facilities but, realistically, these laws certainly do not help.

CAPITAL

As the saying goes, "It takes money to make money." Adequate seed money is needed to encourage and facilitate business start-ups and to attract expanding businesses from elsewhere. Take California, for example. If it were a nation, its economy would make it the world's seventh largest, ahead of Italy, China, Canada, and Brazil. About 100 of the 500 venture-capital firms in the United States are located in California; 80 of them reside in the San Francisco area. Perhaps a quarter of America's venture-capital pool is under California management and maybe 35% to 40% of the invested venture capital in the United States has been put into California start-ups. In fact, the state may now have too much venture capital chasing too few high-potential start-ups. Moreover, California venture capitalists are risk-takers. Californians go in and out of business faster than residents of sister states; in 1983, as the economy recovered from a recession, business bankruptcies declined in the United States as a whole, but they almost doubled in California. One of the most successful and well-known venture capitalists in America, William Hambrecht of Hambrecht & Quist, described the state's entrepreneurial spirit:

> Looking back, I am still amazed at how easy it was to raise money to start Hambrecht & Quist. My partner and I decided to start our firm one evening in San Diego. We wrote a brief four-page business plan on the plane the next day. We visited four prominent San Francisco families that afternoon, and by that evening we had raised a million dollars. I couldn't imagine doing that in New York, Boston, or Philadelphia...here in California, our investors are only one generation removed from the risk-takers who created the capital in the first place. Their willingness to take risks has its cultural roots in the pioneer traditions of this state.[17]

Economic development works best when there are two engines driving it. On the one hand, there is business expansion from existing companies. For instance, a local firm might build a new facility, or a plant may be attracted from elsewhere. On the other hand, there are business start-ups. Commercial banks are heavily into financing the former and venture capitalists heavily finance the latter. Thus, if a community wants to develop full force, it is not enough for it to rely solely on its commercial banking institutions for business capital;

banks are not venture capitalists and should not be—it is too risky in terms of their fiduciary responsibility to depositors. A community may be able to do well by promoting the expansion of existing business but, if it really wants to grow, business start-ups are essential. Burton Morgan, a successful Ohio venture capitalist, was driving at this point when he said, "If we help enough new ventures get started here [Ohio], we can hire engineers from California rather than watch engineers trained here go off to Texas or Massachusetts."[18]

So, capital is an essential ingredient to economic development; a community cannot make "something from nothing." In addition to initiatives for conventional financing of business expansion by banking institutions, some communities or even states might consider such innovations as venture-capital fairs, which are less than a decade old. These fairs, which bring together potential investors with would-be or extremely young companies, are being conducted at locations throughout the United States. At the very least, the movers and shakers in larger communities need to consider the appropriateness of establishing venture-capital funds through investment companies underwritten by both corporations and wealthy citizens.

GOVERNMENT INCENTIVES

The importance of government actions and attitudes toward economic development are not easily embellished. For instance, consider this negative impact: In 1984, IBM was to cancel a planned $50 million expansion in Boca Raton, Florida, because of Florida's then new unitary tax which, based on a formula, taxed multinational companies' worldwide income. Also, Citicorp threatened to back out of plans to expand its Tampa processing base and Sony and Westinghouse reconsidered their plans for Florida expansion. Yet, Florida officials apparently believed that because Florida is such a large market, business must locate there, regardless of the unitary tax.[19] Indeed, the regular 1984 Florida legislative session did not repeal the tax, although it was eventually abolished late that same year in a special legislative session.

On a more positive note, many states have passed enterprise-zone legislation as part of their economic development programs. Their primary goal is to provide special inducements to business in order to get firms to locate in commercially depressed areas so that jobs for the disadvantaged will be created. For example, Maryland provides venture-capital loans and property income tax credits; Kentucky allows for income and sales tax exemptions and deregulation; and Indiana provides employee wage and property tax credits, tax credit to lenders, and a venture-capital program.[20] Similarly, the Edison Electric Institute has identified some 20 utilities in the United States that are offering electric-rate discounts for companies that locate or expand in economically distressed neighborhoods.[21]

ILLUSTRATION 7.1

A creative play on words.

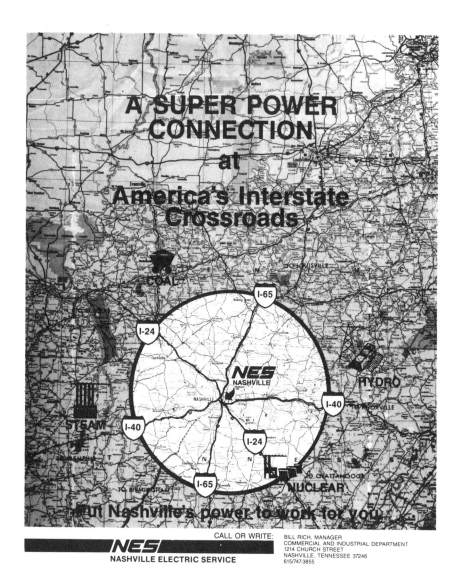

One can argue the pros and cons of government-financed and regulatory incentives. Whether tax abatement, industrial-revenue bonds, deregulation, enterprise zones, and the like are justifiable (and work) for economic development can be debated. And, no doubt, some of these incentives are more effective than others. However, what is not subject to debate is this: Those governments that experiment and innovate with financial and regulatory incentives for economic development are viewed more kindly by business. Such governments get a reputation—a halo effect—for being probusiness, even though some of their individual initiatives may not work in practice. For example, whether enterprise zones will be effective or not is as yet unclear. And, given the choice between locating, expanding, or starting up in a "perceived" probusiness or antibusiness state or community, most business executives will make the obvious choice. The unfavorable results of an antibusiness government tack may not be evident in the next 5 years, for example, but eventually, in the longer term, the results will be painfully apparent. In brief, business likes to locate where it is wanted and appreciated.

INFRASTRUCTURE

Peter Giles, president of the Santa Clara County (California) Manufacturing Group, a coalition of about 85 Silicon Valley companies, remarked in 1984 about California's economic development efforts:

> Five or eight years ago, most people only cared about reducing regulations and taxes. For the first time I can remember, there's a real merger of interests in this state. We all realize that improving the infrastructure is key to our long-term future.[22]

And *Inc.* magazine observed about California, "Oddly enough, most of the pressure for big spending to improve roads and education has come not from Democrats but from conservative business leaders."[23]

These concerns with infrastructure are right on target; they have a sound basis in fact. As Mr. Giles notes, infrastructure is crucial to long-term economic development. Companies put considerable emphasis on infrastructure when evaluating states and locales for facilities. Infrastructure can be looked at as a package of benefits encompassing streets and roads, educational facilities, financial institutions, utilities and the like. This package goes a long way in determining how attractive an area is for doing long-term business. Even a high-tax state such as Massachusetts (Taxachusetts, to some), with a high cost of living to go with it, can often overcome these negatives precisely because of its quality infrastructure, notably premier higher-education institutions and a vibrant downtown Boston.

A number of locales—Palo Alto, California, and Research Triangle, North Carolina, to name two prominent examples—have grown because of industrial or business parks near universities. *Venture* magazine reports that, "Increasingly, land-rich universities see parks as a way to both increase income from their endowments and to foster university-industry linkages."[24] Properly located, run, and marketed, business parks undoubtedly can be important contributors to an area's economic development efforts. They can be full-fledged industrial parks created with funds from the public sector, private sector, or both. Or, they can be quasi-industrial parks along the lines of business incubators to promote start-up ventures.

In short, a state or community can neglect infrastructure in the short term possibly without much discernible effect. In the longer-term scheme of things, a neglected infrastructure will have a tremendous negative effect on economic development. Besides the obvious effects of utilities, education, roads, and so forth, on economic development, aesthetics also matter. Businesses generally do not like to locate in an area wherein, from the looks of the place, its better days are in the past.

INTANGIBLES

Noneconomic factors are important location criteria to businesses, especially at the margins. We mean that given a virtual standoff on economic criteria between or among communities, a company will usually select the one with the best perceived set of intangibles.

Companies look beyond economic criteria, such as labor costs, utilities, and transportation access, for the presence of factors such as a "can-do" community spirit, a probusiness air, and an aura of government goodwill toward business. In the course of conducting research for this book, we have heard executives say time and again that such and such state or city is on the move because of these kinds of intangibles or, alternatively, that a community is stagnant due to a lack of esprit de corps (translation: the community projects the image that it cannot get its act together and really does not particularly care about courting business).

Moreover, the important intangible of executive preference is one that is frequently underestimated. Top managers are not economic automatons; they also look closely for quality of life, particularly where corporate headquarters decisions are involved. In this book, we have cited several instances where the chief executive officer of a company *probably* located headquarters in a community primarily because he or she preferred to live there. Quality of life does matter greatly in corporate-location decisions. One company, a Fortune 500, specifically and openly said that it moved its headquarters to a more-attractive location because it had to pay too high a monetary premium to entice executives to its old location. Thus, when it comes to actually

ILLUSTRATION 7.2

Stressing a high-tech "can do" ambiance.

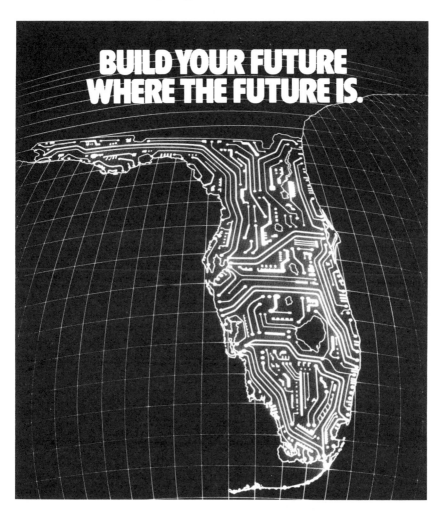

BUILD YOUR FUTURE WHERE THE FUTURE IS.

On January 31, 1958, the future began. On a Florida beach called Cape Canaveral. With the launching of Explorer I – and a technological revolution so sweeping, your company will feel it for years to come.

The scientists, technicians, and managers who created that revolution are still at work in Florida. Assembling more professionals like themselves into an advanced technological base. Accelerating Florida's growth at a pace few other states can match. And, according to a noted economist, making Florida one of three emerging megastates which will shape America's future.

So if your business is affected by technology and planning for the future (and these days, which business isn't?), Florida's a great place to see it grow.

Write Steve Mayberry, Director, Division of Economic Development, Florida Department of Commerce, Suite FB-19, The Collins Building, Tallahassee, Florida 32301. Or call (904) 488-5507.

And don't delay. Because the future belongs to those who prepare for it.

FLORIDA

choosing a community for a company facility, executives go beyond mere objective economic criteria; their "feel" for a situation and their intuition come into play as well. And, of course, their impressions are formed on the basis of what they see, hear, and read about various states and communities. Even so, numerous communities across the United States seem to have an almost suicidal tendency to send out the wrong signals to businesses.

A BIRD IN THE HAND IS WORTH TWO IN THE BUSH

States and communities sometimes alienate businesses in their locales when they attempt to woo companies from other locations. We came across a case where a large city raised the ire of one of its major manufacturing employers by offering a special benefit package (e.g., tax abatement) to get an out-of-state company to locate a plant in the city. The major manufacturing employer did not move in wholesale fashion but, since the incident, has been gradually cutting back the scale of its operations in this particular city.

The point is this: In their zeal to attract new industry, states and communities need to be careful not to so alienate existing businesses that some of them contemplate relocation. This problem is exactly why "home-grown" business start-ups as a way to spur economic development has inherent advantages over attracting businesses from other locales. The director of California's Department of Commerce has addressed himself to just this point:

> Most of our growth [California's] has come from these smaller firms. When you give incentives to one particular company, you're really giving a disincentive to other companies already in the state. Given our size and the attractiveness of our economy, if we started giving out special breaks for companies to locate here, we'd soon run out of money.[25]

This is not to say that states and cities should not court out-of-state industry, because they should. In our judgment, however, the most effective way for a state or city to attract industry, especially over a protracted period of time, is for it to create and maintain an environment conducive to business as a whole, not just to targeted companies. In so doing, the state or city will not drive off existing businesses in pursuit of coveted businesses. Moreover, a probusiness climate will encourage entrepreneurs to *start* and *keep* businesses there.

It has been our experience that if a state or community believes it has to offer special inducements (i.e., those not available to all businesses) to attract new industry, it had better take a hard look at its situation. Why is it that these preferential enticements need to be offered as bait? Is it because the location is generally unattractive to business? If the answer to the latter question is in large measure yes, then broader policy issues come into play. And the state or city powers that be need to develop a plan for making the area more attractive for business per se.

Vignettes

AMERICAN AIRLINES FLIES TO DALLAS*

One of the most publicized corporate relocations ever was American Airlines' 1978 move of its corporate headquarters from New York to the Dallas-Ft. Worth airport. The business reasons cited for the switch included office-space costs, worker productivity, and access to faster-growing Southwest routes. Albert V. Casey, American's CEO, also cited New York's poor "quality of life."

Some observers pointed to other reasons. Several American board members and large stockholders were from Texas, one of whom was chiefly responsible for bringing Casey to American, and an influential member of the airlines' top management was from Waco. And *Business Week* wrote that talk in the airline industry suggested Casey might be frustrated by his failure to become a powerful influence in New York City affairs, and perhaps decided to swim in a smaller pond.

Whatever the reasons, most agree that American's move was due in large part to intangible factors. Even so, a staff member of the North Texas Commission (whose board consisted of the CEOs of 37 Dallas companies) deserves much of the credit for getting the ball rolling in Dallas' favor. While going over an American 10-K report, which the commission's staff did routinely for big companies in search of information that might imply possible relocation, he saw where American's lease was soon coming up for renegotiation. The commission alerted its members and the business people began a letter-writing campaign to get American to Dallas-Ft. Worth. A full-scale marketing campaign was launched shortly thereafter.

---

*Information based on "Dallas Lure for American," *Business Week*, November 20, 1978, p. 144, and several other sources.

THE DIAMOND SHAMROCK EXODUS*

The late 1970s were a tumultuous time for Cleveland; the city went into financial default under the antibusiness populism of then mayor Dennis J. Kucinich. In this period, Diamond Shamrock Corporation moved its headquarters from Cleveland to Dallas. What were the real reasons behind the exodus?

According to Diamond Shamrock's William H. Bricker, president and CEO, there were several reasons:

- We need to be closer to where the [oil and gas] action is going to be in the future [the Southwest];
- The political, economic, and educational climate in Cleveland, and particularly the antibusiness attitude on the part of our city administration, was also something we couldn't ignore. In recent months, several potential key employees decided against joining us, primarily because of Cleveland's negative image...we have continued to have to oversubsidize employees to get them to come [to Cleveland].

Countercharges against Bricker and Diamond Shamrock included resentment over the "gratuitous kick in the teeth [Diamond Shamrock] gave the city as a going away present." Another called Bricker's assertions "a total fabrication." And one author wrote, "Once Diamond Shamrock had become dominated by Texas-based oil interests...its decision to pull out of Cleveland was the end result of a series of investment decisions stemming from the internal dynamics of the company's business." About Diamond Shamrock's overseas operations and "corporate culture," a writer made this biting accusation: "Diamond Shamrock apparently views the business climate as particularly sunny in countries whose military dictatorships have banned unions and stifled freedom of the press."

---

*Compiled from such sources as "Diamond Shamrock Leaving Cleveland for Southwest," *Wall Street Journal*, May 30, 1979 and *Cleveland Plain Dealer* articles of May 30, June 15, and June 16, 1979.

ENOUGH SILICON ALREADY

Perhaps it was originally just the Bay area, but now silicon has seemed to capture everyone's imagination for a couple of decades or more. First, it was Carol Dondo and then it was Silicon Valley, but it did not stop there. The fever spread throughout the land. Every budding or hopeful higher-tech area had to have its own "silicon something."

We have mentioned many of these silicons—Silicon Bayou, Silicon Rain Forest, Silicon Prairie, Silicon Mountain, and so forth. Each has a greater or lesser claim to fame of its own, but the perpetrators of this silicon myth seem unwilling to let their region carve its own unique destiny. Although Route 128 and the Research Triangle have done quite well developing their own image, the newer high-tech locales appear to be riding the Silicon Valley "coattail."

As marketers, we see little value in "me too-ism." Resources spent on image development are too valuable to be employed in such efforts. A famous example in the tire industry a few years ago illustrates what we mean. Goodrich spent a vast advertising budget saying, "We are not Goodyear; we don't have the blimp." When asked about their reaction to the Goodrich campaign, Goodyear executives said, "We hope it continues forever." Why? Wasn't Goodrich increasing customers' awareness that it had been too long confused with Goodyear? The answer is *yes*. Goodyear was so pleased because their *sales and market share* was dramatically increasing. No longer confused, customers were buying the "real thing."

Similarly, every reminder of "silicon" triggers another reinforcement of Silicon Valley and indicates that the other region is merely a pretender. Some of these new silicons are a clever play on words, are cute, and even downright funny. But, the real question is whether they need to play on the reputation of Silicon Valley, and what happens when some of Silicon Valley's negatives begin to rub off as well?

Not to belabor the point, we just say "enough silicon already." We suggest that an area develop its own identity; why not "Timber Top Tech," "Rocky Mountain High," "Cattle Chip Corridor" or whatever, and then it reaps *all* of the pluses a good image can evoke.

REFERENCES

1. Richards, B. (1984, March 29). Prairie promoter, Governor Janklow exhibits strange personal style, but he means business. *Wall Street Journal*, pp. 1, 19.
2. Hamel, R. (1984, October 5). Cities, states scramble for auto plants. *USA Today*, pp. 1B-2B.
3. Robbins, W. (1984, June 24). Cities going where the business is. *New York Times*, p. E3.
4. Bailey, D.M. (1984, September 3). A race for development funds. *New England Business*, pp. 82, 86-87.
5. Alexander Grant & Company. (1983) *The fifth study of general manufacturing business climates of the forty-eight contiguous states of America*. Chicago.
6. Carlson, E. (1984, April 17). Business-climate ratings stir debate over study's methods. *Wall Street Journal*, p. 35.
7. Hillkirk, J. (1984, October 5). Top states for new plant sites hold their own. *USA Today*, p. 5B.
8. U.S. Department of Commerce, International Trade Administration. (1981). *Attracting foreign investment to the United States*. Washington, DC: U.S. Government Printing Office
9. Society of Industrial Realtors and the National Association of Industrial and Office Parks. (1979). *A guide to industrial site selection*. Washington, DC.
10. Society of Industrial Realtors of the National Association of Realtors. (1984). *Industrial Real Estate* (p. 63). Washington, DC.
11. *1979 Site Selection Handbook*. (February) 24 (1), 12-31.
12. *A Guide to Industrial Site Selection*. (1979) p. 9.
13. Donovan, D.J. (1982, July-August). Twelve key questions for site selection decision-makers. *Industrial Development*, pp. 12-15.
14. Isikoff, M. (1984, February 12). Steinbrenner and Lorain sail on stormy seas. *Plain Dealer*, Section E, pp. 1, 9.
15. An ache in the Heartland. (1984, October). *Inc.*, pp. 116-119.
16. Donovan, p. 13.
17. The optimists: A survey of California's economy. (1984, May 19). *The Economist*, p. 62.
18. Gardner, G. (1984, November 19). Sticking his neck out is Morgan's mission. *Akron Beacon Journal*, p. 138.
19. The divisive tax. (1984, January-February). *Industrial Development*, inside front cover.
20. Revzan, L. (1983, December). Enterprise zones: Present status and potential impact. *Governmental Finance*, p. 32.
21. Carlson, E. (1984, October 9). Electric utilities cut rates to spur area development. *Wall Street Journal*, p. 31.
22. Kotkin, J. (1984, October). California: Racing to stay in place. *Inc.*, pp. 119-120.
23. Ibid, p. 120.
24. The industrial park: Ready-made sites. (1984, October). *Venture*, p. 119.
25. Kotkin, p. 120.

8

CORPORATE PERSPECTIVES ON LOCATION DECISIONS

EXECUTIVE SUMMARY

Knowledgeable corporate executives shared their thoughts with us about a number and variety of important location-related questions. These executives represented about 100 companies of all sizes and kinds.

Headquarters-location decisions are naturally much rarer than those pertaining to plant and subsidiary locations. Moreover, the locational influences considered to be most important by corporations vary a great deal depending on whether a headquarters move or a plan or subsidiary location or relocation is under review. Quality-of-life factors tend to be the key ones for headquarters decisions, whereas economic matters, in particular labor costs, are most critical for plants and subsidiaries. But a number of other factors also matter greatly in both headquarters and plant- and subsidiary-location decisions.

All states are, of course, far from equal in terms of their perceived desirability as places for doing business. Corporate executives overwhelmingly prefer the Sunbelt states, some more than others, for a variety of reasons. The majority of these executives see the industrial migration to the Sunbelt continuing, albeit at a slowed pace, for the foreseeable future. But there is a sizable minority view to the contrary.

A state unitary tax device, which assesses a company's shore-to-shore or even worldwide profits, is widely disliked by many companies, although not by all companies. Some domestic-oriented firms see the unitary tax as a means to shift the tax burden to larger companies,

255

mainly multinationals. A unitary tax can be a decisive factor for a company as it determines where to locate a facility. Some notable multinationals, as a matter of policy, automatically reject any state with a unitary tax. States, such as California, which has a unitary tax, are rethinking their positions.

Business is becoming more and more global. As a consequence, states and communities find themselves increasingly competing with foreign nations for business facilities. Knowing what American executives think most important in foreign-location decisions can assist states and their communities at this high-stakes international competition. Political and economic stability and a pro-U.S. business attitude are the key ingredients American executives want in a foreign location for a proposed facility, but other factors also count heavily.

THE *FORTUNE 500s* AND *INC. 500s* SAY . . .

The basis for this chapter is a study we undertook among U.S.-based companies of all sizes and kinds to obtain their "corporate" perspectives on locational-decision influences and tangential matters as reported by executives within these companies whose job it is to locate facilities. The roughly 100 companies that provided us with their attitudes, beliefs, and policies on various location and relocation matters range from *Fortune 500s* to *Inc. 500s*. (The *Fortune 500* is a list of the largest U.S. industrial companies, as determined by their respective sales revenues. The 500 companies are ranked annually by *Fortune* magazine. *Inc.* magazine publishes a comparable annual ranking for smaller companies, which is based on growth rate.) Moreover, their Standard Industrial Classification codes (SIC) revealed that the sample of companies represents a diversity of commercialized products and services. The companies are engaged in such endeavors as

- light manufacturing
- heavy manufacturing
- high technology
- natural resources
- services

In addition, conglomerates, with multifarious product/service mixes, are well represented. Because of the number, sizes, and types of companies that participated in this particular phase of our research, we were able to achieve our objective of obtaining the pertinent views of a true cross-section of American business.

In this chapter, we report our findings in the aggregate whenever there is no discernible difference between the way larger businesses and medium-to-smaller businesses tend to see locational influences and associated decisions. However, when differences do exist, we are careful to point them out. For purposes of clarity, we refer to larger companies simply as *Fortune 500s* and to medium-to-smaller businesses as *Inc. 500s*.

In our next chapter (9), we further our understanding of corporate locational decision making by looking extensively at germane topics as seen by key executives in firms that have actually placed or moved headquarters and plant facilities within the last 5 years, or both. Finally, in our concluding chapter (10), we take many of our findings, recast and simplify them where appropriate, and then integrate our results into a highly focused, realistic, and practical discussion on the *use and misuse* of marketing and marketing programs in economic development.

A couple of caveats about interpreting our findings regarding locational inducements for corporate headquarters and plant and subsidiary decisions are in order. First, we ask the reader not to readily

draw hard and fast conclusions about the absolute or relative importance of the sundry locational influences considered in chapters 8 and
9. Instead, it is more meaningful, from the standpoint of conceptualizing effective marketing strategy for a state or community, to wait until
chapter 10, where we recast and simplify the mass of complex data and
search for useful differences and commonalities between and among
the many possible locational-decision considerations. Second, our
sample of companies includes a diversity of corporations. Thus, our
findings represent a collective opinion regarding locational matters.
Because they do, they can be seen as *general guidelines* for states and
communities to use in formulating programs for attracting and
retaining industry. But it needs to be kept in mind that, as one
executive put it, "Location decisions are always specific to product-
market-labor-skill requirements." In addition, as another executive
commented, "In the end, top corporate management can affect the
decision with personal preferences, no matter how thorough the
[corporation's] study." So, although general location factors are
extremely important to a political entity wanting to attract and keep
industry, it must also pay close attention to the nuances of specific
industries and companies. For example, a high-tech company may be
very interested in whether a city has a scientific community of high
repute, although this location criterion is not a key one across a
diversity of industries. Similarly, environmental regulation will be of
more concern to a steel manufacturer than to a cross-section of
companies which includes nonpolluting kinds of firms. And, a
company's chief executive who is a skiing buff may tilt the location
decision to Colorado Springs, for example, even though Colorado
Springs may rate no better on locational desirability than two or three
other cities.

CORPORATE HEADQUARTERS-LOCATION DECISIONS

Naturally, headquarters-location decisions are infrequently made
when compared to decisions concerning the placement of new plants
or expansion of exisiting plants. Once a headquarters is in place in a
community, a great deal of inertia sets in. Normally, a headquarters
move comes only after some compelling series of events. Nonetheless,
corporations do move their headquarters when given sufficient reason.
And, in our evaluation, the incidence of headquarters moves is on the
increase, no doubt spurred on by the intense competitiveness among
states and communities for growth and jobs.

Any community that harbors the idea, "Corporation XYZ won't move
because it has been here for 100 years," is inviting trouble; communities
and their appeals change over time. This kind of complacent com-

munity mentality has resulted in the departure of numerous companies, many of them major *Fortune 500* firms. In addition, even start-up companies move if conditions are deemed by their respective managements to be "wrong" for them in their original location and "right" for them elsewhere. In fact, start-ups are usually far more mobile than larger companies with more investment and more tradition in a given community.

So, from the viewpoint of the community hoping to retain those corporate headquarters facilities it already has and to attract new ones, the competition from other communities cannot be prudently and lightly dismissed. On the other hand, because of the inertia factor, especially in headquarters decisions, the community wanting to attract corporate headquarters from elsewhere had best offer an overwhelmingly attractive package of inducements. But just what inducements matter most to companies in choosing headquarters locations?

We took a considerable number of typical location-decision factors and asked our respondents to evaluate the importance of each in selecting a headquarters community. Additionally, the respondents were free to provide us with other salient factors that we might not have included. Using a numerical scaling technique, we were then able to classify each locational-decision factor as being of low, medium, or high importance and also to rank order each factor. Moreover, we were able to compare the views of *Fortune 500* companies to smaller *Inc. 500* firms.

Exhibit 8.1 shows what we found. In this illustration, there are three categories of information. First, various location influences in choosing a headquarters community or state are listed, such as tax rates on businesses and cost of living. Second, the table shows how these location influences were ranked as to importance by *Fortune 500* corporations compared to *Inc. 500* companies. For instance, a good labor-relations climate was ranked first in importance by the *Inc. 500* firms and tied for third in importance among *Fortune 500* companies. Finally, the abbreviation HI, MI or LI next to each importance ranking designates whether the location influence is deemed to be of high (HI), medium (MI), or low (LI) importance to a company when choosing a new headquarters location or deciding whether to stay in an existing location. So, each location influence is not only rank ordered in terms of its importance to the *Fortune 500* and *Inc. 500* companies, but it is also labeled in terms of its perceived degree of importance.

A look at Exhibit 8.1 reveals that there are a large number of highly important location influences for both *Fortune 500* and *Inc. 500* companies—16 for the larger corporations and 15 for the smaller firms. There is also a high degree of correspondence between the way *Fortune 500* and *Inc. 500* companies see the importance of the location influences for headquarters decisions. For example, both groups are looking for good transportation facilities for business travel, low tax rates on businesses, existence of a strong work ethic in the community, and the availability of a skilled and educated work force. Nonetheless, there are important differences between the views of the *Fortune 500s* and the *Inc. 500s*. Here are a few especially notable location influences where there is a divergence of opinion:

- The *Fortune 500s* place much higher value on educational systems. They are more desirous than the *Inc. 500s* of locating in a community with a quality primary and secondary school program and with a quality college or university nearby. The *Inc. 500s* are somewhat inconsistent here. They want a skilled and educated work force, but evidently do not correlate its availability with a quality educational system in a community.
- The *Inc. 500s* are more concerned than the *Fortune 500s* with there being a low rate of unionization in the community. Note that both the larger and smaller companies seek a good labor-relations climate (e.g., few incidents of work stoppage), but *Fortune 500s* appear less concerned than the *Inc. 500s* with whether or not the work force is highly organized. It is apparently the *Fortune 500's* belief that heavy unionization and a diminished labor relations climate do not necessarily go hand in hand *for a headquarters work force*. As we see later, a unionized work force for plants is viewed quite differently.
- Locational incentives (industrial-revenue bonds, enterprise zones, etc.) are of far greater interest to the smaller companies. This location influence was considered highly important by the *Inc. 500* firms and ranked eighth. In contrast, the *Fortune 500s* considered incentives to be of medium importance for headquarters locations and ranked it close to the bottom of their list. Again, for plant locations, the larger companies see the incentives influence in a different light.
- The larger companies are less interested than the smaller companies in cost of living.

In general, all the companies are interested in the quality of life for employees, perhaps the *Fortune 500s* more so than the *Inc. 500s* because of the greater value the larger companies place on education availability and ecological factors (e.g., low pollution). We think it instructive that quality of life does not necessarily mean that the companies seek to locate headquarters in a major population center, or suburb thereof, with a rich cultural environment (orchestras, museums, etc.). These factors are only of medium importance. However, recreational opportunities and parks are highly sought after by large and small companies alike. In addition, prevailing wage and

EXHIBIT 8.1

What Corporations Value in a Headquarters Location

Location Influences	Rank and Importance	
	Fortune 500	Inc. 500
Good transportation facilities for business travel	1 HI	2* HI
Availability of skilled/educated work force	2 HI	5* HI
Good labor relations climate (e.g., few incidents of work stoppage)	3* HI	1 HI
Housing availability for employees	3* HI	6 HI
Tax rates on business	4* HI	4 HI
Existence of strong work ethic	4* HI	2* HI
Quality of primary/secondary school system	5 HI	12 MI
Quality college/university nearby	6* HI	14* MI
Community safety	6* HI	10* MI
Tax rates on individuals	7* HI	9* HI
Availability of water and waste system	7* HI	11* MI
Lack of "red tape" by state and local government	8* HI	5* HI
Quality of utilities	8* HI	10* MI
Recreational opportunities and parks	9* HI	9* HI
"Can-do" spirit apparent on the part of community leaders	9* HI	7 HI
Favorable ecological factors (e.g., low pollution)	9* HI	15* MI
Low rate of unionization in the area	10 MI	3 HI
Rich cultural environment (orchestras, museums, etc.)	11 MI	15* MI
In, or a suburb of, a major population center	12 MI	11* MI
First-rate scientific community in the area	13* MI	16 MI
Good transportation facilities for moving goods	13* MI	8* HI
Relatively low cost of living	14 MI	9* HI
Progressive banking institutions	15 MI	8* HI
Relatively low wage/salary levels	16* MI	14* MI
Local/state government programs, other than taxes	16* MI	17 MI
Proximity to the company's major markets	17 MI	13 MI
Moderate-to-warm climate	18 MI	15* MI
$ incentives (industrial-revenue bonds, enterprise zones, etc.)	19 MI	8* HI
Topographical factors	20 MI	19 MI
Proximity to needed raw materials and natural resources	21 MI	14* MI
Plentiful venture capital	22 LI	18 MI

[1] The location factors are rank ordered from most important (1) to least important. Ties are denoted by an asterisk. For example, if the rank order 2 is denoted 2* then there is more than one factor ranked second. The letters HI, MI, or LI by each ranking indicate whether a particular factor is considered by respondents to be of high importance, medium importance, or low importance.

salary levels in a community are not of overwhelming importance; companies are willing to pay more if the "right" kind of skilled and educated work force is present to operate a corporate headquarters.

Ostensibly, proximity to a company's major markets is not a critical location influence in headquarters-location decisions, although it is a reason often cited for public consumption whenever companies move. What is more, whether a community has a warm-to-moderate climate is not a crucial locational influence for corporate headquarters. It could tip the scales if all other things are equal between or among competing communities, but the same can be said of numerous other factors. In our judgment, climate is a grossly overrated decision influence for most companies.

Somewhat surprisingly at first glance, the existence of progressive banking institutions in a community is not terribly important to *Fortune 500s,* but it is to *Inc. 500s.* Yet, upon reflection, it is not so surprising. Commercial banking has become so interstate already that *Fortune 500* companies have ready access to officers of money-center banks. The same national access to venture capital also explains why the availability of plentiful venture capital in a headquarters community is not a prime concern to most *Inc. 500* firms.

It is *significant* that companies of all sizes put high value on two related matters—the existence of a strong work ethic in a community and a "can-do" spirit on the part of community leaders.

We wanted to pursue in more depth the kinds of influences that matter most to a company in locating or relocating a headquarters once the decision process narrows down to but a few candidates. After the company has winnowed down the competing locations to one, two, or maybe three, there is often little to separate the candidates in regards to general economic, demographic, and climate conditions. Therefore, what influences are most likely to tip the scales in favor of one community over another, given parity between the communities in overall economic, demographic, and climatic conditions? Exhibit 8.2 depicts the answers provided by the *Fortune 500* and *Inc. 500* companies.

The *number one influencer,* and it is not even close to the other factors, is quality of life/life-style. So which one of the communities in contention for the headquarters location can supply the best quality of life? Naturally, quality of life is an elusive concept that depends largely

EXHIBIT 8.2

**Headquarters-Location Influences Most Likely to Tip the Scales
Once the Finalists Are Selected**

An Influencer in a Class By Itself	Other Extremely Important Influences	Still More Important Influences
Quality of life/life-style	Transportation access	Competitive synergy (concentration of similar firms)
	University/Educational environment	
		Shipping costs
	Access to present markets/customers	Real estate costs

on one's value judgments. Nonetheless, based upon what corporations told us, we do attempt to define quality of life with some specificity in chapter 10. Besides quality of life, *highly important* influences are also transportation access, so that headquarters employees have easy access to airlines especially; a quality university and educational environment; and easy access to present markets and customers. Inarguably, quality of life might well include a quality educational environment. But the latter is also a business consideration, because it has to do with providing a skilled and knowledgeable work force, and for that reason was separated for reporting purposes and emphasis. Lastly, other important influences that can tip the scales toward one community are a competitive synergy-producing concentration of similar firms (e.g., rubber companies headquartered in Akron, Ohio); and real estate and shipping costs.

PLANT- AND SUBSIDIARY-LOCATION DECISIONS

Regarding these kinds of locations, which are far more prevalent than headquarters moves, three points are abundantly clear from looking at Exhibit 8.3. First, there is a plethora of highly important decision influences whenever companies look for an area in which to locate a new physical facility for expansion. The *Fortune 500s* evaluated 22 locational factors as being of high importance and the *Inc. 500s* identified 23. Second, in contrast to headquarters decisions, when it comes to plant and subsidiary decisions there is a much greater degree of correspondence between the way larger and smaller companies evaluate location influences. Almost item for item as one goes down the list of rankings, there is close agreement between the *Fortune 500* and *Inc. 500* respondents. Of course, there are exceptions. For instance, the larger companies are more interested than their smaller counterparts in the availability of a good, dependable water and waste system. Third, labor factors are dominant in the top rankings. For both the larger and smaller companies, the most important rankings go to such factors as good labor-relations climate, availability of a skilled and educated work force, existence of a strong work ethic in the community, and a low rate of unionization in the area. Without question, labor-related considerations are the driving force in plant and subsidiary decisions. In an advertisement that reads, "What Can We Do For You In Austin," that booming Texas city holds out the allure of a "plentiful right-to-work labor pool" and an "old-fashioned productive work ethic."[1] Companies are much less receptive to what they see as unfavorable labor conditions, particularly unionization, in plant decisions than in headquarters locations, and understandably so. Headquarters labor costs for hourly workers normally pale in comparison to those generated in plants and subsidiaries.

EXHIBIT 8.3

What Corporations Value in a Location for a New Physical Facility for Expansion

Location Influences	Rank and Importance[a]			
	Fortune 500		Inc. 500	
Good labor-relations climate (e.g., few incidents of work stoppage)	1	HI	1	HI
Availability of skilled/educated work force	2*	HI	3	HI
Existence of strong work ethic	2*	HI	2*	HI
Availability of water and waste system	2*	HI	9*	HI
Low rate of unionization in the area	3	HI	2*	HI
Good transportation facilities for moving goods	4	HI	5*	HI
Tax rates on business	5*	HI	2*	HI
Quality of utilities	5*	HI	7*	HI
Housing availability for employees	6	HI	5*	HI
Favorable ecological conditions (e.g., low pollution)	7*	HI	11*	HI
Lack of "red tape" by state and local government	7*	HI	6*	HI
Proximity to the company's major markets	7*	HI	9*	HI
Proximity to needed raw materials and natural resources	7*	HI	11*	HI
Good transportation facilities for business travel	8*	HI	4*	HI
Community safety	8*	HI	9*	HI
"Can-do" spirit apparent on the part of community leaders	8*	HI	7*	HI
Quality primary/secondary school system	9	HI	10*	HI
Recreational opportunities and parks	10*	HI	8*	HI
Relatively low wage/salary levels	10*	HI	8*	HI
$ incentives (industrial-revenue bonds, enterprise zones, etc.)	11*	HI	6*	HI
Quality college/university nearby	11*	HI	14*	MI
Local/state government programs, other than taxes	11*	HI	14*	MI
Tax rates on individuals	12	MI	9*	HI
First-rate scientific community in the area	13	MI	15	MI
Rich cultural environment (orchestras, museums, etc.)	14	MI	14*	MI
Topographical factors	15	MI	16	MI
Moderate-to-warm climate	16*	MI	13	MI
In, or a suburb of, a major population center	16*	MI	12	HI
Progressive banking institutions	17	MI	10*	HI
Plentiful venture capital	18	MI	17	MI

[a] The location factors are rank ordered from most important (1) to least important. Ties are denoted by an asterisk. For example, if the rank order 2 is denoted 2* then there is more than one factor ranked second. The letters HI, MI, or LI by each ranking indicate whether a particular factor is considered by respondents to be of high importance, medium importance, or low importance.

In general, so-called economic factors govern companies' plant-location decisions. In addition to labor costs, companies are concerned with transportation facilities for moving goods, utilities, tax rates on business, lack of "red tape" by state and local government, proximity to needed raw materials and natural resources, and other considerations of this ilk. The plant and subsidiary decision is definitely economically driven. This is not to say that employee-related quality-of-life factors are unimportant. Quite the contrary. As

Exhibit 8.3 shows, a number of these factors are valued highly. Yet, most of the quality-of-life factors are way down the list in terms of relative importance. The inescapable conclusion is this: If a community is not competitive on the crucial labor-related factors, it is not competitive in attracting corporate plants and subsidiaries. In addition, just having a favorable labor climate is far from sufficient; this message must be communicated. Sometimes communities that have worked and improved their labor situations have suffered because they have not been equally successful in changing the widespread historical perception that they are labor-strife communities.

Again, as with headquarters locations, we probed for influences that matter most in tipping the scales once the decision process for a new plant or subsidiary is winnowed down to a very few locations. Holding general economic, demographic, and climatic conditions constant, what are the factors that matter most at the margins. Exhibit 8.4 depicts what the *Fortune 500* and *Inc. 500* companies said. Assuming that the finalists for a plant location are generally equal, and that assumption is a fair and reasonable one for finalists, most companies would select the community that has the best access to present markets and customers. Overwhelmingly, this is the key factor if all other considerations are about equal. Next, if two or more communities provided about equal access to markets and customers, labor relations and costs would be most likely to tip the scale to one community. The communities would obviously have "acceptable" labor relations and costs or else they would not be finalists. Yet, "acceptable" might not be good enough in the final analysis. The company would select the "best" labor climate for its needs. Other important influences at the margins are the relative quality of the university and educational environment in the competing communities; quality of life; shipping costs; and transportation access, particularly airlines for executive travel.

EXHIBIT 8.4

Plant- and Subsidiary-Location Influences Most Likely
To Tip the Scales Once the Finalists Are Selected

An Influencer in a Class By Itself	Other Extremely Important Influences	Still More Important Influences
Access to present markets/customers	Labor relations	University/Educational environment
	Labor costs	
		Quality of life
		Shipping costs
		Transportation access

EFFECTS OF A UNITARY TAX

Now we look solely at a much publicized and debated impediment to attracting and perhaps retaining industry—the unitary tax. Just how much of an effect can a unitary tax have on a state's efforts to encourage companies to locate there?

Predictably, there is a negative reaction to the unitary-tax concept by both larger and smaller corporations. Two-thirds of the *Fortune 500* and *Inc. 500* executives we asked see a unitary tax as a definite negative in a state's ability to attract industry, and the same two-thirds majority feel a unitary tax is also a definite minus for a state in retaining industry. In fact, well over half the *Fortune 500s* and *Inc. 500s* are not just negative, they are *extremely opposed* to the unitary tax and are convinced that it translates into a real inhibitor to a state's economic development thrusts. What is revealing in this regard are two points. First, there is no difference between giant and smaller companies in the way they see the unitary-tax issue; it is largely seen as detrimental. Second, the prevailing sentiment is that a unitary tax is not only harmful to a state in attracting industry, but also in retaining the industry it already has.

Here are some typical verbatim remarks from *Fortune 500* and *Inc. 500* executives about the effects of a unitary tax on a state's competitiveness in attracting and retaining industry:

- "Kills it [the state's competitiveness]."
- "[We] will avoid such states if at all possible."
- "Reduces investment in those [unitary tax] states."
- "Serious negative consequences."
- "It has a very negative effect for a multinational company such as ours."
- "Adverse, especially with large, growing international corporations."
- "This is the worst tax environment for a multinational."
- "Disastrous."
- "Moves firms quickly to another location."
- "Is detrimental to attracting multifaceted, multilined conglomerates."
- "Detrimental."

Of course, not all executives see the unitary tax in this light. A small percentage think that a unitary tax is either a neutral location influence or only becomes important if the location decision boils down to two states, for example, and one state has a unitary tax and the other does not. For instance, one executive says: "Unitary tax becomes instrumental if alternate site is competitive in non-unitary tax state. Unitary tax is a major problem for foreign-owned companies." Additionally, a small percentage of executives think that while a state's unitary tax is a negative in attracting industry, it has little influence in retaining industry, because, once established, companies are reluctant to move.

ILLUSTRATION 8.1

**Differentiating a plant/subsidiary appeal
from a headquarters appeal, by the private sector.**

PICKING
THE RIGHT PLACE
TO PLANT A NEW PLANT

IS A HEAVY
DECISION.

Call RE•DEC.

We're prepared to lighten the load with the
right place and the right kind of help!

RE•DEC

RICHLAND ECONOMIC DEVELOPMENT CORP.

24 W. Third St. • Mansfield, Ohio 44902 • (419) 522-7332

. . . call collect for all vital statistics!

For example, a representative comment was, "Negative in attracting industry, neutral in retaining business, provided there is an equitable method of effecting the change to the unitary concept."

A number of executives, again a minority by far, think of the unitary tax as actually a favorable inducement to some companies to locate or stay in a unitary-tax state. One executive said, "It depends on the company. For as many companies, such as mine, that dislike unitary taxation, there are others which find it most favorable—Silicon Valley, California likes unitary taxes very much. It just depends on whose ox is being gored." In other words, executives with this line of thinking believe that purely domestic companies, or those with a limited international presence, might look favorably on a state unitary tax if it puts the burden on multinationals. In brief, what taxes the multinationals pay will be taxes that domestic companies will not have to pay. The fallacy in this logic is that eventually, if enough multinationals shift operations elsewhere to states without a unitary tax, the domestic companies might well end up paying considerably more in taxes.

A very small number of executives feel that one cannot generalize about the effects of a state's unitary tax on its ability to attract and retain industry. A *Fortune 500* manager says, "Can't generalize—depends on whether it's [the unitary tax] worldwide or shore to shore."

While there is minority disagreement, as noted, one inescapable conclusion flows from our analysis of the unitary tax as it pertains to economic development. That is, in the opinion of a preponderance of "knowledgeable" executives in corporations of all sizes and kinds, the unitary tax is an economic poison. In the short term, it may have no ostensible effect on a state's economic vitality. But over a larger term (perhaps 5 to 10 years), the deleterious effects are likely to begin to manifest themselves. Businesses in a unitary-tax state might not pull up stakes and leave immediately. Yet, they may gradually locate expansion facilities in other "more-receptive" states as time progresses. And businesses not already located in a unitary-tax state are likely to avoid it like the plague. Over time, then, a state's unitary tax is likely to erode the state's economic vitality. Oregon's governor, in discussing his state's elimination of the unitary method of taxation, remarked:

> The Japanese, our neighbors on the Pacific Rim and Oregon's leading trading partners, say 170 of their companies are looking for sites for new plants. But, they have told us bluntly their corporations will not even consider a state that employs the unitary method.[2]

In a speech before the World Affairs Council's International Business Roundtable in Portland, the governor commented that in rescinding the unitary tax "once and for all" he hoped to "position Oregon for unprecedented economic growth."[3]

ALL STATES ARE NOT EQUAL

Much has been written and said about the relative attractiveness of the various cities, states, and regions of the United States to industry. And the ratings that appear from time to time usually create their share of controversy. Places that fare well naturally ballyhoo their favorable circumstances, and places that do not fare so well typically dismiss the rating technique and its results as invalid.

Our respondents from larger-to-smaller companies provided us with their own rankings of the areas of the United States in terms of overall attractiveness to companies. We asked executives to answer from the perspectives of their own industries, so the answers represent a good cross-section of American business.

We intentionally are identifying by name only the states and regions of the United States ranked most desirable. We think it neither necessary nor useful to identify less-desirable states and regions of the country. In fact, the specification of lower-ranked places would be likely to provoke argumentation and defensive reactions, thereby diverting attention away from one underlying question: "What are the elements of success in economic development?" By focusing on places perceived as conducive for doing business, much can be learned about the *mix of ingredients* that companies of all types and sizes look for whenever they are locating facilities.

In the collective opinion of the *Fortune 500* and *Inc. 500* executives, the most conducive location for business is Texas. Following Texas is the southeastern United States (excluding Florida), which consists of such states as Georgia, Louisiana, Alabama, Tennessee, and Mississippi. Next comes the mid-Atlantic region, which we identified as the Carolinas, Maryland, Virginia, and Delaware. The fourth most desirable location was the Southwest, excluding Texas of course, which ranked first by itself. Florida and California tied for fifth place.

These rankings are generally consistent with others we have seen. Moreover, the results unmistakably depict the much-publicized industry bias for the Sunbelt. Indeed, it was not until we got to sixth on our desirability ranking list that a non-Sunbelt region or state showed up—the Great Lakes states. These six top rankings are recapped in Exhibit 8.5.

Note that the states and regions at the apex of the rankings have, in large measure, the key location ingredients shown earlier in this chapter in Exhibits 8.1-8.4. States such as Texas and those in the southeastern United States are widely believed to have a relatively good labor-relations climate, the existence of a strong work ethic, low tax rates, and a "can-do" spirit. To be sure, they have their weaknesses, too, but evidently their good points far outweigh the bad.

EXHIBIT 8.5

**The Six Areas of the United States Most Attractive to Industry,
As Seen By Executives
(in order of importance)**

1.	Texas	4.	Southwest, excluding Texas
2.	Southeast, excluding Florida	5.	California and Florida
3.	Mid-Atlantic (the Carolinas, Maryland, Virginia, and Delaware)	6.	Great Lakes states

Because so much attention in recent years has focused on corporate moves to the Sunbelt, we were interested to see if a representative cross-section of executives think that this obvious trend will continue. Here is what these executives told us:

- 62% said the Sunbelt trend will continue;
- 20% said the Sunbelt trend will continue, but only for a limited time;
- 18% said the Sunbelt trend has already ceased.

Of the executives responding that "yes, the Sunbelt trend will continue," their reasons are captured in these typical excerpted, but verbatim, responses:

- "Labor is more productive and less costly."
- "Moderate climate, growing market, improving quality of life, fewer unions."
- "To serve new and expanding markets."
- "Because of favorable cost environment."
- "As business climate in [a non-Sunbelt region] becomes more oppressive."
- "Better labor relations, more receptive communities, lower costs."
- "We have moved approximately ten plants from the [non-Sunbelt regions] and are well pleased with the results."
- "Higher rate of employee attendance. Many young people, particularly technical persons, attracted to Sunbelt."
- "Strong work ethic."
- "Extensive labor problems in [a non-Sunbelt region]."
- "Because costs are generally lower and Sunbelt attitude toward business is generally more favorable. The Sunbelt market is also growing faster than any other areas."
- "Tax structure, personal and corporate, ability to recruit high potential employees."
- "Lower costs ... land, utilities, labor ... fewer undesirable factors ... labor disputes, weather."
- "Labor related."

- "Available land, available labor, active civic involvement."
- "High taxes such as recently enacted by [a non-Sunbelt state] and organized labor's inability to understand the impact of foreign competition (wages)."
- "Having a right to work law is very inviting, as most Sunbelt states have."

By contrast, the 38% of the executives who said that the Sunbelt trend is either over already or will continue only for a while yet, provided these kinds of thoughts:

- "Sunbelt advantages overrated."
- "[The Sunbelt trend] is fashionable, it gets away from some of the 'unmentionable' problems of the 'welfare states,' and it solves some union problems. But no doubt as the Sunbelt matures, the pendulum will swing back."
- "The quality of the [Sunbelt] work force is not up to the standards of the other areas of the country."
- "Advantages are overstated."
- "Sunbelt does not meet needs of all types of concerns."
- "As long as water holds out [Sunbelt trend will continue]."
- "[Sunbelt] cost and life quality advantages will persist for some time, though diminishing."
- "Already beginning to strain services in those [Sunbelt] areas."
- "Lack of water and the penalties of overcrowding will temper demand."
- "Statistics show that the peak moves have past."
- "Major cities in the North, as well as labor, will react to curb the trend."

As the foregoing statistics and comments on the Sunbelt trend show, there is a strong majority opinion that the trend is irreversible. But, interestingly, one executive foresees the Sunbelt itself falling victim to a trend to offshore manufacturing by U.S. companies. (This kind of competition is precisely what the Japanese fear from the South Koreans and other Third World countries.) In other words, a labor-cost advantage is often ephemeral; a region or even a country's labor-cost advantage can be turned against it in short order. Nonetheless, inarguably the major attractiveness of the Sunbelt *today* is its cost advantages over other regions, particularly regarding labor. These lower labor costs, better labor relations, and an evident probusiness sentiment in the Sunbelt augur the near-term continuation of the Sunbelt trend. No doubt it will be slowed by several factors—the competitive reactions by other regions of the United States; the straining of critical resources, mainly water, needed to support industry and the population; and, as time goes by, a less-favorable labor climate in the Sunbelt than exists today.

FOREIGN-LOCATION DECISIONS

In recognition of the dramatic globalization of American business, we extended our research so that it encompassed foreign-location decision making by U.S.-based corporations, as well as domestic. The vast majority of the respondents in this study were involved in international business, and they provided us with plenty of information and insight on this question: Beyond the normal factors that determine domestic-location decisions by companies, just what additional considerations are paramount in foreign-location decisions? The answers to this query can be of value to states and communities in the United States that compete against foreign nations for business facilities. And, when it comes to states especially, most all of them now compete against foreign countries. In order for a state to be able to present a compelling argument for why a company should locate therein, rather than in another nation, a good empirically-based sense of the competition's strengths and weaknesses is necessary. Put differently, a thorough competitor analysis is called for, so the state can persuasively focus on its own strengths and on the competitions' weaknesses.

According to our findings, U.S. corporations evaluate foreign countries as potential sites for plant, subsidiary, and kindred facilities on several key considerations, as shown in Exhibit 8.6. But, by far the two prime concerns to U.S. companies in evaluating a foreign site are the government's political and economic stability and its attitude toward business in general, and U.S. business in particular.

The political and economic stability criterion fundamentally pertains to a form of government's (democracy, autocracy, etc.) predicted longevity. More broadly, it pertains to a specific political party, or administration, or regime's ability to stay in power and maintain order, a stable currency, and sound fiscal and monetary policies.

A government's attitude toward U.S. business is largely judged by its actions in three areas. American companies are concerned with a government's inclinations regarding expropriation. Moreover, these companies are keenly interested in the government's regulatory policies and how restrictive they are. And a government's posture toward physical security of a U.S. company's human resources and material assets is another component of attitude toward business. Does the government view and treat terrorism and its perpetrators harshly?

If a foreign nation does not have a demonstrably good history on the foregoing concerns, it will have a hard time persuading U.S. business to locate there, irrespective of how favorably the nation stacks up on other locational criteria. Indeed, a state or community in the United States that is competing with a foreign country for a corporate facility can present a devastating argument if the country is historically vulnerable on either or both of the political and economic stability and attitude toward business yardsticks.

ILLUSTRATION 8.2

Creativity in executing a foreign city's strengths.

We make plants GROW into big strong industrial giants

Pietermaritzburg. A city rich in industrial opportunity. With a highly efficient infrastructure supplying some of the most comprehensive facilities in the country. Pietermaritzburg has been designated as an Industrial Deconcentration Point, which qualifies both newly-established and expanding industrial concerns for extensive Government subsidies including:

- Railage rebates
- Relocational allowances (up to R500 000)
- Tender preferences
- Employment incentives
- Rental & Housing interest subsidies
- Training grants

Uniquely situated between the lucrative markets of the Reef and Durban/Pinetown and with easy access to the ports of Durban and

Richards Bay, Pietermaritzburg offers the considerable advantages of a city providing a superb quality of life, together with every conceivable industrial advantage.

For a copy of our brochure "PIETERMARITZBURG THE PLACE TO INVEST YOUR FUTURE" or for further information as to what our beautiful city can offer you, telephone or write to:

The Industrial Promotion Officer
P.O. Box 419
Pietermaritzburg 3200
SOUTH AFRICA
Telephone: (0331) 27031 x 411
or 29214
Telex: 6-43180 SA

Grow with us towards a fertile future.

**PIETERMARITZBURG
SOUTH AFRICA
City with a future.**

EXHIBIT 8.6

**Key Considerations in Corporate Foreign-Location Decisions
(in order of importance)**

1. Government's political/economic stability	4. Taxes on business
2. Government's attitude toward U.S. business	5. Government's profit repatriation policy
3. Labor-related concerns	6. Other concerns: proximity to markets, cost of living, whether English is the country's "working" language

We found labor-related concerns to be the third most important consideration to U.S. companies in foreign-location decisions. Specifically, companies zero in on the country's extent of unionization and the government's degree of balance between industry and unions; for example, whether there are local content laws in force and if plant closings and worker layoffs are extraordinarily bureaucratic and costly. Labor-related concerns also encompass the perceived work ethic and skill levels in the work force.

Taxes on business and the government's policy on profit repatriation are other key considerations in foreign-location decisions by American companies. Matters apparently not as crucial as the ones already mentioned, but nevertheless matters that are often important to U.S. businesses, are the country's proximity to a firm's major markets, the cost of living, and whether the nation's "working" language is English.

With the Iranian revolution firmly in memory and continuing turbulence in a number of low-wage Third World countries, states and communities can often find receptive audiences in companies about to locate or relocate facilities. Recognition and understanding of the factors that U.S. companies look for most in foreign-location decisions can markedly help a state or community to make a better case for itself as an alternate site.

WANTED: A PERVASIVE "CAN-DO" SPIRIT

One executive from a large company made a cogent observation about a state's ability to attract and keep industry: "An overall good climate for business is required, not just at the Governor or Development Director level, but throughout government and the state." How many times has a governor or development director, or both, succeeded in initially interesting a company in the merits of the state, only to have the effort go for naught later when the company's executives visit the state and talk with less-than-enthusiastic representatives from the public and private sectors? The value of the intangible, noneconomic

ILLUSTRATION 8.3

Calling attention to a work ethic.

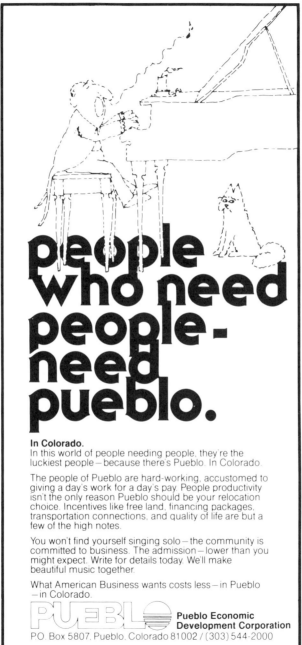

In Colorado.
In this world of people needing people, they're the luckiest people — because there's Pueblo. In Colorado.

The people of Pueblo are hard-working, accustomed to giving a day's work for a day's pay. People productivity isn't the only reason Pueblo should be your relocation choice. Incentives like free land, financing packages, transportation connections, and quality of life are but a few of the high notes.

You won't find yourself singing solo — the community is committed to business. The admission — lower than you might expect. Write for details today. We'll make beautiful music together.

What American Business wants costs less — in Pueblo — in Colorado.

Pueblo Economic Development Corporation
P.O. Box 5807, Pueblo, Colorado 81002 / (303) 544-2000

Wouldn't you rather be in Colorado?

"can-do" spirit cannot be overestimated, but it may take years to develop. It is frequently the case that this aura emerges only after a state (or community thereof) has suffered economically. Only then do enough people from the public and private sectors come to realize that the state cannot keep on shooting itself in the foot indefinitely. It was not, for example, until Oregon's lumber and wood-products industry precipitated much unemployment in the state that Oregon turned a traditional and pervasive antigrowth mentality around. And the results have been rewarding. Unfortunately, from the standpoint of economic development, an attempted turnaround may come too late for many states.

Vignettes

WHERE DOES THE CEO WANT TO LIVE?

Austin, Texas, did a first-rate job of competing for and eventually attracting the Microelectronics and Computer Technology Corporation (MCC). But the city had an edge to begin with; MCC's chief executive officer (CEO) is a University of Texas-Austin alumnus. When Diamond Shamrock Corporation moved its headquarters from Cleveland to Dallas, the major rationale given by the company for public consumption was that it wanted to be closer to its markets. Some individuals close to the situation gave another plausible reason—the company's chief executive was a Texan and wanted to reside there.

According to the *Wall Street Journal,* such examples are not unprecedented. Chief executives sometimes dislike the headquarters city so much that they orchestrate a relocation. AM International was moved from Ohio to California when a Californian took over as CEO; his successor as CEO, a Chicago resident, shifted headquarters from California to Chicago. The West Coast move was attributed to AM International's need to be closer to U.S. high-tech centers. By contrast, the Chicago relocation was ostensibly due to AM International's need to be near its manufacturing facilities. When Greyhound Corporation switched its headquarters from Chicago to Phoenix, it was candid about the reason: Its CEO did not like living in the Midwest. Schering-Plough has moved its headquarters from one New Jersey city to another, yet the distance between them is only 20 miles. Coincidentally, the company's CEO lives in the new headquarters community?*

CEOs are not always successful in moving corporate headquarters. We came across a situation in which a newly appointed CEO attempted to shift corporate headquarters to the city where he had been living and where his family still resides. But the board of directors thwarted the effort.

Regarding headquarters-location decisions, a *Fortune 500* executive told us, "Realistically, the reigning CEO makes the choice for his convenience—the rationalization follows. For those who disagree— the naive—examine the moves of many large companies and the background of a strong CEO!" Another executive, also from a large company, agreed: "Corporate management can affect the decision with personal preferences no matter how thorough the [location] study."

The practice of CEOs moving corporate headquarters to suit their own preferences goes on, as these examples show. Although the practice is far from being pervasive, those cases that have occurred demonstrate without question that the CEO can be a strong influence on location decisions, irrespective of what evidence is adduced by location studies. Additionally, his or her decision criteria may pertain as much or more to subjective and sometimes personal factors than to purely business considerations. The psychological aspects of selling a potential location for corporate facilities, especially a headquarters facility, are considerable.

---

*The information on AM International, Greyhound, and Schering-Plough Corporations is from: Trish Hall, "For a Company Chief, When There's a Whim There's Often a Way," *Wall Street Journal*, October 1, 1984, pp. 1 and 16.

IT'S A SHORT WALK FROM THE
PENTHOUSE TO THE OUTHOUSE

An American border-state city has fallen on hard times, much of which is of its own making. During its heady days of growth, it secured high-paying jobs and an improved standard of living for its populace by making good on efforts to attract several large heavy manufacturing facilities of U.S. companies. But even then, halcyon days they were not; peace and tranquility in labor and management relations were scarce commodities. As time went by, the city suffered a double body blow—basic industry companies sought lower costs in the South and abroad and recession hit hard at those industries upon which the city most depended. The bloom was off the rose.

Some of the city's leaders from the public and private sectors reacted, although belatedly, as jobs and the population dwindled. But instead of being proactive when the early warning signals of impending trouble occurred, they could not get their act together. Because of deep conflict between the business community on the one hand and government and labor on the other, there was not a concerted effort to move the city's economic base away from heavy manufacturing. Even today, as the city desperately strives to diversify its economy, its reputation for labor and management strife haunts it. Its work force is still a national leader in wildcat strikes. Old habits change slowly.

The moral of this story? Economic redevelopment, no matter how well planned, strategized, and financed, cannot compensate for the lack of a consensus community mission of revitalization that cuts across all segments of the population and interest groups.

REFERENCES

1. What can we do for you in Austin. (advertisement) (1984, September/October). *Plants Sites & Parks*, p. 108.
2. Oregon votes to repeal unitary tax. (1984, September/October). *Plants Sites & Parks*, p. 64.
3. *Ibid*

9

THE ONES THAT MOVED

EXECUTIVE SUMMARY

During the last 5 years, many very large and smaller companies have relocated their corporate headquarters or located plants and subsidiaries, or both. Consequently, these companies have a wealth of information about corporate location and relocation decision making. And since their experiences are so recent, they are able to provide accurate perspectives on the events and location influences that entered into their choices. This chapter is based on the knowledge that many of these companies have that was shared with us.

Companies consider many locational influences whenever they are contemplating moving a corporate headquarters or locating an expansion facility. But one overriding influence involves labor. The companies are interested in the quality of labor relations in a prospective state or community, including extent of unionization of the work force and the work ethic in the geographical area under evaluation. Far more often than not, a company looking to move or expand will eliminate from further consideration any area with a less-than-desirable labor climate, irrespective of the area's redeeming qualities on other important locational influences. A good labor climate will not by itself entice a company to locate in a community, but it will often in and of itself cause a company to avoid a community.

As compared to plant- and subsidiary-location decisions, headquarters decisions are based much more on subjective and emotional factors. One giant company we report on opted not to relocate headquarters; its decision went against almost all of the economic, financial, and political factors that objectively pointed to the need for a headquarters relocation.

This chapter elaborates on these subjects and also delves into such topics as how companies go about making location decisions—how many sites they consider and how long it takes them to decide upon a site; and how companies evaluate various economic development organizations and facilitators—state development organizations, private site developers, chambers of commerce, and the like. Also discussed are why corporations move, the major reasons, and what companies look for specifically in a site for a facility—adjacent land use, airport frontage, location in an enterprise zone, and similar considerations.

THE COMPANIES AND HOW THEY
MAKE LOCATION DECISIONS

As we noted, the findings upon which this chapter is developed come from companies with an extrememly high experience base in locating facilities. Many of the firms that provided the information and opinions used in this chapter have recently moved their corporate headquarters. By recently, we mean within the 5 year period preceding our study. And the headquarters moves by a number of the companies attracted considerable publicity. Other corporations in our sample have recently located or relocated plants and subsidiaries. And some of the companies that supplied us with data and insight have current experience in both moving corporate headquarters and in locating plant and subsidiary facilities. This chapter is a cross-check of sorts on the *Fortune 500* and *Inc. 500* responses reported in chapter 8. Even so, fresh and more-specific findings are also presented on location-related matters, as seen by executives in corporations that not long ago underwent a location decision.

These companies range in size from firms with annual sales revenues of less than $100 million to $8 to $10 billion. As to lines of business, again there is diversity. The companies are engaged in endeavors as multifarious as manufacturing, services, and high technology. This kind of size and industry representation makes for a good cross-sectional look at corporate-location decision making.

We found that whenever these companies initiate a location-decision process, almost all of them use an internal corporate site-selection team. The title of this group is likely to vary from company to company; but regardless of its name, the group's purpose is always to act as a corporate site-selection team. More important than title is the composition of the site-selection team. By company title, the executives most often represented in the site-selection group are these:

- Vice presidents of finance, operations or administration, and human resources;
- A vice president or manager of real estate or facilities.

Naturally, these executive titles also vary somewhat across companies.

Chief executive officers and presidents are not normally members of site-selection teams, although they can and often do exert considerable or even total influence on the final decision. Some companies include their CEOs as site-selection team members but, in most cases, CEOs are ex officio members only. Albeit not as commonly seen on site-selection teams as vice presidents of human resources, for example, two other executive functions are represented on these teams often enough to warrant mention—manufacturing and legal. Our inquiries made one answer quite clear: The corporate executive with the highest probability of being involved in site selection is the vice president of finance.

What individuals and groups do the corporate site-selection group consult in helping it to make the right decision? Based on our research, we found:

- 50% use a real estate consultant, either one within the company's employ or an outside consultant;
- 50% contact local or regional development groups in the geographical areas of interest;
- slightly over half use real estate firms;
- 70% employ a labor specialist, again, either one within the company's employ or an outside consultant, to evaluate and advise on labor conditions in the geographical areas of interest;
- about one-fourth consult with financial institutions, mainly banks, in the potential site areas.

In addition, nearly three-fourths of the companies consider a leasing option to be a feasible alternative to buying or building a headquarters or plant or subsidiary facility. In fact, about 42% of them reported that they had recently leased facilities in lieu of purchasing them outright. About 10% of the companies prefer a sale and lease-back arrangement.

EVALUATING DEVELOPMENT ORGANIZATIONS AND OTHER FACILITATORS

In our nomenclature, development organizations include those public, private, and quasi-public or quasi-private institutions whose specific mission it is to attract business to the geographic area in which they are located. Economic development is the raison d'etre of state, regional, city, and county development groups. Other organizations may not be development groups per se, but nonetheless they are often involved in attracting business to a geographical locale. Such organizations as real estate agencies, site developers, and local chambers of commerce are what we call facilitators of economic development.

Whenever a company seeks to locate or relocate a facility, it is usually inundated with information from development-promoting groups. And a company itself frequently initiates information requests. From experience, trial and error, companies have formed opinions about the quality of information typically provided by development organizations and facilitators. Quality means the applicability, credibility, and overall value of information to the location task at hand. One caution: A given type of development or facilitating group can be viewed by corporations as not being especially reliable at supplying quality location information, whereas an individual organization in that category might be a notable exception to the general perception.

So, our findings regarding the impressions the surveyed companies have of the quality of information available from specific categories of development organizations and facilitators are overall perceptions for which plenty of exceptions no doubt can be found. With that qualification made, here is what we found.

EXHIBIT 9.1

How Companies Evaluate Development Organizations and Facilitators as Sources of Information About Potential Locations

Best at Providing Information	Good at Providing Information	Adequate at Providing Information
Local real estate agencies	County development organizations	National real estate agencies
Regional development organizations	Local (private) site developers	Local chambers of commerce
State development groups		City development organizations
Local banking/ Financial institutions		

As Exhibit 9.1 illustrates, the companies we asked think the highest quality information about a geographical area is available from local real estate agencies, regional and state development groups, and local banking and financial institutions. The first three types of organizations mentioned virtually tie as the *best* information sources and banking and financial institutions run a close second.

Viewed by the companies as providing *good* location data, although not the highest quality, are county development groups and private-sector site developers within the local area of interest to a company. National real estate agencies, local chambers of commerce, and city development organizations were seen as *adequate* information sources.

Thus, the companies believe that a number of groups can be helpful sources of location information. Their preferences, however, tend to be for information from state and regional development groups and local real estate agencies and financial institutions.

These findings suggest a two-stage decision process. Initially, a company wants the best information it can get on a *variety* of potential location communities within a preselected area of the United States. Regional and state development groups are in a better position than local development organizations to provide this information. The former groups have more and more balanced information about alternative communities in their states or regions and, further, are understandably less biased than local development groups or facilitators about the relative objective merits of the communities. A state or regional development agency is supposed to be officially indifferent (although exceptions can be cited) as to which community attracts a corporate facility, as long as the facility comes to the state or region. Once a company narrows its choices to several communities, it looks to knowledgeable sources within the community for in-depth, specialized information and insight on possible sites. And the preferred information sources at the community level are local real estate agencies and local financial institutions, mostly banks.

HEADQUARTERS-LOCATION DECISIONS

Of the companies that actually moved their headquarters, the majority of them did not go far. Fifty-six percent relocated in or near the same city, often from a downtown location to a suburb. Thirty-three percent relocated in another part of the same state, although in a different community. And 11% moved their headquarters to an out-of-state location. From the standpoint of a city that loses the headquarters of a major employer, it really matters little economically whether the move is to a nearby suburb or out of state; the lost tax revenue consequences are the same either way. We have come across several city-to-suburb headquarters moves of this kind and, regardless of the reasons cited by the companies for these moves, closer examination usually reveals a company fleeing what it sees as conditions not as conducive for doing business as those offered by a suburb location.

While intrastate headquarters relocations can be of great concern to cities left behind, states, of course, are not much affected. States are concerned with out-of-state headquarters losses. This is another example of where the economic development philosophies of states and their communities do not always coincide.

Because the majority of headquarters relocations were to the same general community, most of them involved a short distance. Even so, a number constituted moves of as much as 500 to 1,000 miles. One company relocated its headquarters over a thousand miles away. While this great a distance is not typical, neither is it rare. Georgia-Pacific Corporation went from Portland, Oregon, to Atlanta, Georgia, and it has not been uncommon for middle-America high-technology companies to leave their origins to relocate near like companies on the West Coast.

Prior to the final site-selection decision, about how many different geographical locations (states or cities) did these companies consider? Three-fourths of them seriously considered no more than three locations. A company that considered only one site was the exception, as were firms that evaluated more than three geographical locations. Occasionally we found that a company may consider as many as six to eight or more different geographical locations. What these findings indicate is that executives undertake headquarters relocations with a very "short" list in mind of acceptable geographical areas for the new headquarters facility.

Once the decision to move a headquarters is made, the site-selection process *normally* takes 5 to 6 months. Nearly 70% of the companies said that it took them this amount of time to search for and make up their minds on a headquarters site. We found the decision process for selecting a headquarters location ranges anywhere from 3 to 4 months to 18 months. Some companies act quickly, others take their time, and most decide within the preferred 5- to 6- month time frame.

The decision to move a corporate headquarters might be years in the making. But, once it is made, the site-selection process is usually carried out with some alacrity. It is typically a 5- to 6-month matter of choosing from among three locations that are not more than 250 miles away.

WHY THEY MOVED

Companies usually leave communities for negative reasons and take up in other communities for positive reasons. A headquarters location is normally sufficiently permanent in the eyes of top management and the board of directors that some compelling negatives have to become almost intolerable before a relocation is considered. As a rule, plants and subsidiaries are moved much more readily than are corporate headquarters. Moreover, they are moved for different reasons. A company may tolerate high prevailing wage and tax rates in a community when its headquarters is involved, but would not do the same for a plant or subsidiary. For example, Route 128 in Boston is a popular place for headquarters facilities for high-technology companies. But as these companies grow and prosper, they are likely to expand their manufacturing facilities in states with a lower wage and tax structure. Indeed, there are indications that this is already occuring.

According to the executives we asked whose companies have actually moved headquarters facilities in recent years, the most important reasons for doing so are these:

- Desire to consolidate operations;
- Outgrown present facilities;
- Desire to locate in an area of the country more attractive to present or potential employees.

This latter reason is particularly germane to high-tech companies that must compete for a scarcity of top-flight scientists, researchers, and engineers.

Exhibit 9.2 identifies these three reasons and also others that are not as frequently cited. Such considerations as poor quality of life, an unproductive work force, and the desire to be closer to like firms, can contribute to headquarters relocations, although they are not the most significant reasons for moving.

We think it wise to reiterate that the reasons that give impetus to a headquarters move may be different from those that cause a company to relocate a plant or subsidiary. Generally, there is more loyalty to a community or state in the headquarters instance.

EXHIBIT 9.2

Importance of Various Considerations in Prompting Headquarters Moves

Most Important Reasons for Moving	Contributory Reasons for Moving
Desire to consolidate operations	Desire to be closer to like firms
Outgrown present facilities	Desire to move closer to present markets
Desire to locate in an area of the country more attractive to present or potential employees	Desire to be closer to raw materials
	Local workers relatively unproductive
	Desire to have better access to transportation
	Desire to leave a downtown location
	Poor quality-of-life factors

WHY THEY ARRIVED

What did these companies that moved headquarters facilities look for most in a new community? Put differently, why did they arrive in their new headquarters location? What were the locational inducements that attracted them most?

Without question, what the companies wanted most in a new headquarters location was a bundle of benefits concerning human resources. Exhibit 9.3 makes this preference quite clear.

Of the first six locational factors shown in Exhibit 9.3, four are labor-related. The companies that moved their headquarters looked for a new location with a good labor-relations climate, a low rate of unionization in the area, the availability of a skilled and educated work force, and the existence of a strong work ethic in the community.

When we asked the companies to provide their number one concern when they were searching for a new headquarters community, the vast

EXHIBIT 9.3

What Companies Look For in a Headquarters Location

Location Influences	Rank and Importance[a]
Good labor-relations climate (e.g., few incidents of work stoppage)	1 HI
Low rate of unionization in the area	1 HI
Availability of skilled/educated work force	2 HI
Tax rates on businesses	2 HI
Existence of strong work ethic	3 HI
Good transportation facilities to business travel	3 HI
Housing availability for employees	4 HI
Quality of utilities	4 HI
Community safety	4 HI
Quality college/university nearby	5 HI
Tax rates on individuals	5 HI
Recreational opportunities and parks	5 HI
First-rate scientific community in the area	5 HI
Relatively low cost of living	6 HI
In, or suburb of, a major population center	6 HI
Favorable ecological factors	6 HI
"Can-do" spirit apparent on the part of community leaders	6 HI
Lack of "red tape" by state and local government	6 HI
Availability of water and waste system	7 HI
$ incentives (industrial-revenue bonds, enterprise zones, etc.)	7 HI
Quality primary/secondary school system	8 HI
Rich cultural environment (orchestras, museums, etc.)	8 HI
Progressive banking institutions	8 HI
Relatively low wage/salary levels	8 HI
Proximity to the company's major markets	8 HI
Local state/government programs, other than taxes	8 HI
Good transportation facilities for moving goods	9 HI
Moderate-to-warm climate	9 HI
Topographical factors	9 HI
Proximity to needed raw materials and natural resources	10 HI
Plentiful venture capital	10 HI

[a]The location factors are rank ordered from most important (1) to least important. The letters HI, MI, or LI by each ranking indicates whether a particular factor is considered by respondents to be of high importance, medium importance, or low importance.

majority of them cited "access to select employee skills." "Quality of life" and the "nature of governmental regulations" were also mentioned prominently.

When one compares the views of the companies that actually moved their headquarters in recent years to the perspectives of the *Fortune 500* and *Inc. 500* companies presented in chapter 8 (Exhibit 8.1), there is a close degree of correspondence. This congruence serves to corroborate what companies want in headquarters locations. However, we do notice two differences worth pointing out. First, the companies that have actually moved place a high importance rating on a greater number of locational influences. Perhaps their recent experiences with a headquarters relocation has made them more attuned to the importance of several factors that were not ranked as highly by the *Fortune 500s* and *Inc. 500s*. Second, although labor factors are ranked highly by all the companies in our studies, they are ranked even higher by companies that have recent experience with headquarters relocations.

Our findings strongly support that *labor problems and issues provide the major impetus to corporate headquarters relocations*. The surest way for a community or area to become intolerable to a company's top management is for it to develop or perpetuate labor problems. Such intolerance, of course, is many years in the making. Because of this distasteful experience, top executives become superconscious of the labor factor and put it right at the top of the list when they start to evaluate potential new headquarters locations.

The conclusion that we have reached is this: Companies seek a variety of benefits, a bundle of benefits, in a new headquarters location. However, if a potential headquarters community is seen as having a poor labor climate, chances are it will not be a viable candidate for many headquarters, regardless of the community's redeeming qualities on other criteria. In brief, labor matters can and do exert powerful influences on a company in its decision to leave one community and to take up in another. Most of the Frostbelt-to-Sunbelt relocations can be largely attributed to perceived and real labor difficulties in the Frostbelt versus labor attractiveness in the Sunbelt.

PLANT- AND SUBSIDIARY-LOCATION DECISIONS

GENERAL LOCATION INFLUENCES

The way companies with very recent experience (within 5 years of our study) in locating plants or subsidiaries, or both, see the importance of various locational factors in these decisions corresponds closely to the *Fortune 500* and *Inc. 500* views that we identified in chapter 8. A comparison of Exhibit 9.4 in this chapter to Exhibit 8.3 in chapter 8 reveals as much. Of course, many of the *Fortune 500* and *Inc. 500* companies that provided us with information for chapter 8 have also had recent experience in locating plants and subsidiaries, but we do not know this to be the case for all of them. In contrast, the companies reported on in this chapter, ranging from large to small, *all* have known experience in locating or relocating plants or subsidiaries within the 5-year period immediately preceding our study. Importantly, the views of the companies in chapters 8 and 9 are corroborative.

Exhibit 9.4 makes it apparent that companies evaluating potential sites for plants and subsidiaries consider a wide range of locational influences. All of the locational factors were evaluated as being of high

EXHIBIT 9.4

What Companies Look For in a Plant or Subsidiary Location

Location Influences	Rank and Importance[a]
Good labor-relations climate (e.g., few incidents of work stoppage)	1 HI
Low rate of unionization in the area	2 HI
Availability of water and waste system	2 HI
Quality of utilities	2 HI
Availability of skill/educated work force	3 HI
Good transportation facilities for moving goods	4 HI
Good transportation facilities for business travel	4 HI
Housing availability for employees	4 HI
Relatively low cost of living	5 HI
Existence of strong work ethic	5 HI
Favorable ecological conditions	6 HI
Quality college/university nearby	7 HI
Lack of "red tape" by state and local government	7 HI
Relatively low wage/salary levels	7 HI
"Can-do" spirit apparent on the part of community leaders	7 HI
Tax rates on business	8 HI
Community safety	9 HI
Moderate-to-warm climate	9 HI
First-rate scientific community in the area	9 HI
Topographical factors	9 HI
Recreational opportunities and parks	10 HI
Quality primary/secondary school system	10 HI
Local/state government programs, other than taxes	11 HI
Proximity to company's major markets	11 HI
Tax rates on individuals	12 HI
$ incentives (industrial-revenue bonds, enterprise zones, etc.)	12 HI
Rich cultural environment (orchestras, museums, etc.)	13 HI
In, or a suburb of, a major population center	13 HI
Proximity to needed raw materials and natural resources	13 HI
Progressive banking institutions	14 HI
Plentiful venture capital	15 HI

[a]The location factors are rank ordered from most important (1) to least important. The letters HI, MI, or LI by each ranking indicate whether a particular factor is considered by respondents to be of high importance, medium importance, or low importance.

importance. Yet, as we saw with headquarters facilities, it is labor-related considerations that are most salient. Concisely put, it is a good labor-relations climate (e.g., few incidents of work stoppage) and a low rate of unionization that companies seek most. Other "factors of production" are important as well—for example, the availability of a good water and waste system, dependable utilities, and more-than-adequate transportation facilities for moving goods and human resources.

As we suggested earlier about headquarters relocations, we believe that in locating plants or subsidiaries most companies look first at the labor-relations climate. If it meets their expectations, then other

ILLUSTRATION 9.1

Stressing key community economic attributes.

QUICK TOUR

Enjoy higher profits with a South Texas building:
You're in low-tax territory!

BUILDING #1
50,800 sq. ft.; formerly used for glove manufacturing; fabricated steel, concrete slab; completed 1976; dock-high loading; 100% automatic sprinkler coverage; all utilities.

BUILDING #2
92,000 sq. ft.; tilt-up concrete, built in 1983 as manufacturing facility; dock-high loading; all utilities; includes 17 acres in an industrial park, with adjoining acreage available. For sale or lease.

BUILDING #3
255,000 sq. ft.; former oil rig manufacturing facility suitable for heavy industry with overhead cranes; all utilities; on 28 acres with high visibility on main interstate roadway. Also available for lease, either in sections or entire building.

You're sure to find the home right for your business in the large selection of buildings now available in South Texas. And you'll gain big advantages from our excellent business climate, starting with lower taxes. Texas has NO unitary tax and NO state income tax, either corporate or personal.

For information about our free site-location services, call (512) 881-5699 or write:

Bruce W. Miller
Manager, Economic Development
Central Power and Light Company
P.O. Box 2121, Department PS-35
Corpus Christi, TX 78403

Advertisement reprinted with the permission of Bruce W. Miller, Manager, Economic Development, Central Power and Light Company, State of Texas.

locational inducements come under scrutiny and evaluation. But, if a community, state, or region does not measure up on the labor criterion, then in the vast majority of cases it is eliminated from further consideration.

SITE SPECIFICS

We found that once the companies have decided to build a new physical facility for expansion, a plant or subsidiary, the actual site-selection process was usually completed within a year. To be more exact, 9% of the companies made their decision in 1 to 2 months, 18% completed the process in 3 to 4 months, 28% made the decision in 5 to 6 months, 18% took 11 to 12 months, and 27% extended the site decision to 12 to 18 months.

Sixty-three percent of the companies considered sites in four states or cities, or both. Thirteen percent looked at three sites, 12% of the companies evaluated five sites, and another 12% looked at six or more possible locations. And company after company said that *labor costs* and *labor relations* were the *most important criteria* to them in selecting from among these potential sites.

Once a general locale for a plant or subsidiary was settled upon—a particular county or city—the companies commenced to search for sites within the locale that met specific development criteria. By far and away, the criterion of most importance was adjacent land use; the companies wanted room to expand their facilities later. Next in importance was that the site be in a planned industrial district, such as an industrial park. But there was sharp minority dissent on this point. Almost as many companies preferred raw land, previously agricultural, that was developable. For them, already cleared and graded land was not all that desirable.

Airport frontage, or at least close proximity to an airport, is another highly attractive characteristic that the companies sought in potential sites. Depending on a company's industry, other favorable site criteria were the availability of a rail siding, waterfront location, and location in an enterprise zone. To reiterate, the importance of these latter criteria varies by industry; some companies need to be located on a waterfront or rail siding, others do not.

SOME SIMILARITIES, SOME DIFFERENCES

In assessing the findings in both chapters 8 and 9, we see several additional noteworthy similarities and differences across the companies. The attitudes and opinions expressed by the companies on locational questions and issues were remarkably alike. The factors that cause large companies to become disenchanted with one community also bother smaller companies. And, irrespective of size, companies tend to look for the same kinds of benefits in prospective communities for relocated or expanded corporate facilities.

Also, regardless of size, companies do put a great deal of emphasis on quality of life. Indeed, once the location decision has been narrowed to several prospective communities, the choice is very likely to hinge on top management's conception of the relative quality of life offered by the communities, especially when a headquarters move is concerned. So-called economic inducements—labor, utilities, taxes, and so forth—are crucial to any type of corporate location, but more so for plants or subsidiaries than headquarters. Quality of life is a powerful rival of economic factors for headquarters-location decisions; in the end, a headquarters location may depend on where top management or even the top manager most prefers to live from among the competing communities.

There are some differences. Although companies do not generally rank such influences as quality of education and the existence of a first-rate scientific community in the area as being of utmost or even top priority, there are exceptions. Notably, these "knowledge" considerations can be extremely influential ones for high-technology companies. Realistically, the research and development component of a technologically-intensive firm often needs to be located in or near an area where there is a concentration of relevantly educated scientists and engineers, and perhaps an area with a top-flight university or research institute with expertise in the high-tech company's specialty. A labor-intensive heavy manufacturing facility can frequently perform well in a low-cost labor area. But the same cannot usually be said for high-technology companies, at least not for their R & D facilities.

Another dissimilarity among companies is the way they see some important aspects of economic development. It is erroneous for anyone to think of a homogenous corporate community with a united view on economic development as it affects them. To be sure, on most economic development issues corporations agree. But there are important exceptions. For example, a state's unitary tax is widely viewed by companies as being equivalent to the state putting out a *Not Wanted Here* sign to industry. Yet, there are some companies that actually like their state's unitary tax laws; they believe it shifts much of the tax burden from them to multinationals. And, in the short-run, it does have this effect. Take another example. Companies normally do not protest vigorously against state or local taxes that are levied against a specific product—cigarettes, liquor, or gasoline, for example. So, how economic development issues are assessed by companies sometimes depends on whose ox is being gored.

DEPARTING ON THE NEGATIVE/ ARRIVING ON THE POSITIVE

Inertia plays a key role in a company's choosing where it wants to locate its facilities. As with people, there is usually a reluctance to pull up stakes and move elsewhere. Detroit is the automobile capital of the United States and it would take a lot to change this fact. Similarly, although not many tires are still made in Akron, the city remains the rubber center of the United States by virtue of the companies head-quartered there. And it is hard to imagine anywhere but New York City being the home of the moneycenter banks.

Nonetheless, it is not all that unheard of for companies to move their headquarters and it is commonplace to see plants and subsidiaries relocated or expanded into new geographic areas. And most of these relocations occur for negative reasons; companies depart from existing locations on the negative. By the same token, they typically arrive in a new location on the positive. That is, they are attracted to a state, community, or, more broadly, a nation, by factors that are seen in a very favorable light. Normally, the locational factors valued most in a new location are those perceived by top management as being the big negatives in the former location.

And, the biggest perceived negative that has accounted for corporate moves from Frostbelt to Sunbelt and from the United States to other nations is labor. The longer-term trends in these regards are difficult to project and hinge on the way a number of questions are ultimately answered. For instance, will the Sunbelt experience a deteriorating labor climate as time goes by? Will organized labor make noticeable inroads in the South? And will competition for economic development cause the Frostbelt to improve its labor climate, especially as a new generation of "never-unionized" workers comes into the work force?

Surely the answer is yes to all these questions, at least to some degree in the long term, perhaps 15 to 20 years hence. In the near term, however, the Sunbelt should continue to have a marked advantage over the Frostbelt with respect to labor climate. The Frostbelt states do have a water advantage, but that is not terribly important to high-tech and knowledge-based service industries. Water availability is most needed in heavy manufacturing, which has been moving anyway to nations with labor-cost savings.

Third World countries will continue to give fits to both the Frostbelt and Sunbelt states on the labor-climate attractiveness criterion. The Sunbelt could be skewered on the same sword of low-cost, nonunion labor that it itself has used so successfully to pierce the industrial base in the Frostbelt.

Vignettes

ONE THAT DID NOT MOVE

Several years ago, a *Fortune 500* company with major interests in high technology seriously contemplated moving its corporate headquarters. A top executive took us behind the scenes in the internal debate that went on and allowed us to publish this vignette, with the proviso that the company not be identified by name.

The company was concerned that the city in which it is headquartered was no longer attractive enough to entice the "best" executives and scientists to locate there. Not only was the company's headquarters in the city, but it had centralized its research and development facility near headquarters. In addition to a not particularly stimulating quality of life, the city was not a probusiness, can-do type of environment.

The company hired a well-known economic development consulting firm to look for a new site for headquarters and the R&D facility, preferably in the Sunbelt location with the appropriate high-tech ingredients, mainly proximity to medical schools.

After considerable study and much discussion and debate by top management and the board of directors, the company decided to stay put. The executive we talked with called this decision one based almost purely on emotion. By financial and most other objective standards, the company should have moved. Yet, management believed that it owed a lot to the community; the company had been founded there and had grown to *Fortune 500* size. The community had been good to them and vice versa. In the executive's words, "the company's headquarters and centralized research facilities will stay in [the city] come hell or high water." However, expansion facilities are quite another matter.

This scenario illustrates one fact of life in corporate decisions concerning headquarters: Emotion plays a key role, maybe even the main role, in top management's decision to keep the headquarters where it is or to move it.

ONE THAT MOVED

In mid-1982, the Georgia-Pacific Corporation (GP) moved its headquarters from Portland, Oregon, to Atlanta, Georgia. The chief executive officer of GP, a Louisiana native, said then that the company's decision to return to the Southeast, where it was founded, "unconsciously was made for us five years ago" when the U.S. Federal Trade Commission brought and won a complaint forcing GP to spin off most of its western operations. The resulting spin-off, called Louisiana-Pacific Corporation, accounted previously for 70% of GP's sales. The FTC action left GP with 17 of its 21 plywood mills in the South. Originally, GP moved West to take advantage of Douglas fir, the only wood then used to produce plywood. But about 17 years ago the company pioneered a process for converting faster growing but pitchy (smeared with pitch or turpentine) southern pine into plywood. According to GP, the scaled-down company derived 75% of its sales and 72% of its profits from its southern and eastern operations.

Before the move from Portland to Atlanta, the travel burden for GP's management was estimated at $6 million a year. But another reason for moving was more compelling. The company felt that the South offered a more attractive business climate. It was concerned with government encroachment in the West. For example, in the late 1970s, 46,000 acres of prime redwood-growing land belonging to several timber companies were appropriated by the federal government under pressure from environmentalists to expand Redwood National Park. These kinds of problems are virtually nonexistent in the South. Instead of a business-government adversarial relationship, there is more cooperation, especially on conservation practices. And, in the Northwest, 75% of the timber is owned by the U.S. Forest Service, while in the South, 95% of forest land is privately held. A forest products analyst noted, "If you want to expand wholeheartedly, you almost have to go South."

The executive director of Oregon's Environmental Council accused GP of "cut-and-run" tactics and of overreacting. And the executive director of Portland's Chamber of Commerce remarked, "We feel demolished and impoverished. We don't ask anyone to come here, but we are insulted as hell when they leave." At a news conference welcoming GP to Atlanta, which was attended by Georgia's political and business hierarchy, GP's CEO commented that, "Most of the time when you build a plant in the western part of the country they say, 'Why are you coming here? You're going to ruin our hunting and fishing.'"

Postscript: GP experienced considerable difficulty in moving their headquarters. Many of the 400 headquarters employees were reluctant to go with the company to Atlanta. In fact, many resigned or retired rather than move. The company even had to schedule seminars in an attempt to disabuse employees of unfavorable notions of what it is like to live in the South. Moreover, the company incurred great expense in constructing the new headquarters building, and in other aspects of the relocation. From Oregon's perspective, it has changed its ways since the GP move. It is now more attentive to company needs and is soliciting new business. To attract high-tech multinationals, Oregon abandoned its unitary tax at a state revenue loss of $23 million a year. Once almost proudly antigrowth, Oregon has changed dramatically as its prosperous timber industry has declined.

---

*Information and quotations derived from various media and corporate sources, but mainly from "Georgia-Pacific Looks Southward to Home," *Business Week*, December 4, 1978, pp. 32-33, and "You Can Go Home Again," *Forbes*, December 11, 1978, pp. 81-82.

MARKETING IS A MUST IN FIGHTING THE SECOND CIVIL WAR

EXECUTIVE SUMMARY

Marketing is an increasingly important element in effective economic development efforts, but not marketing as it is viewed by many in the economic development field today. Rather, we are talking about marketing founded on a "marketing or demand orientation"; one that puts the prospect, the relocating or expanding firm, and its needs *first* in priority. Too often state or city economic development groups focus on what they are willing to "give" or "concede" to the prospect, that is, they adopt a supply-side orientation. Such a marketing orientation recognizes that cities and states find themselves in a heavily competitive struggle and suggests that marketing expertise honed to a fine-edge in a corporate setting may be transferred to industry-attraction efforts.

As an economic development unit begins to move toward a marketing orientation, a city or state must examine its current situation and future goals and objectives. The questions it needs to ask itself through an introspective examination are:

- What is our image? Does it need to be altered, for example, is it consistent with our goals and objectives?;
- What are our competitive strengths and weaknesses?;
- What are our objectives, and are these objectives realistic?;
- What mix of industries is most appropriate for achieving our objectives? What specific firm's needs are compatible with our pluses?;

- Given this *targeting* information and having determined our optimal matches, how can these data be translated into appropriate marketing tactics?

Such considerations are inherent in an economic development effort that is marketing oriented.

Once a marketing-oriented philosophy is adopted, the key to success lies in its implementation. Too often economic development programs are geared to responding to what we call the generic level of "prospect" location influences, that is, what companies in general want from a location. However, the matching process involves a recognition that there are other levels of corporate-location decision making. The more the city or state knows about a prospect's *specific needs*—the criteria that will determine the firm's final location decision—the better its success in developing a package or approach to attract that firm. Even the generic location influences are different, of course, depending on whether or not the location decision involves a corporate headquarters move. (In a corporate headquarters move, companies place more emphasis on community *esprit de corps* and less on *factors of production.*)

How might a marketing orientation be implemented? We offer a marketing strategy and planning schema that economic development units may employ in identifying and then successfully "targeting-in" on prospects. The tactics recommended are quite consistent with our insistence on the city or state, or both, responding to the prospect's needs.

∞

Relatively few individuals involved in economic development programs are trained marketers. This is not surprising because the private sector tends to grab the young graduating marketer and few, if any, college marketing programs have shown any interest in training students for so-called nonprofit careers.

Yet, to someone with an extensive marketing background, the conclusion one would draw from reading the book to this point would be, "What the economic development industry needs is some pure marketing-oriented professionals." Obviously, this is an overstatement, and there are some excellent marketers in this field. However, it is our conclusion from our research that a marketing perspective is seriously lacking in a large proportion of state and city programs.

As we review the typical economic incentive packages, we find that they often are based on a fundamental error. They fail to distinguish between a supply-side and a demand-side market situation. Perhaps we can best explain this difference with an illustration. A few years ago, one of us was giving a talk to a group of Latin business school deans in Colombia on the importance of having marketing in the business school curriculum. These educators came from all over South America—Chile, Brazil, Peru, and so forth. After the presentation, a dean of an Ecuadorian business school mentioned that his university was just exploring the possibility of adding a course in marketing for the first time. He said, "As long as our country's main problem was one of simply trying to supply enough of any given product to meet local needs and goods were always in short supply, we had no need for marketing. In fact, until now we did not have the luxury of competition; people were lucky to find one of something . . . they had *no* choice." What he described was a short-supply situation, a situation in which a supply-orientation was appropriate. Typically, the producer in this "shortage" situation is not really concerned with what the buyer wants; the customer will be happy to take what the manufacturer wishes to offer or, at best, what the manufacturer thinks the buyer may want or tolerate. With competition, however, the producer must become concerned about the buyer and his or her wishes; the producer must be demand- or market-oriented. And, it is in such a market-oriented or demand-oriented situation that the skilled marketer excels.

How is this Ecuadorian illustration relevant to economic development as we see it today? The answer may be too obvious. We see many city, state, and international economic development programs being run with almost total disregard for their prospective buyers. We find their incentive packages and development programs put together on a "what-we-want-to-offer (or can offer)" basis, rather than on a "what-do-relocating-companies-really-want" basis. Further, a devastating assumption made by many is that the company's site-selection decision will be totally financially-driven; the company will take the highest bid. Given this assumption, city councils will argue throughout the evening over "what they can get away with" in terms of tax concessions without any idea whatsoever as to whether these concessions will stimulate new industrial investment. Many seem more concerned with matching competition, which assumes that the competition has some rationale for its offer. And like the crossroads that has four service stations vying for customers through a price war or giveaways, this often merely results in lower tax revenues for all the competing communities, as well as some unhappy local companies which become dissatisfied because newcomers get all the concessions. Our research has identified more than one company that made its initial decision to leave an area when it began to see outsiders receiving all of the tax incentives. However, as the last two chapters have shown, the company decisions are not driven solely by financial bids.

P.T. BARNUM AND THE SATURN WAR

If P.T. Barnum were still alive, he likely would have been awed by the success of CEO Roger Smith and his management team at General Motors. By simply feeding a work-hungry U.S. populace with bits of information and saying "almost every state and community has a chance to land the Saturn project," General Motors created more attention than Barnum's famous Cardiff Giant and generated an unprecedented level of economic development program warfare. Earlier we talked about the Second War Between the States, but would Abe Lincoln and Jeff Davis have debated their relative causes on the Phil Donahue show? Not likely! Yet, Donahue was able to bring the governors of several states to his show and have them try to sell their state to GM representatives who were also present. How was the Saturn site selection orchestrated? Well, GM dropped a little hint here and a little hint there, but stopped short of establishing any real guidelines. For example, Smith was reported to have said rather early in the race that economically-battered states had no chance and that incentives would not be the basis for GM's decision.[1] But, in the same breath a company spokesman repeated the earlier claim that only Florida had been ruled out. The states, buoyed by the prospect of jobs and unsure as to what GM (or any company) really wanted, charged forward with concessions. (And state efforts were magnified by individual city efforts that sometimes complemented, but oftentimes competed, with the states.) "What can we *give* GM" was the watchword of the efforts, and the nature and level of the incentives escalated on a daily basis. It were as if GM wanted to make a point: Most states and cities really do not understand corporate needs at all, and we (GM) are not going to help by pointing them out; let's see how far they will go. The final selection, of course, became anticlimatic to us, because

Saturn itself had provided the best possible raison d'etre for this book. It clearly established that (1) most of the competing states, cities, and so forth, knew little about corporate-location decision making, and (2) most of these economic development groups had not carefully identified those companies or industries that should be their prime targets. They merely were casting a big net in hopes of catching a "keeper" and they would not miss any opportunity regardless of the stakes involved.

ASSUMING A DEMAND-SIDE MARKETING ORIENTATION

To simplify matters, we are going to make several key assumptions about the economic development battleground today. These are:

- The struggle by states and cities for new investment—headquarters moves or plant or subsidiary moves—is fiercely competitive. It is *not* a foregone conclusion that the Sunbelt will always beat the Rustbelt, for example;
- The states and cities need to offer a minimal financial incentive program in order to meet the "table stakes"—in order to play the game. (These include some type of tax incentive program and industrial bonds or financing.) But, few location decisions will be made on financial packages alone;
- The company's traditional checklist approach for sorting out its final location is useful at best for narrowing the competition to two or three locales (states or cities within a state). Qualitative factors become preeminent in the end.

Given these assumptions, the economic development group in any state, city, or county can readily employ many of the marketing tools that have been carefully honed by corporate marketers. Certainly, major corporations do make marketing-related mistakes themselves, as the recent "new Coke" fiasco tells us, and not all are equally proficient. However, marketing insight can even be gained from blunders, as well as success stories. Let us look at Coca-Cola. This major multinational company had really underestimated how success-ful it had been in developing its corporate authority* over the years. The company had developed a strong belief in its basic product (Coca-Cola); it had made Coke appear to be a product that represented the "golden days" of America. America might be having problems with terrorists, the superdollar, and its world-leader role, but one could still count on Coca-Cola never changing. "Coke is it" in fact had been its

---

*(*Corporate authority* is a term that represents a combination of a company's image, awareness, and market share. Companies with high corporate authority not only have achieved a high market share, but have strong levels of awareness and image as well.)

most recent campaign theme prior to the introduction of the new product. To many, Coca-Cola ranked right along with mom, Chevrolet, hot dogs, and apple pie. Then, Chevrolet joined forces with the "enemy" (Japan) to produce an automobile—the Nova. This apparent heresy was closely followed by the announcement of a new Coke taste, an act that was more than many patriotic Americans could swallow. (It was the type of action that would drive the American humorist Jean Shephard to decry our fate.) In a marketing sense, however, what Coca-Cola had done was to take an action that was *inconsistent* with its deeply embedded image. This would be akin to Hawaii saying that they do *not* want to be considered a vacation paradise and that people were wrong to have ever held this perception of the state. Stated simply, Coke's basic error was that it underestimated the strength of its image. An image can be changed, but it requires extensive effort, and becomes an objective in and of itself. Once the "Coca-Cola dilemma" is recognized as a potential problem that can be avoided, economic development groups should not fall into such an image trap, and a useful lesson is learned from a corporate experience.

TRANSFERRING THE CORPORATE MODEL

What can be learned from the corporate marketing model? How might the experience that has made foreign-based producers envious of U.S. marketing techniques and the United States the most marketing-competitive country in the world, be transferred to economic development organizations? In this chapter, we have developed a schema that demonstrates just how economic development groups can apply marketing principles in their industry-attraction efforts.

But, first, let us consider several basic questions that need to be answered by a city or state, as the economic development unit moves toward a marketing orientation.

• What is our *image?* Does our city or state have one, and, if so, how deeply imbedded is it in the public's mind? The more deeply implanted the image, the more difficult will be the credibility problems you will have, if you want to change or alter the image. For example, when Pittsburgh was chosen as America's top metropolitan area (the best place to live) by Rand McNally's *Places Rated Almanac,*[2] a great hue and cry arose from other cities and the research by Boyer and Savageau was challenged. Why? The answer is that this was inconsistent with the public's view of "the Steel City"; it was a credibility issue. Pittsburgh had altered itself physically, but it had not altered America's perceptions of it. Tulsa's city officials, for example, might have accepted Raleigh/Durham, San Francisco, or Boston's higher ratings, but Pittsburgh—no way. Corporate marketers on the other hand are well aware of the credibility problems relating to claiming that you are *something* that the public believes you are *not*. They recognize that image-altering efforts often must precede any claims and that these efforts need to be taken in a progressive fashion. An excellent illustration is provided by Beatrice Foods, which fully recognized that extensive efforts were necessary to support its product claims and embarked on an image-building campaign with the 1984 Summer Olympics that continued at least through mid-1985.

- What are our competitive strengths and weaknesses? This requires a very objective analysis and may, in fact, require an assessment by an outside consultant. Further, it must be remembered that the competition is not simply a neighboring community; Brownsville, Texas, may be competing with Mobile, Alabama, and Tampa, Florida, if a company (or the federal government) wants a Gulf Port city. And, we are talking about all facets of a state or local community including image, existing industry, infrastructure, or community or state attitude. Oregon, for example, has apparently had some difficulty overcoming an earlier reluctance to welcome newcomers, but still has been competitive in attracting Japanese concerns[3] which may, of course, be aware of its earlier image.

- What are our objectives? And, very importantly, are these objectives realistic? Many states and communities want to emulate Silicon Valley and, similarly, we see the rush to be *the* biotechnology center. Few, if any, have the attributes needed to accomplish this sort of objective and, thus, many locales need to be braced for failure. On the other hand, although Henry Cisnero's (San Antonio mayor) trip to Hong Kong to offer a haven to dispossessed Chinese capitalists undoubtedly drew some incredulous stares and comments from his peers, his effort was far from an unrealistic junket. Although San Antonio may have a relatively small Chinese community, Texas and San Antonio certainly were able to offer a capitalistic climate that these Hong Kong business leaders would find appealing. And, whether this was part of Cisnero's grand plan for San Antonio or just part of the opportunistic, can-do spirit so characteristic of the young mayor, the Hong Kong business community does have qualities that would be consistent with the international and border trading environment that has been one of that city's pluses. Another city, Memphis, has placed its bets on distribution, on being *the* distribution center, which on the surface at least is realistic considering its very central location.

- Given our objectives, what mix of industries is most appropriate for achieving them? And, what is the match between our attributes and the requirements of these industries? This is not a simple one- or two-question quiz, however. For example, some cities or states say, "We have water!" Fine, and there are manufacturers who need a huge supply of water. But, a lot of places have water; therefore, that plus just keeps a city or state with available water in the running. Buffalo (New York) and Golden (Colorado) each have water, but one has "mountain water" that matches Coors' needs and the other has access to the Great Lakes with its transport potential. At this point, the next level or levels of industry (relocation or subsidiary-building firms) needs should also be investigated. Business-to-business and consumer product manufacturers do detailed analyses of their potential customers. Further, these manufacturers develop not only quantitative information, but qualitative as well. It is this marketing lesson that must be transferred to economic development groups. For example, who in the firm actually makes the site-selection decision, and how is the decision made?

- Given our *targeting* information and having determined our appropriate matches, we now need to ask how we translate this data into appropriate marketing tactics. What media do we need to employ to reach the right decision makers? What does our product (incentive and other data package) need to include? Where do we need to go overseas and in the United States to establish our onsite offices? What type of sales force do we need; what type of background do they need if we are dealing with the targeted industries? Let us consider a few illustrations here. Memphis is now employing cable television to reach the target market it is seeking, a unique targeting effort. Another medium that is rarely employed to reach specific industries is the trade show, one that is appropriate to these specific fields. This is somewhat surprising when one considers that overseas, states often have representatives at trade fairs. Regarding onsite offices, states such as Ohio, Louisiana, and Missouri have had one or more offices overseas that serve as their base of economic development operations in key foreign markets. (Many of these locations are primarily for trade, rather than for attracting or obtaining foreign investment.) However, how many states have economic development offices in target locations, such as Silicon Valley?

These questions suggest the types of considerations that are (or will become) second nature to an economic development group with a marketing-orientation.

IMPLEMENTATION

In the remainder of this chapter, we will suggest ways that economic development groups can employ marketing strategies and tactics. But, at the outset, we need to sound one caution, one which stresses that there is *no single utopian formula for success in marketing economic development programs,* nor marketing anything for that matter. In fact, pseudomarketers over the years have offered a plethora of false hopes to companies everywhere; the "all-you-need-is-more-motivational-research" type of ballyhoo.

A frustration for any marketer is that no two customers have totally identical reasons for buying a product or selecting a particular site.

ILLUSTRATION 10.1

Changing perceptions.

POINT OF DEPARTURE

The Port of Pittsburgh: the busiest inland port in the United States. It all comes together here.

Transportation. The ability to move products and people between a company and its markets quickly and economically. Business depends on this.

As a city, Pittsburgh offers major facilities in air, highway and rail transportation.

As a port, Pittsburgh offers even more. A Foreign Trade Zone. The 8,954-mile inland waterway system. This

network of canalized rivers stretches through 24 states to New Orleans, providing water linkage to ports around the world.

The Port of Pittsburgh, based at "The Point" in downtown Pittsburgh, is a great point of departure for a dynamic business community. Each year, well over 60 million tons of cargo are shipped on its waterways, more than

any other inland port in the country. And, its location makes it a great point for intermodal shipping, where barge, rail and truck combine to create the most cost-effective transportation available.

But the Port offers more than transportation. It provides every resource you and your company need to grow and prosper...capital, infrastructure, energy, education, sports, culture. It's a place of business where the people live and work at a friendly pace.

The Port of Pittsburgh will make a great starting point for your business. For more information about relocation or new business development,

write or call Marketing Coordinator, Port of Pittsburgh, Allegheny County Department of Development, 100 Fort Pitt Commons, 445 Fort Pitt Boulevard, Pittsburgh, PA 15219, (412) 355-5838 (5841).

A great starting point.

PORT OF PITTSBURGH

This advertisement developed by The Port Authority of Allegheny County with financial support from the Commonwealth of Pennsylvania. Department of Commerce

Advertisement reprinted with the permission of Allegheny County Department of Development.

ILLUSTRATION 10.2

Exemplary recognition of a city's prime potential.

MEMPHIS.
DISTRIBUTION
BULLSEYE.

When you land on Memphis you'll hit the bullseye for multi-region and national distribution. It's uniquely located for multi-region access. It has superb transportation and communications facilities and services, in all major modes. And government, business and the public are zero'd in to the needs of distribution. That's why Memphis is America's Distribution Center for both goods and information.

Multi-region Consolidation Cuts Costs
Because of the enormous costs of carrying duplicate inventories, leading firms are now consolidating at locations accessible to more of their market or to multiple regions. Memphis is a natural "bullseye" for multi-region or national movement. It's the perfect hub for Southeast/Southwest, Midsouth/Midwest and national distribution, more efficiently situated than Dallas, Houston, Atlanta or Chicago. From Memphis, you can reach 60% of the nation's population overnight by truck or rail.

Memphis Transportation Moves Fast
Everything moves fast in Memphis because there are so many ways of moving it...air, rail, river

or road...and year round because of climate. In Memphis, you'll find transportation that matches the need and the speed of your requirements, from guaranteed overnight delivery of small parts to bulk barge river shipments. In Memphis there's no monopoly on service. You'll find 96 fixed route common carriers, six class one railroads, six barge lines, eight major airlines, 42 air freight carriers and the national hub of Federal Express, all in tune with your need for speed and reliability.

Put Us to the Test
Things do move faster at America's Distribution Center. To prove it, call our toll free number as you leave the office this evening—you'll have our complete facts file on your desk tomorrow—guaranteed—showing you how you'll hit the Distribution Bullseye with a move to Memphis, America's Distribution Center.

Call Toll Free:
800-238-1200
America's Distribution Center. c/o Memphis Area Chamber of Commerce, P.O. Box 224-D, Memphis, TN 38101. In Tennessee call 901/523-2322.

MEMPHIS
America's Distribution Center

315

ILLUSTRATION 10.3

Strong testimony of a state's new found concern for a company's specific needs. If effective, this approach leads to a vigorous reinvestment climate.

"Michigan's support gave my business the boost it needed."

Dave Bing, President, Bing Steel Inc.

Things are looking up for business in Michigan. Business and government have left the era of finding fault; instead, we're finding solutions.

Dave Bing is one Michigan businessman who has witnessed the change in our economic climate. And benefited from it.

"The whole way of thinking in Michigan has changed. Michigan's government is actively supporting business, both small and large. And it's not just lip service. There's a strong commitment to making business work here. And that support was exactly what Bing Steel needed."

Working side by side, business and government are finding innovative solutions to the problems faced by businesses like Bing Steel.

Solutions that include tax-abatement and job-training programs. Changes in the securities law that give small businesses easier access to venture capital. A reduction in red tape that has cut down approval time on loans for businesses like Bing

Steel by as much as five months. Though work still remains, Michigan has tackled problem areas with the enthusiasm and commitment needed to get results. And results we have. Just listen to Dave Bing.

"The government's support provided Bing Steel with an important missing link. They didn't just help me secure a loan to purchase and renovate my second plant; they also provided me with the leverage I needed to get financing for the installation of equipment.

"The state has really gone out of its way to participate in and support the development of small business."

Michigan is willing to help your business, too.

For more information, write:
Doug Ross, Director
Michigan Department of Commerce
Lansing, Michigan 48909

YES MICHIGAN

Michigan business, the answer is yes.

Advertisement reprinted with the permission of the Michigan Department of Commerce.

Just as quickly, however, we need to add that it is possible to reduce the areas of difference and to identify as many similarities as possible. In the following section, we discuss the generic location influences that we have identified with our research. These help the economic development organization to better understand what companies in general are seeking, but the economic development group will need to go further. It may be helpful to visualize an inverted pyramid [see page 317] with each "layer" of effort becoming more specific to the company's particular needs. The economic development group, in other words, must seek to develop a better and better understanding of its targeted industries and companies.

Then we will offer a schema that identifies the steps we feel that the economic development organizations need to follow in their marketing efforts. Again, these are general guidelines, but ones that can provide the kind of action plan that is needed today. This schema and its related discussion are what we feel to be the central core of this chapter.

CORPORATE-LOCATION DECISION MAKING

A company's relocation and expansion decision making involves several rather distinct phases. To successfully target specific companies, an economic development group must gain insight into corporate needs at each of these independent levels. As our research has indicated, some of the firm's decision criteria are quantitatively based and comparisons between competing cities or states, or both, are rather easily made. For those that are more subjective (and often even difficult to articulate), however, the job of matching community or state strengths with company requirements is more difficult.

Before proceeding further, consider the nature of each of these decision-making phases, as shown in Exhibit 10.1.

- *Phase I: Evaluation of generic state/community factors.* Generic factors include the traditional elements ranging from climate and other quality-of-life concerns to corporate tax rates. The checklist of factors is extensive and lists include those from such sources as the Society of Industrial Realtors and *Inc. Magazine.* Although firms may assign different weights to each factor or even ignore certain factors, these factors apply to all companies; they are generic to relocation and expansion decisions. Generally, these factors are quantifiable and economists have considered this to be *the* decision level. But, in reality, this phase results in the retaining of two or more states or communities—typically no more than five—for consideration in Phase II.
- *Phase II: Evaluation of specific corporate needs/preferences.* There are a number of related, judgmental factors that play a crucial role in the company's location decision. Some of these company-specific criteria are based on the top management's longer-term goals and

objectives. Others may be based on specific marketing or financial considerations. Such factors in the phase would include: (1) current or desired image compatibility; (2) future sourcing and prospecting objectives; (3) change in geographic orientation; (4) labor leverage goals; (5) key personnel retention/acquisition; (6) capital position (amount of excess capital, desired retained earnings, etc.); (7) predicted competition (long-term competitor analysis results; and (8) acquisition objectives. In fact, it is here that claims that the CEO chose to move to a Sunbelt city to play year-round golf often have validity, but merely as one consideration.** When Phase II is completed, only one state, and one to three adjacent communities, remain in consideration.

- *Phase III: Evaluation of real-property particulars.* Real-property particulars involve all activities relating to the selection of the actual construction site. As the firm's location decision makers enter this phase, they will have already selected a community or metropolitan area. In the case of the latter, there may be more than one political jurisdiction still being considered and the selection will depend on real-property availabilities. (Often a metropolitan area contains an extensive number of small communities, a number of which would be equally attractive, and the decision will rest on the construction

EXHIBIT 10.1

Phases in Site-Selection Decision Making

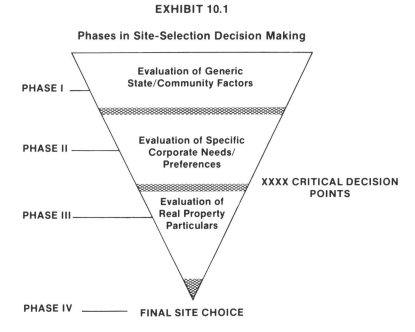

** With some of the factors, the question might be raised that they can be accommodated in Phase I. However, they require deeper, more judgmental *probing* and are less quantifiable than they would be if they were treated in Phase I.

site qualities.) Take, for example, a company that needs, among other things, to have accessibility to a port or good rail service. At the completion of Phase I, only those states or cities with the needed port or rail service will remain under consideration. Now, in Phase III, the company may wish to choose an industrial park in the selected city that has the most direct access to the port or railroad. In this phase, everything from soil composition, drainage, and site preparation costs, to land prices are considered. At the completion of this phase, a construction site has been selected.

- *Phase IV: Final site choice.* The decision is approved and implemented. Some degree of overlap or *blurring* occurs between the phases. That is, the nature of the line (critical decision point) separating the various phases shown in Exhibit 10.1 reflects this blurring. For example, part of Phase I for a given company may involve construction-site considerations (Phase III) if all acceptable states or cities must have an available industrial park with a particular soil composition. However, with such exceptions, the phases described reflect the different levels of corporate-location decision making that were shown by our research.

What does this corporate location decision making approach mean to the economic development unit? Most economic development groups focus their marketing efforts at Phase I, and most industrial realtors direct their targeting efforts toward Phases I and III, principally Phase III. The former is quite similar to the way business-to-business marketers viewed their customers or potential customers for many years; they made the critical error of considering their buyers to be totally economic-oriented—the so-called rational person of economic lore. Now, however, business-to-business marketers devote a good share of their marketing research to obtaining qualitative insights on their prospects (companies and their decision makers) or the equivalent of economic development groups being concerned about Phase II of the decision process. To ignore a vital corporate decision-making step can lead economic development groups to make critical errors in their marketing efforts.

How can (and when should) economic development groups implement their efforts to obtain Phase II data on their prospects, in order to better match their needs and desires? First, we wish to make it clear that we are not proposing that some sort of "corporate espionage" be employed on prospects. Yet, we do feel that it is essential to learn more about a targeted prospect's real goals and objectives than you would typically determine if you focus on Phase I. We suggest a sequence of targeting efforts that we see as realistic, considering the staff and budget level available to most economic development organizations.

- Begin by identifying your target industry or industries and the prospect firms in that industry or those industries.
- Inquire about these prospect firms' relocation and expansion plans.

- Provide *basic* Phase I information to all the initial prospect firms, but particularly to those planning to make a location decision—the "hot prospects."
- Conduct more detailed (qualitative) research on those identified as hot prospects. This step includes secondary research, survey research, and even personal interviews or focus groups where feasible.
- Carefully and objectively assess the strengths and weaknesses of your community or state's profile against the needs and preferences of the hot prospects.
- Where the matches seem competitively close—where you feel that you can make the Phase I cut in the prospect's decision making— develop a special presentation, including incentive package, multimedia, and so forth, that directly speaks to the company's needs. In other words, make it the most appropriate, company-specific type of "offer" you can prepare.

While some may argue that this more detailed and elaborate approach is too costly, the fundamental question remains, "Is this approach more costly than firing a shotgun salvo in the hopes of hitting a prospect?" Or, better still, "Is this too costly when hundreds of jobs are at stake?"

Finally, we add that this same concept can be employed in examining which, if any, local industry expansions should be encouraged and fostered by the public sector. By obtaining Phase II-type inputs from local companies, it is often possible to determine which have the best long-term potential and could provide the sort of employment and tax base enhancement the city or state desires.

GENERIC LOCATION INFLUENCES

In chapters 8 and 9, we discussed corporate evaluations of the importance of various locational influences in selecting headquarters, plant or subsidiary locations. Early on in that discussion, we promised to eventually simplify the mass of complex data presented in chapters 8 and 9. In order to deliver on this promise, we applied the statistical technique known as factor analysis to the plethora of information we obtained from the roughly 100 companies that took part in our study. These companies represented a diversity of industries and, in terms of size, ran the gamut from *Inc. 500s* to *Fortune 500s.*

Factor analysis is a high-powered statistical tool for cutting through data, simplifying it, and thereby making it more understandable. Technically, it is a method for determining the number and nature of the underlying variables among larger numbers of measures. For example, if 30 to 35 locational influences (measures) appear to affect a company's choice of a location for a new plant, into how many categories and underlying variables can these influences be grouped?

Five or six ostensibly independent locational influences may really be perceived by companies as being part of a single more generic influence. Take quality of life. This generic locational influence encompasses numerous and more specific measures, such as culture, education, and recreational opportunities. Factor analysis would tell us which measures are grouped under quality of life when respondents' (100 companies in this case) answers are analyzed accordingly. In factor analysis, the respondents neither explicitly identify generic categories nor which locational influences fall under generic categories; instead, the technique figures it out, so to speak, from the way respondents answer individual questions about the relative importance of location influences.

We want to emphasize that no general listing of generic locational influences is by itself adequate for formulating marketing strategies for economic development programs. A more segmented approach is needed. For instance, high-technology companies are likely to have different "educational" requirements for selecting a community to locate in than will corporations engaged in heavy manufacturing. *Nonetheless, we have found certain generic influences underlie all corporate-location decisions and we believe that attention to these basic influences is the best place for a state or community to begin to conceive an economic development strategy: The influence categories provide a useful frame of reference for conceptualizing and decision making.*

What varies between and among companies across industries is not the generic location influences, but rather the importance weightings that each places on the same generic influences. For example, whereas a chemical manufacturer is likely to be far more concerned than a service firm with infrastructure, the latter would not ignore infrastructure entirely. In other words, infrastructure would be an important decision influence to both the chemical company and the service firm, but not to the same magnitude. A first-rate water or waste system might be a "plus" for the service company, but would be "mandatory" for the manufacturer.

The marketer of economic development needs to begin the marketing task with a fundamental understanding of what generic categories *all companies* look for in potential locations. Second, he or she then needs to appreciate what kinds of more specific locational influences tend to be perceived by companies as being subsets of these generic categories. The marketer also must determine how well his or her state or community fares on each and every generic category, in the eyes of companies locating or relocating facilities, vis-a-vis the competition for economic development—whether it be other states, communities, or even countries. Keep in mind that what is most relevant here is how the state or community is actually perceived by companies or industries it wishes to attract or keep, not how the state or community thinks it is perceived or ought to be perceived. Recently, for example, a newspaper poll of business executives in an industrial city found that, given the opportunity to move elsewhere, one-third of them would do so. The city's economic development director reacted by focusing on why the executives were wrong in their perceptions, instead of addressing why the negativism existed and what might be done to change it.

Our findings pertaining to key generic location influences, as revealed by factor analysis of the responses from the 100 corporations that participated in our study, are depicted in Exhibit 10.2. Note that four of the generic categories are the same for headquarters *and* plant or subsidiary decisions, as follows:

- General economic attractiveness
- Human resources
- Infrastructure
- Quality of life

EXHIBIT 10.2

Key Generic Location Influences

Headquarters Location Decisions	Plant/Subsidiary Location Decisions
1. General economic attractiveness	1. General economic attractiveness
2. Human resources	2. Human resources
3. Infrastructure	3. Infrastructure
4. Quality of life	4. Quality of life
5. Community esprit de corps	5. Factors of production

Typical definitions of these key generic location influences, again as determined from factor analysis of the corporate responses, are given in Exhibit 10.3.

So, for both headquarters and plant or subsidiary location decisions, companies look for a state's or community's general economic attractiveness, its human resource capabilities, the quality of its infrastructure, and its quality of life. However, the fifth generic location influence is not identical for headquarters and plant or subsidiary decisions. As pointed out in Exhibit 10.2, the fifth key influence for headquarters decisions is what we call community esprit de corps, or the presence of a "can-do" spirit on the part of community leaders. For headquarters especially, companies want to be part of a progressive, probusiness environment. Although this subjective "can-do" influence may also be helpful to a community in attracting plants and subsidiaries as well, it is imperative for attracting headquarters facilities.

The fifth key generic influence for plant- or subsidiary-location decisions is embodied in the nomenclature *factors of production.* When it comes to plants and subsidiaries, companies look to locate in areas with the "right" educational and occupational skills existing in the work force. "Right," of course, depends on the industry or company involved. In addition, proximity to needed raw materials and natural resources is another important component of the factors of production category. Apparently companies are more willing to bring in properly skilled and educated workers from elsewhere for staffing headquarters operations than they are for filling jobs in plant and subsidiary facilities.

EXHIBIT 10.3

Typical Definitions of the Generic Location Influences

General Economic Attractiveness	Human Resources
In, or a suburb of, a major population center	Existence of strong work ethic
Local/state government programs, other than taxes	Good labor-relations climate
	Low rate of unionization
Plentiful venture capital	Relatively low cost of living
Progressive banking institutions	Relatively low wage/salary levels
Proximity to the company's major markets	
Tax rates on businesses	

Infrastructure	Quality of Life
Availability of water/waste system	Community safety
Good transportation facilities for moving goods	Favorable ecological conditions
Quality of utilities	Good transportation facilities for business travel
	Housing availability for employees
	Quality college/university nearby
	Quality primary/secondary school system
	Recreational opportunities and parks
	Rich cultural environment
	Tax rates on individuals

Factors of Production	Community Esprit De Corps
Availability of skilled/educated work force	"Can-do" spirit on part of community leaders
Proximity to needed raw materials and natural resources	

In summary, companies tend to evaluate both potential headquarters and plant or subsidiary locations on four key considerations: (1) economic attractiveness, (2) human resources, (3) infrastructure, and (4) quality of life. The fifth key influence for headquarters-facility decisions is community esprit de corps; for plant or subsidiary operations, it is factors of production.

A few qualifications to these guidelines are in order. First, a moderate-to-warm climate is an *instrumental* quality-of-life consideration to *some* companies, but not to most. Second, housing availability for employees is more important for plant or subsidiary decisions than for headquarters moves. The reason for this is simply that plants and subsidiaries are more likely than headquarters facilities to be located in rural areas where there is often less to choose from in housing. Third, being in, or a suburb of, a major population center is usually the preferred choice for a corporate headquarters, which is not necessarily

EXHIBIT 10.4

A Marketing Strategy and Planning Schema for Economic Development

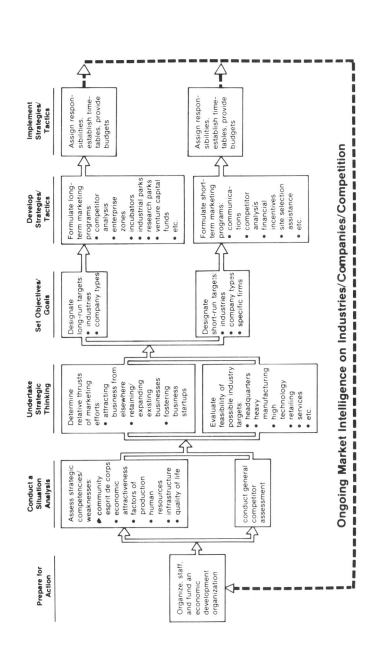

Prepare for Action

Organize, staff, and fund an economic development organization

Conduct a Situation Analysis

Assess strategic competencies/ weaknesses:
- community esprit de corps
- economic attractiveness
- factors of production
- human resources
- infrastructure
- quality of life

conduct general competitor assessment

Undertake Strategic Thinking

Determine relative thrusts of marketing efforts:
- attracting business from elsewhere
- retaining/ expanding existing businesses
- fostering business startups

Evaluate feasibility of possible industry targets:
- headquarters
- heavy manufacturing
- high technology
- retailing
- services
- etc.

Set Objectives/ Goals

Designate long-run targets:
- industries
- company types

Designate short-run targets:
- industries
- company types
- specific firms

Develop Strategies/ Tactics

Formulate long-term marketing programs:
- competitor analysis
- enterprise zones
- incubators
- industrial parks
- research parks
- venture capital funds
- etc.

Formulate short-term marketing programs:
- communications
- competitor analysis
- financial incentives
- site selection assistance
- etc.

Implement Strategies/ Tactics

Assign responsibilities, establish timetables, provide budgets

Assign responsibilities, establish timetables, provide budgets

Ongoing Market Intelligence on Industries/Companies/Competition the case for plants and subsidiaries. Thus, an urban or suburban site is often an additional determinant of economic and quality-of-life attractiveness for headquarters-location decisions. Fourth, as might be expected, the existence of a first-rate scientific community is a far more important human resource influence to high-tech companies than it is to companies in general.

MARKETING STRATEGY AND PLANNING FOR ECONOMIC DEVELOPMENT

Our recommended marketing strategy and planning process for economic development is founded on the considerable amount of research and inquiry underpinning this whole book. We think the process, shown phase by phase in the schema in Exhibit 10.4, provides economic development strategists with an easily-grasped conceptual blueprint for organizing and marshaling their resources in pursuit of their industrial-growth mission.

PREPARE FOR ACTION

Fundamental to any successful economic development effort on a sustained basis is a well-organized, adequately-funded, and competently staffed organization. Show us a state or community without one and we will almost always see mediocre results at best.

What constitutes well-organized varies across situations. New York City and a small community obviously have quite different organizational requirements. For purposes of simplicity, we will talk in terms of larger entities—states and bigger cities—and smaller political subdivisions—medium-sized to small communities, recognizing full well that a continuum from large-to-small exists.

Larger political entities need full-time development organizations. These may be public-sector, private-sector, or, most likely, both. It is common in big cities for taxpayer-supported economic development groups to coexist with private organizations, such as arms of chambers of commerce, growth associations, committees comprised of business and community leaders, and venture-capital funds. Where the best results have occurred are in those places in which the public- and private-sector groups have worked together for the common good of the state or city. These groups coordinate their efforts and view one another not as rivals, adversaries, or even enemies, but rather as partners. The best-laid economic development plans and strategies will not achieve expectations if community bickering between the public and private sector is the case. So much historical evidence exists on this point that it is not arguable.

In a state or big-city development organization there needs to be careful attention and individual, but coordinated, strategies concerning the three main branches of economic development—attracting new businesses from out of state or out of town, retaining and expanding existing businesses, and fostering business start-ups.

We have found instances time and again where a state or city has devoted far too much attention to the strategy of inducing businesses from elsewhere to relocate in the state or city. In the process, the other two branches of economic development have suffered.

Inadequate concern for the strategy of retaining and expanding existing businesses—those already located in a state or community—is a monumental oversight. A state or community generally has a much better chance of getting a business already there to stay and expand, than it does to entice a business from elsewhere to pull up stakes and move or to expand in a community new to them. A certain amount of inertia is involved whenever a company considers a move. So, within an economic development organization, there should be programs and staff devoted largely or exclusively to business retention and expansion. Kentucky, for example, is a state that has done just this. We know of situations, however, where so much has been done for out-of-state or out-of-city business interests that existing businesses have been miffed and eventually moved some or all of their facilities. Before special incentives are offered to coveted businesses, the effects on existing businesses need to be evaluated. And that is where economic development officers who focus on retention and expansion of existing businesses play a vital role.

Similarly, a state or large city should concern itself a great deal with fostering business start-ups. As we have tried to emphasize, businesses that get their start in a place have excellent odds of remaining there. Moreover, these smaller businesses are critical to job creation; they have been responsible for much of the new job creation in the United States. Even in Europe and Japan, which have traditionally looked down on entrepreneurs but whose economies have slowed down lately, there is now, understandably, considerable public- and private-sector emphasis on entrepreneurship. A state's or city's endeavors along these lines might include, for instance, working with the private sector to establish venture-capital funds, incubators to house and counsel business start-ups, and support of small-business development centers at local colleges and universities. One or more people in an economic development office must be assigned to such duties if the job is to get done properly.

What we recommend is an organizational concept borrowed from the private sector and used by such eminent marketers as Proctor & Gamble—the product (or brand) manager form of organization. In this arrangement, each major product—Tide, Dreft, Pringles, Jiffy, and so forth—is under the auspice of a product manager whose job it is to market and shepherd his or her assigned brand. In economic development offices, the three branches of industrial development—attracting business from other locales, retaining and expanding existing businesses, and facilitating business start-ups—could be viewed as three products (or services) to be managed, marketed, and shepherded by their own individual product managers.

Available resources in medium-sized to smaller cities usually cannot support the scope and magnitude of economic development organizations in states and big cities. Nonetheless, organizing around the three major economic development tasks—again, attracting business from elsewhere, retaining and expanding existing business, and fostering business start-ups—is still the most effective way of going about marketing economic development. Making someone responsible for each task is the best way to ensure that the job gets done. Even in small communities with no formal economic development organizations per se, where the mayor and community leaders handle development, efforts are best organized around these three tasks. Otherwise, *all* the tasks are not likely to receive appropriate attention and, most probably, retention or expansion and business start-ups will suffer at the expense of attempts to entice new businesses from other locales.

As for staffing, we suggest that the very best people available be hired for marketing economic development. Oftentimes in the public sector, salary levels are simply inadequate to attract and retain people with the necessary skills and experience. For example, after only two productive years, Ohio lost its dynamic economic development director to a more lucrative position in the private sector. In our view, one way to mitigate this kind of turnover dilemma is for the private sector in a state or community to supplement public salaries for key economic development executives. This tack, in fact, was tried in Ohio but political sentiment against it persuaded the governor to back off. But this need not be the case, indeed should not be the case, if a state or city is to hire and keep first-rate people for marketing economic development. Considerations such as how much economic development officials earn compared to their bosses—governors, mayors, or the like—must be set aside; the economic development job is too vital to let it be understaffed by objections based on ego and jealousy. How a state or city reacts to an innovative approach to staffing economic development offices is in itself a commentary on how serious it is about creating new jobs. It reflects whether the state or city really has a "can-do" spirit.

Traditionally, economic development organizations were heavily staffed with individuals educated and trained in public administration and economics. This is changing more and more as the competition for economic development heats up. Development offices are seeking to hire people with proven marketing backgrounds. We see this trend as a natural outgrowth of a more competitive environment. However, to get and keep experienced marketers, salaries will have to be competitive with the private sector.

Finally, we point out that a state or community economic development office must be well funded if it is to effectively do its job. The most ably staffed and carefully designed marketing program imaginable will fail in implementation if there is not enough money to execute it. Promotion and advertising alone are expensive endeavors. Again, sometimes a combination public sector/private sector approach to funding can get the job done. For instance, a city economic development office could be partially funded by a growth association or chamber of commerce, for example.

CONDUCT A SITUATION ANALYSIS

Assess strategic competencies/weaknesses. The first step in conducting a situation analysis (i.e., determining where we stand today in relation to our environment and competition) is to take a hard and objective look at a state's or city's strengths and limitations. This step requires some sound market research; what a state or city thinks of itself versus what others, in this case corporate executives who make facility-location decisions, think of it may be quite different. Only independent and unbiased market studies can provide the data a political entity needs to assess its pros and cons. So, our suggestion in this regard is for a state or city to retain a competent market researcher, either in-house or on a consulting basis, to collect and report the information necessary for an objective situation analysis. Too many times, a state or city tries to cut corners on market research in order to save money, and ends up with shoddily-done studies that do not yield information one can feel comfortable with in formulating a "game plan" for economic development.

A conceptual frame of reference for a self-assessment study is provided by the six main categories of location-decision factors or variables that we identified earlier in this chapter. To reiterate, they are:
- Community esprit de corps,
- Economic attractiveness,
- Factors of productions,
- Human resources,
- Infrastructure,
- Quality of life.

Detailed inquiries into each of these categories will give insight into where a state or city is doing well and where it needs improvement. For instance, under the quality-of-life heading, there would be data adduced about schools, colleges and universities, cultural activities, recreational opportunities, and related subcategories. Similarly, to evaluate infrastructure, a study would be made of roads, highways, water-sewer facilities, and so on. Even though a number of these kinds of questions could be answered through the use of objective data—for example, relative wage rates in a state or community—it is still advisable to also obtain perceptual and subjective readings on such matters. Perceptions, although they might at times be quite incorrect, can be more important than reality in corporate-location decisions. It does a locale little good, for example, if it has evolved from a "bad" labor-management climate to a more harmonious environment and it still retains its poor image in the corporate community. Bringing facts and perceptions into congruence is, of course, a job for marketers of economic development. First, however, these marketers must know *for sure* that a disparity exists between facts and perceptions. And that is precisely what a thorough and unbiased situation analysis reveals— how corporate-location decision makers perceive a state or other political entity to stack up on the key decision factors.

Conduct general competitor assessment. A second facet of a situation analysis is often overlooked: conducting a broad-brush assessment of competitor strengths and weaknesses, as well as your own. After all, how one measures up on important location-decision factors is not determined in isolation. Instead, a state or city is compared to other states or cities. Such decision factors as quality of life, community esprit de corps, and economic attractiveness are not absolutes; how a city rates is determined by city-to-city comparisons.

At this stage in the marketing strategy and planning process, the competitor analysis is very general. For instance, how does Florida look on important decision variables versus other states in the Southeast? Or, what does Chicago offer versus major Sunbelt cities? Later, when more detailed strategic analysis is developed for specific economic development objectives—for example, obtaining General Motors' Saturn manufacturing plant—the competitor analysis will become quite specific because the major competitors will be known.

UNDERTAKE STRATEGIC THINKING

Determine relative thrusts of marketing efforts. Once a state or city has a fundamentally sound, research-supported situation analysis to guide it and go on, it can more confidently turn its attention to strategic thinking about its future industrial development. At this point, the political entity evaluates its "strategic window" to see what opportunities are in the external environment that it has the competencies, strengths, and wherewithal to seize upon. Additionally, it will want to consider what to do about the weaknesses and limitations that the situation analysis has revealed or confirmed.

As to its window of opportunity, the state or city will want to ponder the three basic economic development options open to it:

- Attracting business from elsewhere,
- Retaining or expanding existing businesses,
- Fostering business start-ups.

Then, going on what it has learned from the situation analysis, the political entity will be in a position to determine which of these options can be most fruitful in the short term and which, because of weaknesses, it had best pursue in the long term. Short-run might well be in the next 1 to 5 years and long-term thereafter, depending on individual situations and how long it will take to complete corrective action on weaknesses. Generally, the state or city will opt for short-run marketing strategies consistent with its strengths, and long-run strategies where remedial action on weaknesses must first be undertaken.

So, the question in this phase of the marketing strategy and planning process is how much relative weight or emphasis is to be placed on the three economic development options. Most economic development organizations, and the political entities or private-sector groups that support them, are not so flush with resources that priorities for spending on industrial development do not have to be established. Therefore, will a third of the available resources be devoted to each of the three options? Will the split be 60%, 20%, 20%, or just what will be the breakdown? Whatever the allocation, the decision needs to be consciously made on the basis of a thorough situation analysis and careful, creative strategic thinking about the future. A one-third allocation to each of the options should be looked at skeptically. It may indicate that resources are being spread so thin that a mediocre job is the best to be hoped for in each case. A state or city might be better off concentrating its resources (attaining the necessary critical mass) on the development option or options that play to its strengths. For instance, concentrating on assisting existing businesses to expand and fostering business start-ups may be far more productive (and realistic) than heavy spending on attracting business from out of state or out of town. Before spending on any one option can work, it must be enough to pass some minimum threshold. This is not to say, however, that any of the three options should be or can be ignored entirely or slighted; only that short-run and long-run priorities need to be established and translated into facilitating strategies.

Evaluate the feasibility of possible industry targets. This second aspect of strategic thinking requires a state or city to determine what kinds of industry it has the best chances of obtaining or incubating. Conversely, it needs to establish which types of industry do not constitute a match with its strengths. Again, answers to these questions tend to flow from the situation analysis.

Realistically, most areas of the country cannot even hope to be high-technology industrial centers. Because of the special needs and wants of high-tech companies, only certain locales will be considered. Likewise, most states and cities do not have the mix of ingredients to be chosen as headquarters communities for large companies. So, for most states and cities to target high-tech industry or corporate headquarters, or both, would be self-delusion. What successes a community might have to showcase probably would not have been worth the time and effort from a cost-benefit standpoint.

Charleston, West Virginia, is a good example of a community that has realized and consequently concentrated on its strengths. Charleston and the Kanawha Valley are the focus of West Virginia's economic development. This area is supported by a manufacturing base from the Kanawha Valley's chemical production. But it also contains a service sector—legal, health care, utility, financial, and distribution services, for example—double the size of manufacturing. More than 50% of the work force is white collar. And, although the Charleston community's forte is not high-tech production, the area is involved in high-tech application.[4]

Whether it be a big city or a small town, economic development strategists need to evaluate objectively the *feasibility* of potential industry targets. Does the locale have the *best chance* of building its industrial base by promoting heavy manufacturing, light manufacturing, services, retailing, headquarters, high-tech, or which mix of these? Charleston, West Virginia, has conceptualized and articulated its fortes, but many states and communities have not. And this strategic thinking process may not yield answers that the state or community necessarily likes; for instance, given first choice, Charleston would probably not choose chemical plants as the underpinning of its economic environment. Chemical plants carry high risks, as the 1984 Union Carbide tragedy in India too painfully illustrated. Yet, while attempting to diversify, Charleston and the Kanawha Valley are not about to encourage Union Carbide to relocate elsewhere. It is simply self-deception at its worst for the vast majority of the states and cities to attempt to develop themselves industrially on "clean" manufacturing and service-type businesses alone.

Several years ago, one of us had occasion to talk with officials of a small midwestern city whose goal was to turn its downtown into a hub of specialty shops and fashion boutiques. Like many places, its central business district had been gutted by the advent of suburban and regional shopping malls. Apparently undeterred by their slim chances for success, the city's officials and chamber of commerce are unsuccessfully pursuing their "dream" rather than shifting to a more plausible plan for revitalization.

SET OBJECTIVES/GOALS

By this time in the marketing strategy and planning process, the state or community is in a position to set long-term and short-term objectives and goals for itself. It has assessed its situation and thought strategically about where it should concentrate its industrial development efforts in the near term and longer term.

It is imperative that the political entity dichotomize objectives and goals into short-term and long-term—and define what short-term and long-term mean in years. The two sets of objectives may turn out to be virtually the same—for example, "We will shoot for a service-based economy now as well as 10 years from now." However, what might not be possible in the short run, the next 3 to 4 years, might be achievable 5 to 10 years out if certain actions are begun pronto. For instance, if a state works with the private sector to establish business incubators in its major cities, a productive round of entrepreneurial activity could result several years hence. Or, if a state dramatically upgrades the engineering school at the public university in its major city, and develops a research park near the university, then it might eventually be able to attract expansion facilities of certain types of high-tech companies.

In the short term, the political entity will need to be precise concerning what its development objectives are for specific industries, company types, and firms. For example, service industries might be the broad objective. At the second level of objectives, the community might more specifically target company types—financial institutions, health-care organizations, sales branches of major corporations a la Atlanta, and so forth. Finally, and with the most specificity, objectives regarding branches of coveted firms would be delineated—IBM, Xerox, Ryan Homes, Humana, New York Life, and so forth.

Objectives and goals for the longer term will be more sketchy. Industries and company types need to be identified and targeted, but probably not specific firms within these broader categories. Importantly, as part of long-term objectives and goals, the state or community should state what it wants to achieve in the next 5 to 10 years, for example, to overcome the shortcomings it identified earlier in its situation analysis. For instance, what are its objectives in terms of improving its infrastructure or the quality of labor and management relations?

DEVELOP STRATEGIES/TACTICS

Once the objectives and goals have been agreed upon and stated, the marketing strategy and planning proceeds to the formulation of strategies and tactics to achieve the objectives. These should be quite concise; as John Welch, the chairman of General Electric has pointed out, a well-thought-out strategy can be summarized in a page or two. Tactical statements—that is, more specific maneuvers—might take longer to summarize, but should not become too complex. Short, concise strategy statements represent "focused" thinking about how objectives are to be achieved.

Short-term marketing strategies and tactics are by nature more operational. They are meant to achieve objectives in the years immediately ahead. These kinds of marketing programs revolve around the marketing mix—the variables the marketer blends together to achieve objectives. Notably, short-term marketing programs for economic development would certainly include communications (advertising, personal selling by governors, mayors, executives from the

332

private sector, etc.), assistance in site selection to targeted companies, financial incentives, and, importantly, provisions for competitor analysis. At this stage, a state or city is often able to identify its major competition for a company's facility. For instance, the major contenders for GM's Saturn plant were known early on. Thus, a *detailed* competitor analysis is possible and indeed essential if a state or city is to design a marketing plan with a fighting chance of winning. Say, for sake of illustration, that Michigan is willing to provide $125 million in financial incentives to GM to get the Saturn plant. Knowing this—and a competitor analysis might reveal it or at least show that large financial incentives are Michigan's typical MO (method of operation)—would be a valuable piece of information for Ohio, Illinois, Indiana, and the other Saturn contenders to have.

Long-term marketing strategies and tactics are much less operational; they typically deal with "structural" concerns rather than with the marketing mix per se. Long-run strategies often address a state or city's competitive shortcomings. Some of the structural changes that a political entity might pursue to make itself more attractive as a place for doing business are:

- Establishing enterprise zones;
- Promoting the formation of incubators for start-up business;
- Encouraging or sponsoring industrial parks and research parks, or both, contiguous to or near a university;
- Working toward better infrastructure;
- Upgrading education;
- Fostering the formation of private-sector venture-capital funds.

In long-term economic development strategies, the manner in which the state or community intends to accomplish its long-range objectives and goals is mapped out. Because long-term objectives are couched in terms of the industries and company-types the political entity has targeted, the strategies delineate what needs to be done to make its business climate receptive to them. A shotgun approach is not usually indicated; instead, the state or city needs to rifle in on strategies that have the best chances of achieving the objectives. A wealthy state such as Texas can pursue sundry kinds of industries and businesses; incubators, industrial and research parks, venture-capital funds, enterprise zones, and massive financial incentives are not beyond its wherewithal. However, most states and locales are not so fortunate, and most establish reasonable priorities pertaining to where their economic development efforts and resources will be expended.

IMPLEMENT STRATEGIES/TACTICS

Many plans fail not because they are conceptually flawed, but rather because they are improperly executed or implemented with a poor sense of timing. For this reason, we suggest that first of all, short-term and long-range objectives or goals and strategies be committed to writing in a formal plan. Additionally, who (what economic development officials) is responsible for what (strategies or tactics) needs to be quite clearly specified as well. It is also critical that these tasks and duties be budgeted for. Unless action plans are budgeted for, they will not get done except through happenstance. In brief, there needs to be *close linkage* between plans and budgets. Moreover, each objective or goal and strategy or tactic should be framed in time. That is, "By when do we want to achieve the objective and over what period of time is the strategy accompanying the objective to be executed?" Lastly, objectives and goals need to be as quantified as possible so there can be some judgment made eventually about whether or not they have been attained. The objective of "completing work on a $10 million industrial park on the Smith property by 1992" is certainly more measurable and useful than the objective of "eventually building an industrial park in our city."

ONGOING MARKET INTELLIGENCE ON INDUSTRIES/COMPANIES/COMPETITION

The final phase in the marketing strategy and planning process is one that is never truly complete, not even for a moment. Only via continual and systematic market-intelligence gathering and interpretation can a state or city economic development group stay on top of what is happening in its environment. Some mechanism—an internal capability, consulting services, or both—needs to be provided for if this all-important job is to be done right. Otherwise, a state or community can be blindsided by environmental events it does not see coming. Simply put, a state or city that does not maintain a keen sense of what is happening in the environment, as well as what the future augurs, is not going to be successful in economic development on a sustained basis.

SOME PARTING THOUGHTS

We have stressed the importance of taking a marketing orientation in state and city economic development efforts. The whys that we noted relate as much to philosophy and style, however, as they do to substance. Many states and cities employ marketing tools and techniques, such as advertising, sales promotion, "branch" locations, and marketing research, without having a marketing or demand-side orientation. In short, their philosophy is more supply-side oriented— "What we are willing to offer?"—than demand-side—"What do the companies we seek to attract really want and need in their new site?"

In contrast, a marketing-oriented philosophy focuses on the prospect, the company that is planning to relocate, to expand locally, or to build a subsidiary (warehouse/plant/sales office) facility. Such a marketing-oriented economic development group will (1) recognize it has tough *competition,* (2) target its highest-potential prospects, and (3) take the necessary steps to present itself in terms of these prospects' *needs and wants.* Integral to this process is a determination of its *image,* and objective assessment of its strengths and weaknesses and an understanding of the needs of firms in particular industries.

We have suggested a comprehensive marketing strategy and planning schema for economic development and, further, have identified the generic factors that influence corporate site selection. We have provided the place for city or state economic development organizations to start and have given them a road map to follow. However, in the final analysis each community is unique, as is each company's closing decision factors. As the process of reducing the number of potential sites (states and/or cities) progresses, the company sifts through a new level of considerations (a process not unlike what Thomas Bonoma has referred to in business-to-business marketing as "nesting"). If the economic development group has effectively targeted its prospects, it will (1) understand the companies' priorities and (2) have positioned itself to stay in the race to the end. Ongoing marketing intelligence is a necessity, as a company's needs may change even during the location-decision process and the competitions' strategies may also be varied. Further, our research has shown that the factors important to a headquarters relocation differ from those appropriate to a plant or other subsidiary site-selection effort. Thus, flexibility in approach is a real necessity for an effective marketing plan; it is worth the extra effort to tailor your approach to the prospect's needs. Why? Because, the level of competition will require it.

To conclude, we turned to Roy Harris, the Industrial Development Commission of Mid-Florida, Inc. president and an individual we came to greatly respect during our research. We asked him to comment on the competitiveness issue; here is his answer:

Q: How competitive do you see economic development groups becoming in the next decade? Will cities and states become more or less competitive and will this competitiveness be more professional?

A: There has always been heated competition in the economic development arena, whether on a state or local level. That heated competition has recently been fanned into a raging fire, spurned by a national economy that focuses on economic recovery and expansion. I predict this fire will rage for many years to come.

It is plain to see why economic development will become even more important in the next decade. Communities that encourage and enjoy a diversified economy are the ones that remain stable during times of country-wide strife; it's just like a healthy investment portfolio. No investment counselor in the world would recommend you put all of your money into one particular investment. Instead, your portfolio should be diversified. It's the same in development. A community with all of its eggs in one basket risks watching the fall of its economy should that industry see troubled times. Conversely, a diversified economy can withstand, and even continue to prosper, during troubled times.

The focus on economic or industrial development means that states and regions will do whatever it takes to get to the top. They'll start new programs as incentives to business to locate there; they will hire the best people they can to develop better, more professional programs. Many economic development groups are taking a hard look at the way they present their region to prospects. If they seem fragmented, with several groups doing the same job, they may miss an opportunity to win a relocation or expansion. So what we've seen is that parochialism is being put aside in many regions, with many groups combining resources in order to do a more professional job of "selling" their region.

It's going to get tougher, and only those regions with many attributes and someone sharp that can carry that message will prosper.

(Roy Harris, IDC of Mid-Florida president)

Roy has articulately pointed out the significant challenge that lies ahead for economic and industrial development groups. As he suggests, only those with the strongest battle plan and the best people will likely succeed, and we feel it will be those that can employ a true *marketing perspective*.

Vignettes

McALLEN: CHOOSING YOUR STATS

City economic development organizations are faced with many temptations when putting together the information packet to send to inquiring firms. One is the tendency to be a bit overzealous in describing their community's attributes; for example, a high school theatrical club becomes a semiprofessional little theater offering Broadway-quality entertainment, and a local river becomes a "sailing paradise." What these enthusiastic copywriters forget is the importance of having a credible message.

Similarly, the organization's economist or economists are tempted to overburden prospective new companies with statistics. "The more the better" seems to be the motto that is followed and the mounds of data that result tend to provide the prospects with more information than they would ever wish to know (or care to receive). A point that is ignored in all of this overzealousness is that the company may simply feel that the community is offering evidence of a "lack of understanding of business needs" or that it is too difficult or troublesome, or both, to sift through the materials in order to find the cogent data they want to include in their decision making.

Perhaps the best packaging of city economic data we have seen was provided to us by McAllen, Texas. A single 40-page publication presents in a clear, easy-to-read, and "time-sensitive" format the economic picture of McAllen. As the accompanying illustration shows, highlight statistics were presented on each page to assist the busy reader.

We asked Karin Richmond, who was Director of Economic Development at McAllen's chamber of commerce at the time, to give us her philosophy in preparing such materials. She told us:

When developing our economic promotional material, we simply recognized that time is a crucial element for the CEO when screening pertinent community data. We implemented this philosophy by presenting the most salient bit of data top-and-up front so if the CEO did nothing but scan our report, he or she would capture our community strengths in less than 30 seconds time.

ILLUSTRATION 10.4

Recognizing in statistical presentation business readers' time limitations.

COMMERCIAL CONSTRUCTION

■ **TOTAL VALUE OF COMMERCIAL CONSTRUCTION PERMITS INCREASED 91% IN 1983**

1980	$14.2 MILLION
1981	$50.9 MILLION
1982	$32.2 MILLION
1983	$61.6 MILLION

■ **AVERAGE COST PER SQUARE FOOT OF NEW COMMERCIAL LEASE SPACE IS $0.74**

RETAIL	$0.74
OFFICE	$0.79
WAREHOUSE	$0.47

■ **1983 COMMERCIAL SPACE USAGE BREAKDOWN**

RETAIL	40%
OFFICE	33%
WAREHOUSE	27%

■ **COMMERCIAL CONSTRUCTION**
Source: City of McAllen, Code
Enforcement Division

■ **QUARTERLY COMMERCIAL BUILDING PERMITS VALUE**

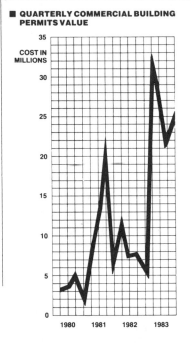

	1983 UNITS	COST	1982 UNITS	COST	1981 UNITS	COST	1980 UNITS	COST
RETAIL	34	34,008,972	40	9,289,860	44	13,830,341	34	4,146,400
OFFICE	14	10,545,100	33	7,854,535	28	3,575,000	24	2,046,623
WAREHOUSE	185	7,522,291	237	9,830,537	264	15,797,287	191	5,371,843
PUBLIC	75	9,515,888	66	5,313,332	101	17,705,344	97	2,663,020
TOTAL	308	$61,592,251	376	$32,288,264	437	$50,907,972	346	$14,227,886

Annual Economic Report material reprinted with the permission of Tommy Joyner, President, McAllen (Texas) Chamber of Commerce.

THE GREAT LAKES PROFILE:
INTERSTATE COOPERATION AT ITS BEST!

An inhibiting factor in most efforts to achieve interstate cooperation on economic development is finding an appropriate forum to bring a regional state group together. In the midwest, the Great Lakes Commission stepped forward to provide just such a vehicle and has found considerable interest among its eight-state constituents. In particular, recent cooperative efforts led to a 264-page economic resource book/overview, *The Great Lakes Economy; A Resource and Industry Profile of the Great Lakes States,* that was first unveiled at the Commission's annual meeting held in Indianapolis in October, 1985.

To say that the *Profile* represents merely a cooperative effort of the Commission, the Federal Reserve Bank of Chicago and the states, would be a gross understatement. When James Fish, Executive Director of the Commission, enlisted the interest and support of the Chicago Fed, the end result was a study that marked a first in presenting the strengths and attributes of the Great Lakes region in a single document. An Economic Trends Review Task Force was established by the Commission in eary 1985 including representatives of the Chicago Fed and the economic development offices of the eight states that make up the Commission's coverage area, i.e., Minnesota, Indiana, Illinois, Ohio, Michigan, Wisconsin, Pennsylvania, and New York. This Task Force established the objectives and the overall format for the study, which was then prepared by David R. Allardice, a vice president of the Chicago Fed, and his staff during the summer of 1985. A sample page of the report appears in Exhibit 10.5.

What can be learned from such a project? Just as the Industrial Development Commission of Mid-Florida, Inc. has shown how local interests can be unified in a most positive effort, the Great Lakes Commission has taught us several lessons on state cooperation. First, some type of ongoing suprastate body is needed ... particularly one that has demonstrated its successes in the past and has the combined support of various states' leadership. Second, each state must see the effort as having importance to it ... a positive self-interest. In this instance, the *Profile* is useful as both a planning and promotion tool. And, third, each state (officials) must feel involved in the process.

On September 16, 1985, the Task Force held its final meeting regarding the study; a wrap-up session to make some final changes in the format and wording of the publication. What was evident from the members' comments was that the *Profile* was just the beginning of many future joint efforts to enhance these states' economic development programs.

EXHIBIT 10.5

Employment shares by major sector: 1969 and 1984

(In percent)

(Great Lakes Region vs. The United States)

	1969		1984	
	Great Lakes Region	United States	Great Lakes Region	United States
Construction	4.3	5.1	3.4	4.6
Manufacturing	33.1	28.7	23.1	20.6
Durables Manufacturing	21.6	16.9	14.9	12.2
Nondurables Manufacturing	11.4	11.8	8.3	8.4
Transportation & Public Utilities	6.1	6.3	5.2	5.5
Retail Trade	14.6	15.3	16.8	17.6
Wholesale Trade	5.4	5.6	5.4	5.9
Finance, Insurance & Real Estate	5.4	5.0	6.4	6.0
Services	15.4	15.9	22.8	22.0
Government	15.2	17.3	16.0	16.9

Note: Does not total to 100 percent due to absence of mining sector and rounding.

Source: U.S. Department of Labor, Bureau of Labor Statistics, Employment and Earnings.

This Exhibit is taken from The Great Lakes Economy: A Resource and Industry Profile of the Great Lakes. The study is available from Harbor House Publications, Inc., Boyne City, Michigan.

REFERENCES

1. Stepanek, M. (1985, March 19). Poorer states no good for Saturn, GM hints. *Akron Beacon Journal*, p. B5.
2. Boyer, R., Savageau, D. (1985). *Places rated almanac.* p. 417. Chicago: Rand McNally and Company.
3. Sharp, K. (1985, June 16). Why Japan is coming to 'Silicon Forest'. *New York Times*, p. F17.
4. Charleston report: Economic development. (1984, November/December). *Pace*, p. 13C.

SELECTED BIBLIOGRAPHY

NOTE: Specialized publications, such as *Business Facilities, Plants Sites & Parks* and *Industiral Development,* contain numerous useful articles on economic development. Only a few of these are noted here—the ones we have found particularly useful in our research. However, the reader will also find it helpful to review back issues of these publications.

Government

An Assessment of U.S. Competitiveness in High Technology Industries. Washington, D.C.: Department of Commerce, International Trade Commission, February, 1983.

Attracting Foreign Investment to the United States. Washington, D.C.: U.S. Department of Commerce, International Trade Administration.

Choosing a Future. Menlo Park, CA: SRI International for Ameritrust Corporation, 1984.

General Manufacturing Business Climates of the Forty-Eight Contiguous States of America. Chicago, IL: Alexander Grant & Company, 1983.

A Guide to Industrial Site Selection. Washington, D.C.: Society of Industrial Realtors of the National Association of Realtors, National Association of Industrial and Office Parks, 1979.

Impact of Transportation Policy on the Spatial Distribution of Retail Activity. Washington, D.C.: U.S. Department of Transportation, Research and Special Programs Administration, 1984.

A Local Impact Study of a Foreign Direct Investment in the United States: Noranda Aluminum, Inc. Washington, D.C.: U.S. Department of Commerce, International Trade Administration, 1982.

Technology, Innovation, and Regional Economic Development. Washington, D.C.: Congress of the United States, Office of Technology Assessment, 1984.

Books

Boyer, Richard, and Savageau, David. *Places Rated Almanac.* Chicago: Rand McNally & Company, 1985.

Industrial Real Estate. Washington, D.C.: SIR Educational Fund, 1984.

Rogers, Everett M., and Larsen, Judith K. *Silicon Valley Fever.* New York: Basic Books, 1984.

Silver, A. David. *Venture Capital, the Complete Guide For Investors.* New York: John Wiley & Sons, 1985.

Smilor, Raymond W., and Kuhn, Robert L. *Corporate Creativity.* New York: Praeger Publishers, 1984.

Wilson, John W. *The New Ventures: Inside the High-Stakes World of Venture Capital.* Reading, MA: Addison-Wesley Publishing Company, 1985.

Articles

Adams, Anne L. "USA Firms Hurt by Their Plants Going Abroad." *USA Today,* January 11, 1985.

Adams, Jane Meredith. "Westborough Picked for High-Tech Center." *The Boston Globe,* May 31, 1984.

Ady, Robert M. "Shifting Factors in Plant Location." *Industrial Development,* November/December 1981, pp. 13-17.

"Airport's Chief Asset Is Luring High-Tech Firms." *Air Travel Journal,* April 6-20, 1984, p. 5.

"America Rushes to High-Tech for Growth." *Business Week,* March 28, 1983, pp. 84-90.

Anderson, Kevin, and Lewyn, Mark, "Technology is Erasing National Boundaries." *USA Today,* April 12, 1984.

Anderson, McTier, and Kelley, Donald E. "Forum—The Product Life Cycle." *PACE,* November/December 1984, pp. 25-27.

Anderson, Robert V. "Corporate Real Estate and Review Appraising." *Industrial Development,* September/October 1982, pp. 24-27.

Antilla, Susan. "Irvine, California, goes Biotech." *USA Today,* March 29, 1984.

Ashyk, Loretta. "Growth Association Team Hopes to SWAT Firm's Troubles Away." *Crain's Cleveland Business,* August 5, 1985, p. 1.

"Associations Play Major Role in States' Economy, Political Future." *Austin Business Executive,* April 1985, pp. 27-31.

Austin, Danforth W., and Beazley, J. Ernest. "High-Tech Track: Struggling Industries in Nation's Heartland Speed Up Automation." *The Wall Street Journal,* April 4, 1983, p. 1.

Bailey, Douglas. "The Next Industrial Boom." *New England Business,* September 17, 1984, pp. 96-102.

_____ . "A Race for Development Funds." *New England Business,* September 3, 1984, pp. 82-87.

Baum, Laurie. "Dade Cities Must Cooperate to Boost Tourism, Officials Say." *Miami Herald,* June 4, 1984.

Benedetto, Richard. "Governors Court Saturn on TV." *USA Today,* February 25, 1985.

Beucke, Daniel A. "Cracks in Silicon Mountain." *The New York Times,* June 30, 1985.

Beynon, Roger. "The High Tech Race: Not to the Penny Pincher." *Texas Business,* June 1985, p. 14.

Biermann, Wallace W. "The Validity of Business Climate Rankings: A Test." *Industrial Development,* March/April 1984, pp. 17, 23-25.

Blaine, Charley. "With Help, Firms Build Strong Base." *USA Today,* June 5, 1984.

Blankenhorn, Dana. "High-Tech, Southern Style." *Sky,* February 1984, pp. 12-23.

Blundell, William. "Economic Recovery Bypasses Coast of Northern California." *The Wall Street Journal,* August 21, 1984, p. 29.

Bodec, Ben. "North and South Battle for Industry." *Marketing and Media Decisions,* June 1981, pp. 66-69, 140-42.

Bond, Gary. "Boom in High Tech Is Just Beginning." *Advertising Age,* August 23, 1982, pp. M12-M13.

"Boomtown, USA." *World Business Weekly,* December 15, 1980, pp. 29-42.

"Boston's High-Tech Highway." *Management Today,* January 1984, pp. 62-67.

Brennan, Kevin, and Miller, Randall. "Spain Outlines Ambitious Plan for Its High-Tech Industries." *Business America,* July 9, 1984, pp. 27-28.

Brennan, Peter J. "Picking the Place: Choice of Location for Your Company May or May Not be Crucial." *Venture,* October 1984, pp. 112-31.

Bronte, Stephen. "Wall Street Woos the High-Techs." *Euromoney,* July 1983, pp. 78-82.

Brooks, Andree. "Connecticut: Too Much of a Good Thing." *The New York Times,* May 13, 1984, p. 33.

Browning, E.S. "Seoul Seeks High-Tech Self-Sufficiency." *The Wall Street Journal,* September 7, 1984, p. 24.

Burns, James J. "International Siting Priorities for a High Technology Firm." *Industrial Development,* May/June 1984, pp. 10-12.

Carlson, Eugene. "Business-Climate Ratings Stir Debate over Study's Methods." *The Wall Street Journal,* April 17, 1984, p. 35.

_____. "Colleges Alight in New Areas to Exploit High-Tech Market." *The Wall Street Journal,* June 25, 1985, p. 31.

_____. "Electric Utilities Cut Rates to Spur Area Development." *The Wall Street Journal,* October 9, 1984, p. 31.

_____. "Florida's Plan for the Future: More Questions Than Answers." *The Wall Street Journal,* February 19, 1985, p. 31.

_____. "Great Lakes Governors Split over Truce on Industry Raids." *The Wall Street Journal,* July 12, 1983, p. 35.

_____. "Great Lakes to Other States: Don't Go Near Area's Water." *The Wall Street Journal,* February 5, 1985, p. 35.

_____. "Industrial Midwest's Recovery Belies Predictions of Its Demise." *The Wall Street Journal,* July 3, 1984, p. 23.

_____. "It's the Land Tax, By George, That Sets Pennsylvania Apart." *The Wall Street Journal,* March 12, 1985, p. 33.

_____. "Local Governments Still See Secession as a Remedy for Ills." *The Wall Street Journal,* May 29, 1984, p. 29.

_____. "Los Angeles's Growth Differs from Other Cities." *The Wall Street Journal,* January 15, 1985, p. 31.

_____. "Massachusetts Deftly Handles Volatile Issue of Plant Closings." *The Wall Street Journal,* June 26, 1984, p. 29.

_____. "Midwest Gets Blunt Advice on Ending Economic Slump." *The Wall Street Journal,* April 10, 1984, p. 31.

_____. "New England's Big Recovery: The 'Most Spectacular' Event?" *The Wall Street Journal,* December 18, 1984, p. 35.

_____. "Steady High-Tech Job Drain Doesn't Upset New York City." *The Wall Street Journal,* May 1, 1984, p. 37.

_____. "Taxes in State of Washington Are Hurting Fledgling Firms." *The Wall Street Journal,* August 7, 1984, p. 29.

_____. "U.S. Cargo—Preference Rules Penalize Ports on Great Lakes." *The Wall Street Journal,* May 15, 1984, p. 33.

_____. "Value Added Tax Is Providing Revenue Stability in Michigan." *The Wall Street Journal,* September 25, 1984, p. 37.

_____. "Virginia Plans Research Site to Serve Its High-Tech Firms." *The Wall Street Journal,* June 5, 1984, p. 37.

_____. "Why Sir Run Run's Donation Had to be Everyone's Business." *The Wall Street Journal,* September 17, 1985, p. 31.

Carpentier, Michel. "Toward a New Kind of Community." *Europe,* May/June 1984, pp. 28-29.

"A Cautious Nod to Industrial Policy." *Business Week,* March 19, 1984, p. 15.

Celli, Raymond. "A Case for Strategy in Fixed Asset Planning." *Industrial Development,* September/October 1982, pp. 28-31.

"The Checklist of Expansion Planning and Site Selection Factors." *Site Selection Handbook,* February 1979, pp. 12-31.

Coffin, Donald A. "Property Tax Abatement and Economic Development in Indianapolis." *Growth and Change,* April 1982, pp. 18-23.

Cook, James. "We Started from Ground Zero." *Forbes,* March 12, 1984, pp. 98-106.

"Corporate Real Estate Investment: The Undiscovered Road to Higher Profits." *Site Selection Handbook,* February 1983, pp. 10-14.

"Dallas Lure for American." *Business Week,* November 20, 1978, p. 144.

Davis, Bob. "Electronics Hits Boston's Chinatown." *Wall Street Journal,* August 21, 1984, p. 29.

Days, Michel. "Baltimore Realty Firms Buck Trend To National Networks." *The Wall Street Journal,* January 16, 1985, p. 23.

DeGeorge, Gail. "Piper Hoping New Owners Will Help It Take Off." *The Miami Herald,* June 4, 1984.

Demuth, Jerry. "What Can Incubators Offer?" *Venture,* November 1984, pp. 78-84.

"Diamond Shamrock Leaving Cleveland for Southwest." *Wall Street Journal,* May 30, 1979, p.22.

Diemer, Tom. "Celeste Makes Plea on TV for Saturn Plant." *The Plain Dealer,* February 27, 1985.

Dolan, Carrie. "Washington State Takes a Tip and a Bit More from Oregon." *The Wall Street Journal,* July 16, 1985, p. 29.

Donovan, Dennis J. "Twelve Key Questions for Site Decision Makers." *Industrial Development,* July/August 1982, pp. 12-15.

Drucker, Peter F. "Europe's High-Tech Delusion." *The Wall Street Journal,* September 14, 1984, p. 24.

Due, John F. "The Surprising Roles of the State and Local Governments in Preserving Rail Freight Service." *State Government,* Spring 1985, pp. 7-13.

Ehrlich, Dan. "British Real Estate Lures U.S. Investors." *USA Today,* January 15, 1985.

Fallon, Richard. "University as Venture Capitalist." *Forbes,* December 19, 1983, p. 82-93.

Feder, Barnaby J. "Britain's Science Corridor." *New York Times,* April 24, 1983, p. 8F.

Fikac, Peggy. "White: Valley Should Get Enterprise Zone." *Valley Morning Star,* December 18, 1983.

Flanagan, James. "Israel's High Technology Growth Benefits American Manufacturers." *Business America,* March 19, 1984, pp. 28-29.

"Floating Rates Blamed for Economic Ills." *The Orlando Sentinel,* December 23, 1984.

Friedman, Jon. "Silicon Valley: Hard-won Millions." *USA Today,* August 30, 1984.

Gabe, Vernon D. "An Outline of a Corporate Site Location Procedure." *Industrial Development,* September/October 1983, pp. 23-25.

"Georgia-Pacific Looks Southward to Home." *Business Week,* December 4, 1978, pp. 32-33.

Gibson, Richard. "Minnesota Moves Help Thaw Once-Chilly Business Climate." *The Wall Street Journal,* July 31, 1984, p. 33.

Glover, Tony. "Myth of High-Tech." *The Accountant,* February 10, 1983, pp. 19-22.

Goodman, JoEllen. "Chicago Image Poor among Execs: Study." *Crain's Chicago Business,* September 17, 1984, pp. 1, 77.

"Graham Signs Bill Ending Unitary Tax." *The Orlando Sentinel,* December 21, 1984.

Greenhouse, Steven. "The Fragile Middle West." *New York Times,* June 23, 1985.

"Growing Pains: Trying to Lure High-Tech Industries; Austin Expands Fast, But Some Residents Are Irked." *The Wall Street Journal,* September 11, 1984, pp. 1, 17.

Guenther, Robert. "Foreign Investors Are Making New Moves into U.S. Market." *The Wall Street Journal,* December 17, 1984, p. 37.

Hack, George D. "The Plant Location Decision Making Process." *Industrial Development,* September/October 1984, pp. 31-33.

Halberstam, David. "Robots Enter Our Lives." *Parade Magazine,* April 10, 1983, pp. 17-19.

Hall, Matthew. "Governor Celeste's Mid-Term Review." *Ohio Business,* January 1985, pp. 40-45.

Hall, Trish. "Executive Style: For A Company Chief, When There's a Whim There's Often a Way." *The Wall Street Journal,* October 1, 1984, pp. 1, 16.

Hallquist, H. Basil. "The Strategic Plan: Facility Management in Context." *Industrial Development,* July/August 1984, pp. 32-33.

Hamel, Ruth. "Cities, States Scramble for Auto Plants." *USA Today,* October 5, 1984.

Harding, Charles F. "Business Climate Studies: How Useful Are They?" *Industrial Development,* January/February 1983, pp. 22-23.

Hartley, Tom. "Corporate Streamlining Likely in Cities." *USA Today,* June 9, 1984.

Hatras, Dora. "Silicon Capital; Staying Close to the Federal Government." *High Tech Facilities,* February 1985, pp. H14-21.

Hayes, Thomas C. "Dealing with Overseas Job Competition." *The New York Times,* March 25, 1984, pp. 5, 16.

Hedman, William. "Strategy for Seeking a New Facility." *Industrial Development,* July/August 1982, pp. 24-26.

Herman, Phyllis Messer. "FTZ Areas Report New Operations." *Plants Sites & Parks,* September/October 1985, p. 1.

"The High-Tech Renaissance in Southern California." *Business Week,* September 17, 1984, pp. 142-44, 148.

Hillkirk, John. "Austin: Next Silicon Mecca?" *USA Today,* April 13, 1984.

_____. "Colorado Weighs Hi-Tech Price Tag." *USA Today,* October 23, 1984.

_____. "Oregon Seeds Hi-Tech." *USA Today,* October 30, 1984.

_____. "States Find It Hard to Recruit Firms" *USA Today,* November 13, 1984.

_____. "Top States for New Plant Sites Hold Their Own." *USA Today,* October 5, 1984.

Hodge, Scott A. "Spurned by Saturn, Illinois Must Rethink Its Technique." *Crain's Chicago Business,* September 16, 1985, p. 11.

Hooper, Mary. "Mentor on the Move." *Crain's Cleveland Business,* October 22, 1984, p. F-1.

350

Houx, Cynthia. "Enterprise Zone Aims To Be Best in Nation." *Business First,* August 20, 1984, pp. 1, 24.

Huey, John. "Executives Assess Europe's Technology Decline." *The Wall Street Journal,* February 1, 1984, p. 26.

Inman, William H. "The Texas Draw." *Texas Business,* December 1984, pp. 49-52.

Isikoff, Michael. "Steinbrenner and Lorain Sail on Stormy Seas." *The Plain Dealer,* February 12, 1984.

Jacobs, Sally. "Some Rare Criticism of High Tech Industry by Bay Street Group." *New England Business,* May 21, 1984, p. 56.

Johe, Sara; Sole, Diana; and Walters, Mona. "Charleston Report." *PACE,* November/December 1984, pp. 1C-66C.

Johnson, Robert. "Iowa Villages' Tourism Boom Brings Questionable Progress." *The Wall Street Journal,* May 8, 1984, p. 31.

Jones, Robert Snowden. "Florida Rated Southeast's Top Hi-Tech Center." *The Atlanta Journal and Constitution,* February 12, 1984, p. 2-E.

Karle, Delinda. "State Nod Could Fund Polymer R&D Center." *Crain's Cleveland Business,* July 9-15, 1984, p. 1.

Kay, Michele. "Over There? No, Over Here!" *Texas Business,* March 1985, p. 11.

Knecht, G. Bruce. "Benjamin Duke Holloway: Equitable's Player in the Real Estate Sweepstakes." July 1, 1984, p. F-7.

Konrad, Walecia. "The Wrong Medicine." *Forbes,* March 12, 1984, p. 95.

Kotkin, Joel. "Will Japan Again Copy the U.S.?" *Akron Beacon Journal,* May 13, 1984, p. C1.

_____ and Critsen, Greg. "Capital Ideas". *Inc.,* October 1985, pp. 96-98, 103-104.

Kuhn, Tom. "Phoenix Media's Battle for Dominance Escalates." *Advertising Age,* August 23, 1982, pp. M-16 - M-19.

Lancaster, Hal. "Raising the Ante: Competition by States to Lure Firms Turns into a Fierce Struggle." *Wall Street Journal,* December 28, 1983, p. 1.

Langhart, Victor D. "Computer Age Technology For Facility Planning." *Industrial Development,* September/October 1984, pp. 23-25.

Latham, William R. III, and Hockersmith, Paul J. "Investor-Owned Electric Utilities as Information Sources." *Industrial Development,* March/April 1984, pp. 30-36.

Leonhardt, Derr. "Environmental Aspects of the Site Location Decision." *Industrial Development,* July/August 1984, pp. 23-27.

"Let's Swap; Ever the Middleman, South Florida Plans to Get Rich Off Counter Trade." *Miami/South Florida Magazine,* June 1984, pp. 116-20, 125.

Lewin, Tamar. "Putting Industry Policy to a Vote." *The New York Times,* June 10, 1984.

Lewis, Paul. "Europe Gears Up for World Class Technology." *The New York Times,* April 17, 1983.

Lindsey, Robert. "State Tax Fight with Global Implications." *New York Times,* July 7, 1985.

"Low Rankings, High Ambitions." *The Economist,* September 14, 1985, pp. 34-35.

Lowe, Roger. "Celeste Pushes Ohio's Saturn Quest; No Development Chief Appointed Yet." *Crain's Cleveland Business,* February 18-24, 1985, p. 1.

Lublin, Joann S. "Foreign Tourists Are Wooed to Take Roads Less Traveled." *The Wall Street Journal,* February 26, 1985, p. 37.

McCoy, Charles. "High-Tech Prosperity, Basic Industry Gloom Mingle in the Rockies." *The Wall Street Journal,* August 3, 1984, pp. 1, 5.

MacDonald, Douglas, "Incubator Fever." *New England Business,* September 2, 1985, pp. 62-70.

MacDonnell, Arthur. "How Silicon Valley Lures 128 Engineers with Sports, Arts." *New England Business,* May 21, 1984, p. 45.

McNamara, Mark W. "Trading Credit for Commerce." *Miami/South Florida Magazine,* June 1984, pp. 77-78, 126.

Magarrell, Jack. "Governors Warned about Weaknesses of Colleges in High Technology Areas." *The Chronicle of Higher Education,* March 9, 1983, pp. 1, 8-10.

Margolis, Nell. "Report on the States." *Inc.,* October 1985, pp. 90-93.

Markow, Paul. "Relocating to Enhance the 'Quality of Life.'" *Business Week,* April 17, 1978, pp. 134B-134I.

Marlowe, Dick. "Industry Can Locate Anywhere—Tourism is What Central Florida Does Best." *The Orland Sentinel,* December 23, 1984.

"Mazda Car Firm May Build in U.S." *The Plain Dealer,* March 17, 1984.

Meadows, James B. "Snappy Slogans, Financial Incentives Highlight." *Rocky Mountain Business Journal,* March 26, 1984, pp. 20-23.

Miller, Jay. "National Real Estate Giants Explore Local Turf," *Crain's Cleveland Business,* February 4, 1985, p. 1.

Morgan, Howard. "How Chicago Has Shed Its Dreary Outpost Image." October 15, 1984, p. 11.

Mullen, Frank. "Metro Counties Scamble for Share of 'Pie'." *Rocky Mountain Business Journal,* March 26, 1984, p. 18.

Oppenheimer, Andres. "Are Florida Firms Exporting Jobs?" *The Miami Herald,* December 24, 1984, pp. 1, 8-10.

Oser, Alan S. "Building Tempo Picks Up Across Country." *The New York Times,* May 13, 1984, pp. 8-9.

Ostroff, Jim. "A Ghost Town Comes Alive." *Venture,* July 1984, p. 100.

Padda, Kuldarshan. "Report Card on the States." *Inc.,* October 1981, pp. 91-98.

Peterson, Eric. "Enterprise Zones: There's Nothing to Lose by Trying Them." *Business Facilities,* May 1985, pp. 53-58, 99-103.

Posner, Bruce G. "Report on the States". *Inc.,* October 1984, pp. 108-29.

Rebello, Kathy. "More Japanese Firms Invest in USA Factories." *USA Today,* April 13, 1984.

Reinhold, Robert. "Houston Tightens Reins on Growth." *The Plain Dealer,* September 16, 1984.

Revzan, Lawrence. "Enterprise Zones: Present Status and Potential Impact." *Governmental Finance,* December 1983, pp. 31-37.

Richards, Bill. "Governor Janklow Exhibits Strange Personal Style; But He Means Business. *The Wall Street Journal,* March 29, 1984, pp. 1, 19.

Robbins, William. "Cities Going Where the Business Is." *The New York Times,* June 24, 1984.

Roth, Stanton F. and Shapiro, Charles A. "Current Trends in Corporate Relocation." *Corporate Design,* November/December 1983, pp. 25-26.

Rowan, Geoffrey. "Tech Center Tilts to Westboro." *The Boston Herald,* May 30, 1984.

Saiter, Susan. "Everyone's Trying to Start the New 'Silicon Valley'." *The New York Times,* March 27, 1983.

Samuels, Lori Young. "Productivity Rate Baffles Economists." *Plant Sites and Parks,* March-April, 1983, pp. 1-4, 27, 34, 76-77.

Saporta, Maria. "Foreigners Welcome in Dixie." *The Atlanta Journal and Constitution,* February 12, 1984, p. 16-E.

Schmidt, Peggy. "The Greening of Research Parks." *The New York Times,* October 14, 1984.

Schuh, Scott D. "Oregon Votes to Abandon Unitary Tax in Victory for Multi-national Companies. *The Wall Street Journal,* August 1, 1984, p. 10.

"Session Boosts Education, Angers Business." *The Miami Herald,* June 3, 1984.

Shaffer, Richard A. "Talking Mail...Lisa's Sales...Tracking Trucks from Space." *The Wall Street Journal,* July 20, 1984, p. 17.

———. "Venture Capitalists Pay Less to Invest In High-Tech Firms." *The Wall Street Journal,* May 4, 1984, p. 19.

Shaw, Webb. "Feighan Joins Effort for Saturn Plant." *Akron Beacon Journal,* February 2, 1985.

———. "Ohio Is Investing in the Future with Research, Training Centers." *Akron Beacon Journal,* May 20, 1985.

Shaw, Webb and Hershey, William. "Akron Not among 20 Saturn Bidders in Ohio." *Akron Beacon Journal,* February 1, 1985.

Sheridan, John H. "Industry's View of the South...Fruitful but Flawed." *Industry Week,* February 28, 1977, pp. 49-58.

Silver, Deborah. "Quest for Space: Why Local Firms Move." *Crain's Chicago Business,* August 2, 1982, pp. 15-16.

Simon, Jane. "Poor Image Problems Blamed in Defeat of R.I. 'Greenhouse'." *New England Business,* August 6, 1984, pp. 36-37.

Skur, Julie. "County Eyeing Female Enterprise Unit." *Crain's Cleveland Business,* October 15, 1984, p. 4.

Smith, Larry A. and Gruber, Maurice. "Planning a Location Study with the Aid of PERT." *The Real Estate Appraiser and Analyst,* Spring 1983, pp. 22-31.

"Southeast." *The Atlanta Journal and Constitution,* February 12, 1984, p. 6E.

Stepanek, Marcia. "First GMF Robotics Plant Could Assure a City's Future." *Akron Beacon Journal,* October 30, 1983.

———. "Poorer States No Good for Saturn, GM Hints." *Akron Beacon Journal,* March 19, 1985, p. B5.

Stipp, David. "Growing Pains; Austin, Texas, Keeps Courting High Tech, Irks Some Residents." *The Wall Street Journal,* September 11, 1984, p. 1.

Thompson, Robert W. and Harding, Charles F. "The Environmental Regulator and Industrial Development." *Environmental Management,* 1982, pp. 27-33.

Thurow, Roger. "New Vigor Is Infusing Small-Business Sector of German Economy." *The Wall Street Journal,* August 28, 1984, pp. 1, 14.

Townshend, Bickley. "The Sunbelt and How It Grew." *The Wall Street Journal,* May 24, 1984, p. 26.

"University Proposes 1st Software Library." *The Plain Dealer,* March 18, 1984.

Van Dam, Laura. "A Plant Relocation Out of Connecticut Engenders a Debate." *New England Business,* June 17, 1985, pp. 55.

Wald, Matthew L. "Back Offices Disperse from Downtowns." *The New York Times*, May 13, 1984.

Warnick, Marta. "Japanese Auto Plant Is a Boom to Small Tennessee Town." *Lexington Herald-Leader*, June 24, 1984.

Wilkening, David. "Stakes Are High in the Relocation Game." *Orlando Magazine*, December 1984, pp. 54-64, 114-117.

Wood, Allen R. "IDRC: A Review of Services for the Facility Planner." *Industrial Development*, January/February 1984, pp. 34-35.

Wynter, Leon E. "Congress Is Debating Federal Role in Setting Technological Priorities." *The Wall Street Journal*, August 1, 1984, p. 21.

"You Can Go Home Again." *Forbes*, December 11, 1978, pp. 81-82.

Zaslow, Jeffrey. "So the Act Isn't Bruce Springsteen; Aruba Isn't Exactly Paradise Island." *The Wall Street Journal*, June 25, 1985, p. 31.

"The Zinger of Silicon Valley." *Time*, February 6, 1984, pp. 50-51.

Zschau, Ed, and Ritter, Don. "Encourage Innovation Instead of Industrial Lemons." *Wall Street Journal*, August 1, 1984, p. 18

INDEX

356

358

Ministry of International Trade and
Industry, 198
Minnesota, 85, 93, 100, 201
Mississippi, 77, 97, 269
Missouri, 312
Montana, 78
Montgomery County Office of
Economic Development, 126
Morgan, Burton, 243
Multinational Corporation, 54-56

Naisbitt, John, 44, 54
Nashville, Tennessee, 244
National Association of Industrial
and Office Parks, 18, 167,
237-238
National Association of Real Estate
Investment Trusts, 171
National Association of Realtors,
237
National Association of State
Development Agencies, 171
National Cash Register (NCR), 220
National Development Council, 233
National Governors Association
Committee, 203
National League of Cities, 233
Nebraska, 78
Nestle, 149
Netherlands, 36, 39
New Jersey, 78, 170
New Mexico, 121
New York, 16, 52, 73, 76, 79, 127
New York City, New York, 297
New York Times, 56
North Carolina, 85, 88, 93, 201, 234,
246, 269
North East Tier Advanced
Technology Center, 105
North of England Development
Council, 101
North Texas Commission, 251
Northeast-Midwest Congressional
Coalition, 1

Oakland, California, 117
Objectives, 330-331
Ohio, 7, 10, 51, 57, 77-78, 81, 93,
116, 145-146, 149-151, 163,
194, 243, 267, 312, 326
Oklahoma, 49, 97, 202
Omaha Economic Development
Council, 152
Omaha, Nebraska, 152
Orange and Rockland Utilities, 16

Oregon, 40, 47, 75-76, 236, 268, 276,
302
Orlando, Florida, 125, 153-159, 168
Overseas Development Offices, 19

Palm Court, Florida, 118
Pennsylvania, 10, 50, 73-74, 310, 313
Phillips, Phillip D., 186-187
Phoenix, Arizona, 195
Pietermaritzburg, South Africa, 273
Pittsburgh, Pennsylvania, 74, 310,
313
Plant Location Decisions, 175-176,
255, 263-265, 283, 292-297
Plants, Sites, and Parks, 20, 57, 93,
122, 125-126
Port of Brownsville, Texas, 15
Private Land Developers, 167
Private Research, 45, 47-48
Proctor & Gamble, 325
Product Life Cycle, 24-27
Promotion, 122
Pueblo, Colorado, 275

Quality-of-Life Considerations, 235,
255, 260, 262, 263, 296, 321-
322, 324

Railroads, 165-166
Ranking Systems, 234-235
Real Estate, 18
REIT Report, 171
Relocation, 21-23
Reseach and Science Parks, 211
Research and Technical Centers,
211
Research Triangle, 192, 246, 253
Research Triangle Institute, 209
Retention Strategy, 233
Reuther, Walter, 197
Rhode Island, 97, 124
Rhodes, James, 57
Richland Economic Development
Corporation, 267
Richmond, Karin, 339
Rochester, New York, 17
Rogers, Everett, 221
Route 128, 192, 201, 213, 253
Rubicon Group, 53
Rustbelt, 309

San Antonio, Texas, 116-122, 311
Saturn, 7, 33-35, 51, 73, 174, 176,
179, 184-185, 308-309, 328,
332

In addition to those persons mentioned in this index and elsewhere in the book, the authors wish to especially acknowledge the valuable assistance provided by the following individuals: Connie Bekez, Ronald Dornin, Kim Dunlap, Judy Fritsch, Kim Kasenow, Bernadette Messina, Linda Poje, Tamara Rynearson, Susan Snyder and Cricket West.

ABOUT THE AUTHORS

John K. Ryans, Jr., and William L. Shanklin have been involved in consulting and executive development with organizations ranging from *Fortune 500* companies to small entrepreneurial ventures. Their associations have included such premier companies as Digital Equipment, General Electric, GenRad, Georgia-Pacific, Goodyear, Master Builders, Prime Computer, Xerox, and commercial banks in the United States and abroad. Mr. Ryans has been a consultant to the Great Lakes Commission (GLC) on marketing the Great Lakes and has served on the Federal Reserve Bank of Chicago-GLC task force that developed a profile of the Great Lakes economy. Mr. Shanklin has counseled a number of cities and chambers of commerce on downtown revitalization strategies; this work has encompassed the design and execution of supporting marketing studies.

Messrs. Ryans and Shanklin are sought-after speakers. They have addressed the Association of National Advertisers, Biomedical Marketing Association, chambers of commerce, Institute for Constructive Capitalism, M.I.T. Enterprise Forum, Research Directors Association of Chicago, and a plethora of similar organizations. Additionally, they have been called upon by various companies for special in-house presentations to executives.

Among their publications are the acclaimed recent books *Thinking Strategically* (Random House, 1985) and *Marketing High Technology* (Lexington Books, D.C. Heath & Company, 1984). Their articles have appeared in the *Harvard Business Review, Business Marketing, Research Management, California Management Review, Strategy & Executive Action, Directors & Boards,* and many other periodals.

In addition to their consulting practice, speaking, and writing, Mr. Ryans is Professor of Marketing and International Business and Mr. Shanklin is Professor of Marketing, both in the Graduate School of Management at Kent State University in Ohio. The authors hold doctorates in business administration (marketing), Mr. Ryans from Indiana University and Mr. Shanklin from the University of Maryland.